Tax Incentives
and Economic Growth

Tax Incentives
and Economic Growth

BARRY P. BOSWORTH

THE BROOKINGS INSTITUTION
Washington, D.C.

3 8 9 2 9 8

Library of Congress Cataloging in Publication data:

Bosworth, Barry, 1942–
  Tax incentives and economic growth.
  Includes bibliographical references and index.
  1. United States—Economic policy—1981– .
2. Tax incentives—United States. 3. Supply-side
economics—United States. I. Title.
HC106.8.B66 1984   338.973   84-9625
ISBN 0-8157-1036-4
ISBN 0-8157-1035-6 (pbk.)

9 8 7 6 5 4 3 2 1

THE BROOKINGS INSTITUTION is an independent organization devoted to nonpartisan research, education, and publication in economics, government, foreign policy, and the social sciences generally. Its principal purposes are to aid in the development of sound public policies and to promote public understanding of issues of national importance.

The Institution was founded on December 8, 1927, to merge the activities of the Institute for Government Research, founded in 1916, the Institute of Economics, founded in 1922, and the Robert Brookings Graduate School of Economics and Government, founded in 1924.

The Board of Trustees is responsible for the general administration of the Institution, while the immediate direction of the policies, program, and staff is vested in the President, assisted by an advisory committee of the officers and staff. The by-laws of the Institution state: "It is the function of the Trustees to make possible the conduct of scientific research, and publication, under the most favorable conditions, and to safeguard the independence of the research staff in the pursuit of their studies and in the publication of the results of such studies. It is not a part of their function to determine, control, or influence the conduct of particular investigations or the conclusions reached."

The President bears final responsibility for the decision to publish a manuscript as a Brookings book. In reaching his judgment on the competence, accuracy, and objectivity of each study, the President is advised by the director of the appropriate research program and weighs the views of a panel of expert outside readers who report to him in confidence on the quality of the work. Publication of a work signifies that it is deemed a competent treatment worthy of public consideration but does not imply endorsement of conclusions or recommendations.

The Institution maintains its position of neutrality on issues of public policy in order to safeguard the intellectual freedom of the staff. Hence interpretations or conclusions in Brookings publications should be understood to be solely those of the authors and should not be attributed to the Institution, to its trustees, officers, or other staff members, or to the organizations that support its research.

Foreword

BY MOST STANDARDS the U.S. economy performed very poorly during the 1970s: both inflation and unemployment increased, and the growth of real incomes slowed substantially. The causes of this poor economic performance are the subject of sharp debate among economists. Those subscribing to supply-side economics blame excessive government in the form of regulation, taxes, and spending. In particular, supply-side economists have argued that increased tax rates have seriously eroded incentives to work, save, and invest.

The role of incentives has long been explored by economists from both theoretical and empirical perspectives. But there is renewed interest in the subject as a result of the large expansion of government's role in the economy and growing concern with the slow growth of labor productivity. Unfortunately, discussions about incentives have often been marked by conflicting claims, stridency, and overstatement. This has obscured points of agreement and disagreement and has made it difficult to identify areas where the empirical evidence is strong and those where it is weak.

In this study Barry P. Bosworth, a senior fellow in the Brookings Economic Studies program, attempts to clarify the basic analytic issues about incentives and to summarize the empirical evidence. He relates these to a discussion of the need for policies that focus on the supply side of the economy and the alternative forms they might take. While the sharp decline in U.S. productivity growth is a central motivating factor behind the debate over the need for supply-side policies, the causes of that decline and the role of capital formation, technological change, and the quality of the work force are subjects of continuing dispute. In addition, the debate over the specific policy actions that should be taken is dominated by differing views about the effectiveness of taxes in altering incentives for saving and work effort. The author examines the difficulties of coordinating tax incentive measures with fiscal and monetary policies.

Several of the specific issues under discussion in this book have been the subject of previous Brookings publications. The causes of slow productivity growth have been examined in *Accounting for Slower Economic Growth,* by Edward F. Denison, and a series of articles in *Brookings Papers on Economic Activity.* Specific aspects of the relationship between taxes and economic activity were also evaluated in *How Taxes Affect Economic Behavior,* edited by Henry J. Aaron and Joseph A. Pechman. Finally, the basic theme of supply-side economics, calling for a reduced role of government in the economy, stands in sharp contrast to proposals for the development of an industrial policy in the United States. That side of the policy debate is discussed in *Can America Compete?* by Robert Z. Lawrence.

For helpful comments and suggestions the author is grateful to Henry J. Aaron, Alan J. Auerbach, Martin N. Baily, Gary Burtless, Edward F. Denison, Harvey Galper, Patric H. Hendershott, Joseph A. Pechman, Rudolph G. Penner, and Eugene Steuerle. Shannon P. Butler and Michael K. Kuehlwein provided research assistance. Computational assistance was provided by the staff of the Social Science Computation Center. Kathleen Elliott Yinug provided secretarial assistance. Nancy Davidson edited the manuscript and William O. Lively prepared the index.

The views expressed here are those of the author and should not be ascribed to the trustees, officers, or staff members of the Brookings Institution.

BRUCE K. MAC LAURY
President

April 1984
Washington, D.C.

Contents

Index   205

Tables

Figures

CHAPTER ONE

The Supply-Side Debate

UNDER THE LABEL of "supply-side economics," the determinants of the productive capacity of the economy and policies to increase its level and growth have become major policy issues in recent years. Specifically, the current discussion reflects an increased awareness of and concern about the effects of government actions on economic incentives in the private sector.

The term *supply-side economics* is often used in two different senses: (1) a broad interest in the determinants of aggregate supply—the volume and quality of the capital and labor inputs and the efficiency with which they are used—and (2) a narrower focus on tax reductions as a means of increasing the supply of saving, investment, and labor. This book is primarily about supply-side economics in the broad sense: How is the productive capacity of the nation affected by government policy? What is known about the effects on growth of changes in tax and transfer programs? In the process of reviewing these issues the discussion will also examine the narrower contention of the supply-side "purists" that reductions in tax and transfer benefits will bring about very large increases in supply.

Several forces explain the increased interest in these supply-side issues at this time. First, during the 1970s the traditional policies of demand management failed to reduce inflation without causing widespread unemployment. This failure initiated a search for alternatives; policy proposals that promised to curb inflation through expanded supply rather than depressed demand were particularly attractive. Second, and of more relevance, there has been increasing doubt about the adequacy of the current rate of capital formation as a source of gains in productivity. The collapse of productivity growth threatens to still the historical trend of rising standards of living and reduces the competitiveness of U.S.

goods in world markets. In addition, the enormous growth of the labor force during the 1970s was not matched by a similar expansion of industrial capacity, which led to questions of whether the existing capacity is sufficient to allow full employment of the work force. Finally, the experience with the social programs enacted since the 1930s has raised questions as to whether the design of these programs reduces efforts to seek employment in the private sector and thereby contributes to inflation, unemployment, and the slowing of productivity growth— potentially exacerbating the social problems they were intended to correct.

In part, supply-side economics reflects an understandable and desirable effort to measure responses to a variety of government programs that intentionally or inadvertently influence the activities of individual markets. In earlier decades, such programs were rare. There were few transfer programs, and taxes were used principally to raise the modest revenues required in peacetime or the larger sums required only temporarily for war. They were not instruments for altering the distribution of income or affecting the allocation of resources. During the 1960s and 1970s the government used taxes and transfers more and more for these purposes. When these means seemed inadequate, it even resorted to off-budget tools to achieve specific goals, such as special loan programs and social regulations to protect the environment or improve health and safety. Government has lacked an analytical framework to assess the effects of these policy actions on microeconomic decisions.

The role of incentives is not new to economics in either theory or empirical work. But the vastly increased range of government action and the changing nature of the problems have strengthened interest in the effect of such incentives. Unfortunately, renewed interest in these fundamental analytical problems has been marked by stridency, overstatement, and contradiction, making it difficult to identify the areas where the evidence is strong and where it is weak and the points of agreement and conflict.

Supply-side economics also has strong political overtones because the conclusions about the effects of taxes and transfers on incentives to work, save, and invest influence perceptions of the desirable degree of relative taxation of different economic groups, the appropriate means of distributing the fruits of the economic system, and the benefits of growth in the overall system.

The Evolution of Macroeconomic Policy

The relative importance of supply and demand factors in the evolution of economic systems is a long-standing source of controversy among economists. According to classical economists, involuntary unemployment would not exist in an economy that is characterized by competitive "flexprice" markets. Adjustment of prices to equate demand and supply would result in a situation of continuous market clearing. While a decline in demand in one market might initially be reflected in unemployment, the excess of supply would quickly cause the price to fall and would induce a combination of an offsetting rise in demand within that market and a shift of supply to other uses where rewards were greater. Classical economics emphasized the flexibility of prices within competitive markets in adjusting to changes in demand and supply (as illustrated by the auction market for wheat) and the efficiency of a decentralized price system, together with the signals and incentives it provides, in directing resources to their most productive uses.

In one sense, supply was viewed as creating its own demand since the adjustment of prices provided a means of equating demand to any level of supply. Thus, for the classical economists, demand was not a problem, and they emphasized the importance of promoting the growth of supply through saving, investment, and innovation.

The Neoclassical-Keynesian Synthesis

The contribution of John Maynard Keynes was to recognize that reduction of demand in one market could, through its impact on the incomes of the newly unemployed and the consequent reduction in their purchases from other industries, outweigh the effect of any decline in prices and create a cumulative move away from full employment. Thus he rejected the classical assumption that prices adjust to clear all markets continuously and argued instead that the sluggish response of prices to changes in demand and supply—particularly in labor markets—created the potential for a substantial gap between demand and supply.

The events of the Great Depression and the development of Keynesian economics led to a belief that supply and demand, for the economy as a whole, would not always remain in equilibrium at full employment and that market price adjustments alone provided too weak an equilibrating mechanism. Hence there was a need for government to intervene through the combined use of fiscal and monetary policies to set demand at a level consistent with the full utilization of available resources.

Within this framework supply was not forgotten; but the focus on stabilizing cyclical fluctuations in demand did lead to an interpretation of aggregate supply as a relatively exogenous, trend-dominated target for demand policies. This interpretation was most evident in the development of the concept of potential gross national product—the level of GNP corresponding to the full employment of labor. Potential GNP was projected to expand in line with the trend rate of increase in the labor force plus labor productivity.

Yet it is wrong to believe that economic research or economic policy ignored the issue of supply in the postwar period. The reference of Alfred Marshall to supply and demand acting as "two blades of the scissors" became a cliché; economic growth and the determinants of capital formation were among the more active subjects of economic research; and the postwar history of economic policy in the industrial countries is replete with efforts to encourage faster growth of aggregate supply. Economists were also well aware that changes in government tax and transfer programs involved, in addition to an income effect, a change in relative prices that could alter decisions to work, save, and invest. In that sense the analytical and prescriptive framework remained highly classical in its view of the determinants of growth of potential output, while adopting a Keynesian perspective on demand.

The focus on demand-side issues in policy nonetheless reflected a belief that the effects of relative price changes on aggregate supply are generally small and that government policies cannot sharply alter the growth path of potential GNP in the short run. For individual markets or regions of the country, the growth of supply can be very sensitive to relative prices because resources can be shifted from one market to another where the returns are greater. For the overall economy, however, supply is limited by the growth in labor and capital and the efficiency with which they are used.

At the same time, studies of the sources of economic growth in the United States and other industrial countries found that increased amounts of capital and labor could account for only about half of the gains in production. Economies of scale, improved resource allocation, education, and a residual of advances in knowledge were of equal importance.[1] This broader view of the growth process was evident during the postwar period in the efforts of governments to reduce trade barriers as a means of expanding markets and in the emphasis on public financing of education and research.

The neo-Keynesian or neoclassical synthesis—bringing together long-held views of the determinants of supply and Keynesian views on the need to manage aggregate demand—has provided the framework for the discussion and conduct of economic policy for the last several decades. And, at least in the early 1960s, both blades of the scissors were clearly visible as government policies focused on measures to expand both demand and potential output. On the demand side, fiscal and monetary policies were aimed at moving actual output closer to potential and avoiding the fluctuations that had been so costly in the past. On the supply side, new tax incentives and an accommodative monetary policy were major elements of an effort to encourage new investment.[2]

However, as the U.S. difficulties with inflation mounted throughout the late 1960s and the 1970s, demand management became the focal point for most of the discussion of policy options, and issues of supply creation were relegated to a minor role in the formation of aggregate economic policy. Economists, for example, focused their attention on a debate over the relative efficacy of monetary and fiscal policy as tools of demand management.

The Breakup of a Policy Consensus

The surge of interest in supply-side economics (or what the classicists would view as a resurgence) in recent years reflects a large number of different themes.

PUBLIC DISSATISFACTION. For the general public, supply-side economics helped in the search for a villain that could be labeled as responsible for the poor performance of the economy over the last decade—and they found it in government, or, more specifically, taxes. In that sense,

1. See, for example, Edward F. Denison, *Accounting for Slower Economic Growth: The United States in the 1970s* (Brookings Institution, 1979); and the studies cited in footnote 2 of chapter 2 of this volume.

2. See, for example, *Economic Report of the President,* January 1962, especially chaps. 1 and 2.

supply-side economics was a political movement based on popular thought rather than the outgrowth of academic ideas.

Certainly the performance of the economy in the 1970s did not compare well with prior decades. Unemployment rates approximately doubled from the late 1960s, inflation worsened, and productivity growth fell off to less than half the postwar trend of 3 percent annually. The weekly earnings of the average factory worker (adjusted for inflation) actually declined slightly over the decade. The growth of family incomes was sustained only by a rapid shift to dual-income families as women entered the work force in large numbers.

The initial receptiveness of the public to supply-side economics also reflected a view, heard with increasing frequency, that the redistribution of income through the tax and transfer system had gone too far, eroding incentives and depressing efficiency in economic activities—a shift of emphasis in the continual conflict between the concern for equity versus that for efficiency.[3] From this perspective the general decline in economic performance was explained as a direct result of the growth in government and transfer programs.

As a theory, neo-Keynesian economics cannot be blamed for all these problems. The excessive degree of fiscal stimulus during the mid-1960s was largely the outgrowth of political difficulties surrounding the financing of the Vietnam War. The resulting pressure on demand was a major force in initiating inflation and undermining coordination between fiscal and monetary policy. Similarly, disruptions in world food and energy markets during the 1970s created problems for domestic economic policy that would have been severe regardless of the economic policies that might have been followed.

INFLATION. The experience of the last decade, however, did reveal a major inadequacy of the neo-Keynesian model: the explanation of inflation. The key to the breakup of the policy consensus of the 1960s was the failure to control inflation. That failure involved two elements: (1) economists underestimated the complexities of the inflation process and the difficulties of achieving a satisfactory balance with unemployment; and (2) the application of the analysis forced a choice between inflation and unemployment that neither the public nor its representatives wanted to face.

3. Arthur M. Okun, *Equality and Efficiency: The Big Tradeoff* (Brookings Institution, 1975).

Even in the early 1960s there were serious doubts that inflation could be constrained simply by the adjustment of demand to avoid the extremes of excess demand and recession. The notion of a stable trade-off between inflation and unemployment, as embodied in the empirical formulation of the Phillips curve, lacked a solid theoretical basis and always appeared to be a bit of "ad hockery." In its earliest version it was too simple a formulation that overlooked the role of price expectations.[4]

The emergence of inflation as a serious problem during the 1970s sharply shifted the direction of economic policy. In the 1960s the emphasis was on offsetting fluctuations in private demand to maintain a steady economic expansion. In the 1970s the government was forced into the position of actually generating recessions to slow inflation, only to face strong pressures to reverse the policy as a result of the rise in unemployment. By stressing monetary and fiscal restraint, economists claimed to provide policymakers with a solution to inflation, but the costs in terms of unemployment were extremely high. Throughout the decade economic policy came to resemble a roller coaster as it fluctuated between stimulus and restraint in response to shifting concerns between inflation and unemployment. Dissatisfaction with the resolution of the inflation-unemployment conflict within the neo-Keynesian framework created an atmosphere conducive to the emergence of alternative theories to guide macroeconomic policy.

CHANGING VIEWS ON TAX POLICY. Sustained high inflation during the 1970s increased effective rates of taxation, particularly those on reported income from capital. The income tax system, with its particular definition of taxable income and a graduated tax rate structure, had been designed for an economy of relative price stability. Throughout most of the postwar period both marginal and average tax rates were relatively constant; thus they did not play a central role in anyone's explanation of changes in the economic situation. But the inflation of the 1970s sharply distorted the measure of taxable income earned from capital—primarily because of the failure to adjust capital gains, interest income and expenses, and depreciation allowances for changes in the price level. In some situations taxpayers paid taxes on nominal capital gains when in fact the value of their assets had declined after adjustment for

4. Milton Friedman, "The Role of Monetary Policy," *American Economic Review*, vol. 58 (March 1968), pp. 1–17; and Edmund S. Phelps, "Phillips Curves, Expectations of Inflation and Optimal Unemployment Over Time," *Economica*, vol. 34 (August 1967), pp. 254–81.

inflation. Inflation also pushed all taxpayers into progressively higher marginal tax brackets. As a result there were substantial variations in effective tax rates over the decade and among different income classes and types of income.

The variation in tax rates caused by inflation served to stimulate the research effort (at both the theoretical and empirical levels) devoted to determining the effect of taxes on the supply and allocation of resources. This research focused on the impact of taxes on the choice among economic alternatives (such as work or leisure, saving or consumption, and the choice between capital and labor in production); and it contrasted with the earlier emphasis on the effects of taxes on total income, aggregate demand, and income distribution.

The theoretical studies have improved the understanding of how in principle taxes should affect the allocation of resources in the presence of inflation. And the empirical studies, while they may not provide definitive measures of the magnitude of the impact on actual economic decisions, have reopened the issue of the significance of taxes and after-tax rates of return in determining growth in the supply of capital and labor and the efficiency of their use.

THE EMERGENCE OF A PRODUCTIVITY PROBLEM. Even within the framework of the neo-Keynesian model, the changed nature of today's economic problems would justify a vastly greater emphasis on policies that affect the supply side of the economy.

The concept of productivity growth has always been a confusing one. On the positive side, it is identified with increases in living standards, because a rise in output per hour means that the economy can produce more with the same amount of work effort. On the negative side, it is identified with automation and raises the fear that the same level of output will be produced with fewer workers: that is, more unemployment rather than more output. Historically workers have readily accepted technical change in industries where demand for output is growing rapidly and at times when overall employment opportunities are good; resistance intensifies in industries with declining demand and during periods of high levels of overall unemployment.

The slowdown in productivity growth has been a problem for over a decade. In the early 1970s the annual rate of growth averaged only about 2 percent, compared to a postwar trend of 3 percent. Initially, this slowdown was viewed as temporary, the result of cyclical fluctuations in the economy and a shift toward a younger, less experienced work force. But the continuation of the slowdown in the last half of the decade, with an annual average growth of less than 1 percent, points to more fundamental problems. In the period between 1977 and 1982, output per man-hour in the private nonfarm business economy actually failed to grow at all.

As mentioned earlier, this productivity slowdown was reflected in a sharp falloff in average wage gains (adjusted for inflation) during the 1970s, but its implications for family incomes were camouflaged by the rise in the labor force participation of married women. In addition, the growth of incomes was affected by a rapid expansion of transfer payments—primarily social security—not matched by tax increases.

These offsets cannot be sustained into the 1980s. Demographic factors will not contribute to further large increases in the proportion of the total population in the labor force. Concerns with inflation in the management of economic policy will limit the growth in aggregate demand and job opportunities. And competition for government revenues has already begun to force a slower growth of transfer incomes.

A pattern of little or no growth in productivity and general living standards, if it continues, is likely to have major implications for a heterogeneous population of competing racial, ethnic, and social groups, such as that of the United States. In the past a portion of each year's productivity dividend was used to improve social security programs, expand private health and retirement benefits, and raise the relative incomes of the most disadvantaged; yet room remained for a significant general increase in average real incomes. Mediation among competing groups could be accomplished by promising more to some without actually reducing the incomes of others. From that perspective, slow productivity growth is an almost certain prescription for increased social conflict.

In addition, it complicates the effort to achieve a sustained reduction in inflation. It is not easy to restrain nominal wage demands when workers perceive that their real earnings are falling. From an economist's perspective, inflation and slow productivity growth are distinctly different problems. In the minds of the public, however, the distinction is blurred: they view the situation in both cases as one in which higher prices for the things they buy erode their own hard-won wage gains.

Alternative Views on Supply-Side Economics

Both among the general public and within the economics profession, then, there is a growing consensus that the supply side of the economy deserves greater emphasis. Conflicts emerge out of the evaluation of alternative means of achieving that objective. These conflicts reflect differences in the diagnosis of the cause of the basic problems and in the effectiveness of the prescriptions to effect a cure. In addition, the policy prescriptions are complicated by the need to integrate proposals to expand potential output with policies to reduce inflation. While a concern with inflation implies a need to hold down demand by restrictive fiscal and monetary policies, an emphasis on capital formation and aggregate supply growth implies an expansionary policy of tax cuts and low interest rates.

The current disarray of advice on economic policy is primarily a reflection of divergent views on two issues: (1) the sensitivity of wages and prices to changes in demand and (2) the responsiveness of supply to changes in wages, prices, taxes, and government benefits.

The first is simply the old debate over the extent to which the economy can be viewed as an aggregation of "flexprice" versus "fixprice" markets—the subject of dispute between Keynes and the classical economists. But a judgment on this matter is critical to the question of how much policymakers can focus on measures to expand supply while ignoring the consequences for demand. If the economy is dominated by flexprice markets, inflation is a monetary phenomenon and can be held in check by a restrictive monetary policy without serious implications for real output and employment. If monetary policy can control inflation without depressing production, then fiscal policy is free to pursue the goal of increasing incentives for capital formation without the need to worry about the management of overall demand.

A fixed-price view of the economy, on the other hand, would anticipate that a shift to monetary restraint would reduce total production and employment as prices fail to fall (or decelerate) with sufficient speed to clear all markets. The resulting combination of idle existing resources and high real rates of interest would sharply curtail capital formation. In this view inflation is not just a monetary phenomenon; and thus no simple dichotomy between fiscal and monetary policies is possible.

There are few signs that this difference in viewpoints is moving toward resolution. The fixed-price view is a better description of the day-to-day behavior of the economy. Clearly, wages and prices do exhibit a considerable degree of rigidity, and monetary restraint does result in unemployment. Much of that rigidity, however, seems to reflect adjustment lags, and it is possible that the flexible-price view is a good description of the equilibrium path toward which the actual economy is driven. Neither the fixprice nor flexprice interpretation of markets can be accepted as a complete description of the economy's response to changed policies. There is a tendency to characterize fixed-price models as short-run analysis and flexible-price models as long run, but without any agreement on the boundary between the two or the strength of the competitive forces pushing the economy toward an equilibrium.

The second issue—the sensitivity of supply to changes in prices—is a debate over the magnitude of the effects. How central a role do rates of return or relative prices play in the determination of saving, investment, and the choice between work and leisure? These are subjects on which most economists agree as to the appropriate theoretical model; but, despite a proliferation of empirical studies, they do not agree about the quantitative importance of relative price changes for such basic choices.

Disagreement about these two issues is responsible for much of the divergence of advice as to what government economic policies should be. The diversity of views and their implications for policy are illustrated by examining four different perspectives on the current slow growth of supply in industrial countries.[5]

The Keynesian View

The Keynesian model relies heavily on a fixed-price interpretation of markets; and analysis with such a model leads to an emphasis on the growth of demand, or the utilization of current capacity, with its implications for investment incentives, as a key element in determining the growth of future supply. Economists who use such a model point to the instability of the economy during the 1970s as a major cause of the productivity slowdown. That instability was caused in turn by the magnitude of the disruptions in international commodity markets during the last decade and the vacillations in economic policy as governments struggled to control inflation.

---

5. As a pedagogical device the following sections use specific labels (such as "Keynesian," or "neoclassical") to identify basic themes or schools of thought. It is a mistake to identify individual economists as falling into a specific category: most economists will use different models or combinations of models to analyze different questions. This is particularly true for the synthesis of Keynesian and neoclassical views that developed in the postwar period.

Although Keynesians concede that a rise in effective tax rates on capital income could erode investment incentives, they argue that business cycle recessions and insufficient demand are more important as factors that depress actual and expected rates of return. With respect to saving, they emphasize motivating factors other than expected rates of return (for example, provision for retirement and protection against unexpected future interruptions of income). In effect, both saving and investment are strongly affected by changes in income, but less so by interest rates.

Since the Keynesian model assigns market rates of interest a relatively small role in the short-run decisions of both savers and investors, interest rate adjustments are a relatively ineffective mechanism for realigning investment with a changed level of saving. In fact, there is some ambivalence about the desirability of a higher saving rate: it implies a decline in consumption, production, and expected future demand unless it is matched by a coincident rise in investment demand. Policies to expand saving are desirable only if they are combined with similar policy actions on the investment side.

The Keynesian analysis, therefore, leads to a long-run growth policy based on maintaining a strong growth of demand with high utilization of existing resources and a mix of fiscal-monetary policy that combines a tighter government budget to raise national savings with an expansionary monetary policy emphasizing low interest rates to promote investment. To some extent it is a view that demand creates its own supply, because of the importance it attaches to a sustained growth of demand in line with that of potential GNP if policies to shift the composition of total output toward capital formation are to succeed. Because difficulties in restraining inflation have been the most frequent factor forcing the government to depart from expansionary demand policies, an effective means of resolving the inflation-unemployment conflict emerges as the most important requirement for faster growth.[6]

The American Neoclassical Model

The neoclassical analysis emphasizes the after-tax rate of return on capital as the driving force in the process of economic growth. A decline

6. Elements of this view are reflected in James Tobin, "Stabilization Policy Ten Years After," *Brookings Papers on Economic Activity, 1:1980*, pp. 19–71. (Hereafter *BPEA*.) These policy prescriptions are a reflection of the postwar Keynesian-neoclassical synthesis rather than a strictly Keynesian interpretation of the supply-side issues.

in this rate of return during the late 1960s and 1970s is viewed as the basic cause of a decline in the growth of capital and thus the growth of potential output.

The fall in the return on capital is interpreted as the result of the interaction of inflation with the tax structure, which sharply raised effective rates of taxation on capital income. Inflation, in turn, is regarded as the product of a rapid expansion of the money supply, which created an excessive level of demand. Thus the poor performance of the economy over the last decade, in terms of both inflation and slow productivity growth, can ultimately be traced to mistaken government policies.

Believing that markets are characterized by flexible prices, American neoclassicists argue that the current economic problems can be solved by adopting a more restrictive monetary policy to lower inflation and by reducing the taxation of capital income to eliminate the wedge between before-tax (social) returns and after-tax (private) returns on income from capital. In that view domestic saving is the constraining influence on capital formation, and flexibility of interest rates will ensure that a higher saving rate will be translated into increased investment rather than a decline of total demand.

While conceding that monetary restraint will cause a temporary loss of production and employment, neoclassical economists criticize the Keynesian analysis for an excessive preoccupation with the short run. Demand fluctuations are only a short-term concern, as the failure of markets to clear immediately is the result of transitory informational lags and other institutional factors that slow, but do not prevent, the adjustment of prices.[7]

The recommendations for fiscal policy differ among economists who use the neoclassical analysis, depending upon their perceptions of the magnitude of the effect of tax rates on private saving incentives. Those who believe that interest rates have a small effect on saving emphasize reducing budget deficits as a means of increasing the volume of national

---

7. The academic literature on the neoclassical view has expanded rapidly during the last decade. A nontechnical statement of the differences with Keynesian economics is provided by Martin Feldstein, "The Retreat from Keynesian Economics," *The Public Interest*, no. 64 (Summer 1981), pp. 92–105. Many economists would view his exposition of the Keynesian view as something of a caricature, but it is useful in highlighting the differences. The emphasis on monetary restraint and tax reductions for capital as the policy prescriptions are provided in Martin Feldstein, "Tax Rules and the Mismanagement of Monetary Policy," *American Economic Review*, vol. 70 (May 1980, *Papers and Proceedings, 1979*), pp. 182–86.

saving available for private investment. A reduction in government borrowing rather than efforts to encourage higher private saving is seen as the most effective means of supplying resources for private capital formation. Alternatively, if tax reductions are thought to have a large effect on private saving, total saving will be expected to rise as a result of tax reductions because private saving will rise by more than the increase in the government deficit (dissaving) that accompanies the tax reduction.[8]

In addition, because tight monetary policy has a strong depressing effect on homebuilding, the combination of monetary restraint to reduce residential investment and tax cuts to encourage business investment is seen as shifting the mix of capital formation toward the business sector. Such an approach can be contrasted with a policy that aims to increase the share of output devoted to capital formation by combining a restrictive fiscal policy (to reduce consumption, both public and private) with an easing of monetary policy. In any case, neoclassicists argue that a tax reduction program should favor capital income over labor income and saving over consumption.

The European Neoclassical View

Like their American counterparts, European neoclassical economists emphasize the rate of return to capital as the key element in the growth process. They differ, however, in their explanation of the cause of the decline in the return on capital in European economies during the 1970s. They place less reliance on the proposition that wages and prices are fully determined by market forces (the flexprice view). Instead, they believe that the rise in real wage rates in excess of productivity growth increased labor's share of national income, reduced profit margins, and weakened incentives to invest in those economies.[9] The surge of real

8. One can, of course, believe in both the importance of low tax rates to promote private saving and reductions in government deficits and thereby emphasize the importance of shrinking the size of the public sector. Such a recommendation also involves a judgment about the social value of public services—a judgment involving political-sociological as well as economic issues.

9. This European perspective is most clearly enunciated by Herbert Giersch, "Aspects of Growth, Structural Change, and Employment: A Schumpeterian Perspective," *Weltwirtschaftliches Archiv* (*Review of World Economics*), vol. 115, pt. 4 (1979), pp. 629–52. It is also reflected in the economic analysis in Organization for Economic Cooperation and Development, *OECD, Economic Outlook* (Paris: OECD, various issues, 1977–80). It is examined in detail in Jeffrey D. Sachs, "Wages, Profits, and Macroeconomic Adjustment: A Comparative Study," *BPEA, 2:1979*, pp. 269–319.

wage increases in the early 1970s is attributed to greater union militancy, sustained high-employment policies, the indexing of wages to changes in the cost of living, and a catch-up of wages that had been constrained by income policies in the 1960s. The competitive pressures from the world market prevented a pass-through of these costs into producer prices and placed a squeeze on profit margins.

The wage-cost pressure could not be offset by depreciation of the currency because of a propensity to negotiate wages in real terms, fully adjusted for consumer price inflation: the fall in a country's exchange rate raised import prices and led to a compensating increase in domestic wages. In addition, the overvaluation of the U.S. dollar in the 1960s led to excessive reliance within Europe on export industries. Thus the realignment of currencies in 1971 initiated a transitional period of structural adjustment in which the traditional export industries were forced to contract.

European neoclassicists share some of the doubts of the Keynesian analysis that monetary restraint can succeed in reducing real wages. But they are equally doubtful that inflation, devaluation, and expansion of demand offer an effective means of restoring profit margins. Thus they have a classical interpretation of unemployment as the result of excessively high real wages, but they do not believe that normal market forces will easily restore a balance. They emphasize instead the need for structural reforms to provide an added one-shot boost to productivity, thereby reducing unit labor costs, restoring profit margins, and strengthening investment incentives. They do not agree that government tax policy is the cause of the fall in the return to capital and thus the slowdown in potential output growth. They do frequently identify excessive unemployment insurance as a major cause of unemployment and the high real wage. This European viewpoint is particularly evident in the resistance within the Organization for Economic Cooperation and Development (OECD) to repeated efforts by the United States to induce other countries to adopt more expansionary policies during the mid-1970s.

In the closed-economy (no foreign sector) analysis used by many American economists, high real wages lead firms to substitute capital for labor and thus increase domestic investment. Within the open-economy perspective of Europeans, high real wages (relative to productivity) depress profit margins and divert capital to other economies, reducing domestic investment.

Supply-Side Purists

As a school of thought, supply-side economics represents an extension of the American neoclassical school. Its proponents argue that there
is a very large response by supply (capital and labor) to changes in
relative prices. In the case of capital formation the relevant price is that
of future versus current consumption—the after-tax rate of return on
saving. For the choice between work and leisure, the relative price is
the after-tax wage rate. In both cases, a small increase in the price calls
forth a large increase in supply. At this level, the distinctive element of
the supply-side school is strictly an empirical issue: supply-side purists
speak of a tax cut unleashing a flood of increased entrepreneurial
innovation and a greater intensity of work effort.

Many supply-side advocates go further, however. They argue that
fiscal policy has no direct impact on aggregate demand in either the short
or long run. That is, no distinction should be made, as Keynes did, in
evaluating the demand implications of an increase in government expenditures financed by borrowing as opposed to those of an increase
financed by taxes.

In the Keynesian aggregate demand analysis, tax changes (and changes in
government expenditures) are identified in terms of their effects on the amount
of income available to the affected persons or businesses. In the "supply-side"
analysis the initial effect of any tax or government spending change is identified
as a change in the actual or implied price of something(s) relative to that of
others. In the technical terminology, the distinction is between first-order income
effects or first-order relative-price effects respectively.[10]

There are several situations that would justify the supply-siders' view
that fiscal policy has no direct income effect on aggregate demand. First,
if the economy is characterized by fully flexible prices and wages that
quickly clear all markets, all resources are continuously fully employed.
By definition, *real* demand cannot be increased in such circumstances.
In this sense, supply-side economics represents the application of the
long-run, full-employment analysis of neoclassical economics to the

10. Norman B. Ture, "The Economic Effects of Tax Changes: A Neoclassical
Analysis," in *Stagflation: The Causes, Effects, and Solutions*, vol. 4 of *A Special Study
on Economic Change*, Joint Economic Committee, 96 Cong. 2 sess. (Government
Printing Office, 1980), pp. 318–19.

short run.[11] It denies the existence of the problem that Keynes tried to address—involuntary unemployment, a mismatch between aggregate demand and supply.

This criticism of the Keynesian emphasis on involuntary unemployment is not restricted to supply-side economists. It is echoed in much of the modern neoclassical analysis—particularly the combination of rational expectations with the assumption of market-clearing prices. This new classical macroeconomics argues that aggregate demand departs from supply only because of information errors and lags introduced by contracts and other institutional barriers to market-clearing behavior. In this world, demand-management policies of the government can affect the economy only to the extent that they lead to errors in forecasts by private economic agents. The systematic or anticipated elements of demand management have no impact on real output or employment.[12]

Alternatively, the supply-side view that fiscal policy would have no effect on aggregate demand, real or nominal, could be justified if the public's demand for money were absolutely insensitive to interest rates. In that case, aggregate nominal GNP would be fully controlled by monetary policy, and public expenditure would simply crowd out private spending through higher interest rates. This view of the monetary mechanism is mentioned in an article by Ture, but other supply-side discussions of the interaction with monetary policy do not imply such a rigid interpretation of the monetary mechanism.[13]

Finally, it is possible to argue, in an ultrarationality sense, that taxpayers foresee the future tax implications of a current budget deficit

11. The assumption of full employment is not stated explicitly by the major proponents, but that inference follows from the argument that changes in the amount of inputs to production can result only from changes in their real price. More explicitly, "the supply-side analysis, on the other hand, holds that government actions have no direct initial impact on *real* demand and, indeed, affect nominal aggregate demand only as a consequence of changes in the stock of money." See Norman B. Ture, "Supply Side Analysis and Public Policy," in David G. Raboy, *Essays in Supply Side Economics* (Heritage Foundation, 1982), p. 13.

12. The neutrality of stabilization policy is a theme developed by many authors. The issues are surveyed in Bennett T. McCallum, "Rational Expectations and Macroeconomic Stabilization Policy: An Overview," *Journal of Money, Credit, and Banking,* vol. 12 (November 1980, pt. 2), pp. 716–46; and William Fellner, "The Valid Core of Rationality Hypothesis in the Theory of Expectations," *Journal of Money, Credit, and Banking,* vol. 12 (November 1980, pt. 2), pp. 763–87.

13. Norman Ture, "Supply Side Analysis and Public Policy," p. 13.

and immediately adjust their own saving to pay for it; thus private spending adjusts to offset government dissaving without the need for a rise in interest rates.[14] This argument is not stressed by supply-side advocates and it does not seem to be central to their argument against Keynesian economics.

In summary, the central feature of supply-side economics, with respect to tax (and perhaps expenditure) policy, is its emphasis on changes in price incentives as opposed to changes in income flows. At the theoretical level, it reflects a return to the analytical framework of classical economics: continuous clearing of markets is assumed to maintain the economy at full employment. At the empirical level, its distinguishing feature is the magnitude and speed with which the incentive effects are assumed to operate. Both of these tenets are evident in the supply-siders' interpretation of their major historical illustration of supply-side policy: the 1964 corporate and personal income tax reductions.

Keynesian analysis attributes the surge of economic activity following the 1964 tax reduction to the rise in after-tax incomes and consumer spending. The increased spending had further multiplier consequences as it induced higher levels of production, employment, investment, and income. The higher level of private income subsequently provided for a partial recovery of tax revenue. The level of private saving was increased both because of the rise in the level of income and because the short-run marginal propensity to spend out of income is less than the long-run average. The expansion of demand, without inflation, was made possible by the prior existence of substantial unemployment and idle capacity.

According to the supply-side view, however, the increased supply of labor and capital, which made the higher level of production possible, would not have been forthcoming without a reduction in marginal tax rates. Resources were fully employed at the time of the tax reduction, and any unemployment must have been voluntary. With the lower tax rates, individuals offered more hours of work for a higher after-tax wage. More important, saving was made more attractive and it financed increased investment. Since flexible prices ensure full employment of available resources, supply-side economists make no distinction between actual and potential output, and they attribute all of the rise in output to increased incentives to supply more resources.

14. Robert Barro, "Are Government Bonds Net Wealth?" *Journal of Political Economy,* vol. 82 (November–December 1974), pp. 1095–1117.

The implications of supply-side economics for policy are similar to those that follow from the neoclassical model: monetary restraint to reduce inflation and reductions in marginal tax rates to stimulate capital formation and the supply of labor. Whereas the neoclassical school might foresee some short-run increase in unemployment as a result of monetary restraint, supply-siders foresee no such conflict as long as the change in policy is gradual and the participants are convinced that the appropriate monetary policy will be sustained in the future.

In addition, most proponents of the neoclassical school believe that, while a reduction in tax rates will induce an increase in private saving, the rise in the government deficit will be larger. Thus they advocate matching expenditure reductions to ensure that there is a net increase in funds for private investment. Some supply-siders, however, believe that the rise in private saving plus the secondary recovery of taxes from a higher level of income will more than cover the initial deficit, and thus tax cuts should not be conditional on expenditure reductions.

Issues in Supply-Side Economics

The disputes among economists over the most effective policy to expand aggregate supply reflect a multitude of different issues that greatly complicate the discussion of policy. All aspects of the debate cannot be resolved in this study. The primary objectives are to identify the major issues, indicate those on which there is some consensus among economists who have examined the empirical evidence, and provide some explanation for the continuing controversy over others.

The disagreements begin at the most basic level of accounting for past economic growth. To what extent has economic growth been the result of increased supplies of capital and labor, and to what extent the result of technological gains that raised the efficiency of their use? And to what extent is productivity growth to be interpreted as an endogenous process responsive to economic incentives as opposed to being a reflection of largely autonomous trends of technological change?

As a further complication, some economists believe that the growth in labor productivity is closely tied to the growth of the capital stock because the growth in the latter influences the speed with which new technologies are introduced. Others deny that the embodiment of new technology in new capital is an important issue in practice and regard productivity growth as a more exogenous process not easily altered by broad policy measures.

These issues arise most directly in connection with the slowdown in productivity growth during the 1970s and the debate over the effectiveness of increased capital formation as a solution. If the productivity slowdown is a major motivation for enhanced interest in supply-side economic policies, it would be helpful to have a consensus as to its causes. Unfortunately, as will be seen in chapter 2, that is not the case. Second, there are substantial disagreements about the importance of relative prices as incentives affecting the growth of capital and labor. How important are expected rates of return in decisions to save and invest, and is the choice between work and leisure affected to a significant degree by changes in the after-tax real wage rate?

These might appear to be straightforward empirical issues that economists should be expected to resolve among themselves. In fact, the issues are quite complex, as illustrated by the simple example of an individual who currently takes one afternoon a week off from work. If his tax is reduced, he is affected in two offsetting fashions. On the one hand, he has an incentive to give up his afternoon off and return to the office, because he receives a higher hourly income after tax. This *substitution effect* pushes him in the direction of more work because of the higher opportunity cost, or forgone income, of leisure. On the other hand, the increase in his after-tax income at existing levels of work effort implies that he can afford more leisure. Thus the *income effect* of the tax reduction pushes in the direction of less work. All of us probably know some individuals who would give up their leisure, some who would take more, and many who would show no noticeable response. Economists are asked to predict the average net response, but without the opportunity to conduct a controlled laboratory experiment where other factors can be held constant.

Similarly for savings, the income and substitution effects pull in opposite directions, and the direction of the net effect on the individual, much less the economy, cannot be resolved without empirical analysis. A reduction in the tax on income from capital has a substitution effect of encouraging the individual to reduce his current consumption to take advantage of the higher after-tax return on saving. Alternatively, the increased lifetime income that will be earned because of the higher return on previously planned saving argues in favor of increasing current as well as future consumption. This income effect is likely to be particularly important if the individual saves to achieve a specific goal, such as a minimal retirement income.

For investment, the direction of the response to a change in the rate of return is unambiguous: a reduction in taxes on capital increases the incentive to invest by reducing the cost of using capital versus labor. There are, however, sharp differences of view with respect to the possibilities of substituting capital for labor in choosing among alternative production processes. Some economists perceive the situation as one in which, at a particular time, one specific production process (combination of capital and labor) is likely to dominate others over a wide range of relative factor prices, so that a change in the price of capital relative to labor will have a minor influence on business decisions. The magnitude of this potential for substituting capital for labor in production is critical to the evaluation of tax incentives.

The effect of transfer programs on labor supply is of special interest because both the substitution and income effects operate in the same direction. The higher initial level of income provided by the transfer reduces the need for work, and the reduction of the transfer payment as private earnings rise reduces the net realized wage rate. Differing views on the magnitude of the labor supply response to these transfer programs lie behind much of the controversy about unemployment programs and other forms of low-income assistance.

The empirical evidence on the importance of incentive effects is examined for saving and investment in chapters 3 and 4 and for labor supply in chapter 5. The empirical studies, to date, have not resolved these questions; but substantial progress has been made in narrowing the range of plausible values and in reconciling some of the differences among the studies. This is particularly true in the area of labor supply because of the opportunity to monitor the response of individuals to some of the transfer programs introduced during the 1970s.

Finally, even if it were possible to agree on the above issues, major disagreements about the design of policy would remain—particularly tax policy. In part, this is the result of the obvious fact that efficiency is not the only objective of government policy; equity issues also affect the choice between alternative tax and transfer systems. In addition, however, there are difficult problems of integrating supply-side concerns with demand-management policies, particularly during the period of transition. Neoclassical and supply-side economists, through their emphasis on the efficacy of private market adjustments, may minimize the problem or advocate a dichotomy of responsibility between fiscal and monetary policy. But for economists with a more Keynesian perspective, the coordination of fiscal and monetary policy plays a critical role in the process. They would, for example, argue that a program of monetary restraint to slow inflation is, of necessity, in conflict with a simultaneous effort to expand supply. These issues of policy are the subject of the final chapter.

CHAPTER TWO

The Role of Capital Formation

THE heightened concern with capital formation in recent years is a reflection of several developments. First, the sharp slowing of productivity growth, with its implications for smaller gains in real incomes, has emerged as a major economic problem. Although there is considerable disagreement on the extent to which lower rates of capital formation contributed to the shortfall of productivity, increased investment is often proposed as the cure. In addition, there is a concern that the United States lacks the industrial capacity to employ a work force that has expanded rapidly in the last decade. As a result, future efforts to provide enough jobs may be frustrated by the inflationary consequences of shortages and capacity constraints, particularly in the basic materials industries.

Second, there is a fairly widespread perception that investment has slowed over the last decade. Even that seemingly straightforward factual issue is the subject of substantial debate, however. Those who deny that such a slowdown has occurred point to the rise in the gross investment share of nonfarm business output, shown in the first two lines of table 2-1. Even the share of output devoted to net investment (the addition to the capital stock after deduction of depreciation of existing capital) is low only in comparison to the last half of the 1960s. The evidence of a capital shortfall, on the other hand, is most striking if the growth of the stock of plant and equipment is contrasted with the increase in the work force. Because the rapid expansion of the labor force during the 1970s was not matched by a similar acceleration of investment, the capital-labor ratio grew at an average annual rate of 0.6 percent between 1975 and 1980, compared with a 1950–70 average growth rate of about 3.5 percent (see last line of table 2-1).[1] The capital-labor ratio is highly

1. The shortfall of the capital-labor ratio from its trend growth reported in table 2-1 is substantially less than that reported in several other studies. The difference is largely accounted for by the emphasis here on the nonfarm economy. The shift of employment from farms to the nonfarm sector, which essentially ended in the mid-1960s, sharply

23

Table 2-1. *Alternative Measures of the Trend in Capital Formation of the Domestic Business Sector,*[a] *Five-Year Averages, 1951–80*

Measure	1951– 55	1956– 60	1961– 65	1966– 70	1971– 75	1976– 80
Gross fixed nonresidential investment as a percentage of gross output						
Current dollars	11.4	12.2	12.1	13.6	13.7	14.6
1972 dollars	11.7	11.9	12.3	13.9	13.6	14.5
Net fixed nonresidential investment as a percentage of net output						
Current dollars	3.8	3.5	4.0	5.6	4.4	4.3
1972 dollars	3.9	3.5	4.2	5.8	4.5	4.3
Net fixed nonresidential investment as a percentage of net capital stock[b]	4.1	3.5	4.2	5.7	4.0	3.8
Percentage change in the ratio of net capital stock to total business hours[b]	3.3	3.5	2.9	4.3	3.2	0.6

Sources: U.S. Department of Commerce, Bureau of Economic Analysis, *The National Income and Product Accounts of the United States, 1929–74 Statistical Tables,* a supplement to the *Survey of Current Business* (Government Printing Office, 1977), and subsequent reports, tables 1.9, 1.10, 5.2, 5.3, and 6.8B; and the Bureau of Labor Statistics.
a. Private business sector, excluding housing.
b. The nonresidential stock of equipment and structures valued in 1972 dollars.

sensitive to business cycle fluctuations, however; and on a cyclically adjusted basis the decline is somewhat smaller—a 1975–80 growth rate of 1.3 percent.

Finally, many economists have pointed out that taxation of capital income drives a wedge between the private (after-tax) return on capital and the social (before-tax) return. If saving and investment decisions are sensitive to their yield, the existence of taxes on capital income reduces the stock of capital available to the economy as a whole. Such an argument is less dependent upon evidence of a slowdown in investment because its advocates argue that investment in the United States has always been too low in comparison with other countries. Concern with this issue motivates proposals to exclude capital income from taxation. The supply of labor, however, is also influenced by taxes on wage income; and because the reduction of taxes on capital must be offset by

increases the pre-1970 growth in employment within the nonfarm sector relative to the total economy. The exclusion of the farm sector has little effect, however, on the growth of the capital stock. Inclusion of farms increases the magnitude of slowdown in the capital-labor ratio by about 0.8 percent annually during the 1970s.

greater taxation of labor, such changes in the tax system cannot be evaluated simply by considering the benefits of more capital.

This chapter concentrates on several interrelated issues that surround the question of the adequacy of the current rate of capital formation and the role of capital in economic growth. What role has capital played in the productivity slowdown? Is there a significant capacity problem? How much would productivity rise if the investment share of total output were increased? Do trends in the return on capital support the argument of an inadequate rate of investment? This chapter thus evaluates the economic arguments in favor of a higher future rate of capital formation. The question of whether government policies can influence capital formation is postponed to the following chapters.

A Slowdown in Productivity Growth

The slowdown in the growth of productivity has been documented by many studies.[2] The rate of increase in output per man-hour, after averaging about 3 percent annually during the 1950s and most of the 1960s, fell off to about 2 percent annually in the early 1970s, diminished further in the middle of the decade, and actually turned negative after 1978. It has been more difficult, however, to agree on the causes of that slowdown, and, of particular importance here, to identify the contribution of capital.

Most of the major issues can be highlighted by focusing on the private nonfarm nonresidential sector of the economy. Thus, farming, government (where no measures of productivity are available), nonprofit institutions, and all housing (tenant and owner-occupied) are excluded.[3]

2. Edward F. Denison, *Accounting for Slower Economic Growth: The United States in the 1970s* (Brookings Institution, 1979); Barbara M. Fraumeni and Dale Jorgenson, "Capital Formation and U.S. Productivity Growth, 1948–1976," in Ali Dogramaci, ed., *Productivity Analysis: A Range of Perspectives* (Martinus Nijhoff Publishing, 1981), pp. 49–70; John W. Kendrick, "Productivity Trends and the Recent Slowdown: Historical Perspective, Causal Factors, and Policy Options," in William Fellner, ed., *Contemporary Economic Problems, 1979* (American Enterprise Institute for Public Policy Research, 1979), pp. 17–69; J. R. Norsworthy, Michael J. Harper, and Kent Kunze, "The Slowdown in Productivity Growth: Analysis of Some Contributing Factors," *Brookings Papers on Economic Activity, 2:1979*, pp. 387–421. (Hereafter *BPEA*.)

3. These definitional issues are important in measuring rates of growth in output, labor, and capital, where relatively small differences can be meaningful.

Table 2-2. *Rates of Growth in Output and Factor Inputs, Nonfarm Nonresidential Business, Selected Periods, 1948–80*

	Average annual rate of change		
Item	1948–67	1967–73	1973–80
Output	3.8	3.9	2.1
Factor inputs[a]	1.9	2.5	2.2
Capital and land[b]	3.6	4.3	4.0
Labor	1.2	1.8	1.7
Total factor productivity	1.9	1.4	−0.1
Capital-labor substitution	0.7	0.7	0.5
Labor productivity	2.6	2.1	0.5

Sources: Gross output and man-hour data are from the U.S. Department of Labor, Bureau of Labor Statistics. The stock of plant and equipment (excluding nonprofit institutions) and inventory data were obtained from the U.S. Department of Commerce, Bureau of Economic Analysis; they are midyear averages of the gross and net stock series. The physical stock of land is assumed to be unchanged over the period. Details of the calculation are provided in Barry P. Bosworth, "Capital Formation and Economic Policy," *Brookings Papers on Economic Activity, 2:1982,* pp. 273–317.

a. The index of total outputs is a weighted average of capital and labor inputs with factor income share weights.

b. The capital stock includes fixed nonresidential capital, inventories, and land with weights based on their shares of capital income. It differs from the definition in table 2-1 because of the inclusion of inventories and land.

A summary of productivity trends in this sector is shown in table 2-2. The choice of periods for comparison follows that of prior studies that found some evidence of a slowdown in productivity emerging after 1967 and a dramatic reduction after 1973. The analysis ends with 1980 because the subsequent deep recession introduces a large cyclical influence into the data.

The slower growth of labor productivity (output per man-hour) is clearly evident in the drop from an annual growth rate of 2.6 percent between 1948 and 1967 to 0.5 percent in the 1973–80 period. The error of associating that slowdown with capital alone, however, is immediately evident in the measure of multifactor productivity—output per unit of input where the inputs include capital, land, and labor. Such a measure avoids the mistake of identifying the substitution of one input for another with a change in efficiency per se. The contribution of capital-labor substitution, in fact, appears to have fallen only marginally, about 0.1 to 0.2 percentage point annually—from 0.7 to 0.5 percent.[4]

Trends in labor productivity growth can also be examined on a more disaggregated industry basis, as in table 2-3. The broad-based nature of the slowdown is evident in all the major industries except communica-

4. The role of capital formation is a critical issue that will be taken up in more detail in a later section. In addition, the extent of the productivity decline is overstated because 1980 was a recession year.

Table 2-3. *Rates of Labor Productivity Growth by Major Industrial Sector, Selected Periods, 1947–80*

Industry	Percentage of output (1972)	Average annual rate of change[a]		
		1947–67	1967–73	1973–80
Mining	2.1	4.2	1.5	−5.0
Construction	6.6	2.6	−1.4	−2.3
Manufacturing	32.7	2.7	3.4	1.7
Durables	19.3	2.3	2.8	1.7
Nondurables	13.3	3.2	4.4	1.7
Transportation	5.1	2.3	2.2	0.6
Communications	3.3	5.4	4.7	5.6
Utilities	3.2	6.2	3.5	0.8
Trade	22.3	2.5	2.5	1.0
Wholesale	9.3	2.9	3.6	0.4
Retail	13.0	2.2	1.8	1.2
Services	11.0	1.6	1.4	0.4
Government enterprises	2.0	−0.6	−0.2	1.3
Finance, insurance, and real estate	11.7	1.0	0.0	0.2
Private nonfarm business	100.0	2.6	2.1	0.5

Source: U.S. Department of Labor, Bureau of Labor Statistics.
a. Average annual percentage growth rate computed by least squares trend.

tions and suggests a common causal factor.[5] The declines in mining and construction, however, stand out.[6] Mining contributed 0.2 and construction 0.3 percentage point to the overall slowdown of output per manhour after 1973. The drop in labor productivity within mining was in part the result of higher energy prices, which stimulated the exploration of more marginal situations. Within the petroleum industry, for example, there was a sharp rise in the number of oil wells drilled, but a fall in the ratio of new reserves per well drilled; and production is declining in old wells. Labor costs per unit of output have, therefore, increased substantially. In addition, new health and safety regulations in the 1970s increased labor requirements in underground mining. The coal industry

5. This conclusion is reinforced by data at the more detailed level of the three- and four-digit Standard Industrial Classification. The U.S. Bureau of Labor Statistics reports that three-fourths of its sample of industries had slower growth in labor productivity during 1974–79 than in 1947–74. See U.S. Department of Labor, Bureau of Labor Statistics, *Productivity Measures for Selected Industries, 1954–79,* Bulletin 2093 (Government Printing Office, 1981), p. 2.

6. The distribution of the productivity slowdown among industries is examined in Martin Neil Baily, "The Productivity Growth Slowdown by Industry," *BPEA, 2:1982,* pp. 423–54.

was also plagued with poor labor-management relations, reflected in wildcat strikes that frequently disrupted production.

The sustained decline of output per man-hour in the construction industry is more puzzling. If the data are correct, labor productivity in construction has fallen to the levels of 1953. Suspicions about the accuracy of the data, however, are strengthened by noting that data revisions in 1981 eliminated two-thirds of the decline that was previously estimated for the 1967–73 period. Revisions of this magnitude are possible because the estimate of the value added by each industry requires the computation of both gross output and purchased inputs on a constant-dollar basis. Errors in estimating inputs or outputs of one industry can distort the estimate of others even though they cancel in the aggregate data. Concern with this problem has limited most studies of productivity to the aggregates, and great caution is required in the use of any detailed industry statistics.

A recent study of trends in output and productivity growth in different regions of the United States also found a pervasive slowing of productivity growth after 1973. While rates of manufacturing output growth varied substantially among nine major regions, those differences were almost fully explained by differences in the growth of capital and labor inputs. Multifactor productivity has grown at least as fast in the Snow Belt as in the Sun Belt. On the other hand, the slowdown of productivity growth after 1973 is common to all.[7]

Causes of the Slowdown

While existing studies have documented the magnitude and pervasiveness of the slowdown of productivity, they have been unable to provide a full understanding of its causes. The studies have been useful, however, in highlighting both the complex process by which gains in efficiency are achieved and the multitude of contributing factors Most of the existing studies have used an accounting framework that groups the determinants of labor productivity growth into five major categories:

1. Improvements in the quality of labor, including education, health, and work experience;

7. Charles R. Hulten and Robert M. Schwab, "Regional Productivity Growth in U.S. Manufacturing: 1951–78," *American Economic Review*, vol. 74 (March 1984), pp. 152–62.

Table 2-4. *Estimates of Sources of the Productivity Slowdown in the Nonfarm Nonresidential Business Economy*[a]

Source	Average annual percentage change
Factors contributing to the slowdown	
Capital-labor substitution	0.1–0.2
Labor quality	0.1–0.2
Regulation	0.2–0.3
Research and development	0.1–0.3
Energy	0.1–0.2
Sectoral shifts	0.0–0.1
Residual	1.0–0.5
Total decline in trend growth	1.6
Cyclical influence	0.5
Total decline in labor productivity growth	2.1

Sources: Table 2-2 and text.
a. The slowdown is defined as the difference in the average annual growth of labor productivity between 1948–67 (2.6 percent) and 1973–80 (0.5 percent), as shown in table 2-2.

2. Increases in the quantity of capital per worker (broadly defined to include land and other natural resources);

3. Technological advances, which may or may not be embodied in new capital;

4. Improved resource allocation, including the shift of labor to higher productivity sectors; and

5. Economies of scale and other management aspects of production, including changes in the regulatory environment.[8]

Those studies have provided a partial list of the identifiable factors responsible for the productivity growth slowdown. The factors are shown in table 2-4, together with an estimate of the change in their contribution to the change in labor productivity growth during 1973–80 compared to

8. The growth accounting framework was developed in its most detailed applications by Edward F. Denison. The data used in this presentation differ from those of Denison's study because he uses national income per worker rather than gross product per man-hour. He also favors a smaller cyclical adjustment. As a result, he obtains a larger total decline in productivity growth and a residual of 1.6 percentage points compared to the 0.5 to 1.0 range reported in table 2-3. I have used the gross output concept because of its greater comparability to other studies. The estimated magnitude of the contribution of the noncyclical factors is very similar to those reported by Denison. For a recent set of estimates see Edward F. Denison, "The Interruption of Productivity Growth in the United States," *The Economic Journal,* vol. 93 (March 1983), pp. 56–77.

1948–67.[9] Of the total slowdown in the annual growth rate of 2.1 percentage points, about half can be traced to identifiable factors and half remains as a residual, a source of debate and a measure of economists' ignorance. The key factors are as follows.

CYCLICAL INFLUENCES. Output per man-hour fluctuates widely over the business cycle because firms do not fully adjust their work force to short-run changes in production. As a result, the growth in productivity must be measured over periods with end points in years of equivalent resource utilization, or else the data must be adjusted to remove the cyclical factor. This issue is of small concern over a span as long as 1947–67, but cyclical factors dominated the path of the economy between 1973 (a boom year) and 1980 (a year of recession). A recent study by Baily used a simple regression to derive a cyclically adjusted productivity series, using the unemployment rate as a measure of cyclical conditions.[10] The estimates in table 2-4 extend his methodology through 1980.

CAPITAL INPUTS. The rapid growth of the labor force during the 1970s was not matched by an acceleration in the rate of capital accumulation. The growth of the capital-labor ratio within the nonfarm business economy slowed from 2.4 percent annually in 1948–67 to 2.2 percent in 1973–80. Weighted by capital's share in total income, the slower growth of the capital-labor ratio contributed only about 0.15 percentage point to the slowdown in labor productivity growth (table 2-2). Because 1980 was a recession year in which employment declined relative to capital, the secular slowing of the capital-labor ratio is understated. A cyclical adjustment that parallels that for labor productivity raises the estimate of the contribution of capital to the productivity slowdown to 0.2 percent annually.[11] This estimate still is substantially smaller than that found in

9. This approach follows the presentation in William D. Nordhaus, "Policy Responses to the Productivity Slowdown," in *The Decline in Productivity Growth*, conference series no. 22 (Federal Reserve Bank of Boston, 1980), pp. 147–72. The actual values are different because this study focuses on the nonfarm business sector rather than the total private economy, and there is a slight difference in the time period.

10. Martin Neil Baily, "Productivity and the Services of Capital and Labor," *BPEA*, *1:1981*, pp. 2–5. His methodology appears to yield a somewhat larger estimate of the cyclical factor during the 1973–80 period than the techniques of Denison and others.

11. The measure of the slowdown in the capital-labor ratio is much smaller than reported in table 2-1 for the 1975–80 period. In part, the difference is due to the period of measurement. There is a larger cyclical employment gain if the period of measurement begins with the 1975 recession. In addition, the measure of capital reported in table 2-2 includes inventories and land, and the plant and equipment data are adjusted for changes in the durability of the capital being purchased. See Barry P. Bosworth, "Capital Formation and Economic Policy," *BPEA*, *2:1982*, pp. 277–85.

several of the studies that were surveyed and will require more comment in a later section.

LABOR QUALITY. The shift in the composition of the labor force toward younger and less experienced workers is often cited in discussions of the productivity issue. As Denison points out, however, the changing composition of the labor force is not a sudden development. It has held down the growth of productivity throughout most of the postwar period, and it contributes very little to the explanation of the break in productivity growth in the 1970s. Furthermore, these demographic shifts have been offset by continued gains in education and other aspects of labor quality.[12]

On balance, the Denison study concluded that changes in labor quality did not contribute to the slowdown. Baily, on the other hand, attributed 0.3 percentage point to a decline in labor quality. The difference lies in their interpretation of the influence of education, with Baily arguing that increases in years of schooling did not imply equivalent increases in labor productivity.

REGULATION. Government regulations to improve the environment and worker health and safety have increased business costs without being fully reflected in the measured value of output. Current output may be understated, or past output overstated, by the negative value of environmental damage. Either way, it is difficult to make such a quality adjustment to output. Most efforts to measure the effect of regulations on productivity have concentrated on the added capital and labor input costs. A few studies have looked at productivity growth in specific industries that are heavily affected by regulation. In general, the studies suggest a contribution to the slowdown of 0.2 to 0.3 percentage point.[13] The studies have not gone beyond measuring the extra input costs; the new regulatory environment may also impose costs in terms of delay of new projects and licensing costs.

12. The measures of productivity used in this study are based on hours paid rather than hours worked. There has been a growing gap between these two concepts, as workers receive longer paid holidays and sick leave; but again the available data indicate that the trend is not accelerating. The computation of productivity on an hours-worked basis would yield a higher estimated growth rate in all periods, but it would not alter the magnitude of the slowdown significantly.

13. Denison, *Accounting for Slower Economic Growth*, pp. 67–74, 127–31; Gregory B. Christainsen and Robert H. Haveman, "Public Regulations and the Slowdown in Productivity Growth," *American Economic Review*, vol. 72 (May 1981, *Papers and Proceedings, 1980*), pp. 320–25; Robert W. Crandall, "Regulation and Productivity Growth," in *The Decline in Productivity Growth*, pp. 93–111; and Norsworthy, Harper, and Kunze, "The Slowdown in Productivity Growth," pp. 404–05.

RESEARCH AND DEVELOPMENT. It is extremely difficult to quantify the influence of research and development (R&D) on productivity. Many studies have simply included it in the residual. Yet a slowdown in technological innovation seems to have captured the public's fancy as a convenient explanation of the shortfall of productivity growth. Data are available to measure total R&D expenditures, but much of that activity is undoubtedly directed at the development of new products; little is known about the proportion of the expenditures that is directed toward enhancing productivity. The public component is also dominated by defense research, where efficiency of production is not a major objective. Expenditures on R&D rose throughout most of the postwar period, peaked in 1964 at about 3 percent of GNP, and slowly declined thereafter as a share of GNP to about 2 percent in the late 1970s.[14] The decline is due exclusively to lower R&D for defense and space exploration: expenditures for both private R&D and government civilian projects have continued to rise relative to GNP.

Some studies treat R&D expenses as being comparable to capital. That is, annual outlays on R&D are cumulated to form a stock, and the stock is combined with an estimate of the rate of return to obtain an estimated flow of productive services. Both Kendrick and Griliches have undertaken studies based on such a methodology.[15] Kendrick concluded that the slower growth of R&D had reduced the growth of productivity by about 0.3 percentage point and that an overall slowing of advances in knowledge contributed 0.6 percentage point. Griliches found a much smaller effect of only about 0.1 to 0.2 percentage point in manufacturing.

These differences can be traced to Kendrick's use of a very broad definition of R&D (including defense), his assumption that it is all directed to productivity enhancement, and his use of an estimated rate of return of 50 percent before 1966 with a decline to 40 percent after 1973. Public-sector R&D—included in the Kendrick data—declined sharply as a share of GNP, yet it probably has the weakest link to productivity growth. In addition, the assumed reduction in the rate of return after 1973 implies a

14. John W. Kendrick, "International Comparisons of Recent Productivity Trends," in William Fellner, ed., *Essays in Contemporary Economic Problems: Demand, Productivity, and Population* (American Enterprise Institute for Public Policy Research, 1981), p. 157.

15. Kendrick, "Productivity Trends and the Recent Slowdown," pp. 37–39; and Zvi Griliches, "R&D and the Productivity Slowdown," *American Economic Review*, vol. 70 (May 1980, *Papers and Proceedings, 1979*), pp. 343–48.

20 percent decline in the flow of services from any given stock of R&D. The measurement of the rate of return, much less the extent of any decline, is based on very tenuous data. Kendrick's procedure probably overestimates the contribution of reduced R&D to the productivity decline.[16]

The evaluation of technological trends also should take account of a wide range of information other than total R&D expenditures. One such review found a very mixed picture:

It is possible to paint a uniformly negative (or positive) picture of U.S. industrial innovation only through a selective use of indicators. . . . The use of a broad range of innovation indicators demonstrates the complexity of innovation and its socioeconomic effects, and underscores the futility of identifying a single innovation problem.[17]

ENERGY. Higher energy prices are another popular explanation for the slowdown because the major breaks in productivity growth correspond with the surge of energy prices in 1973 and 1979. And, at least potentially, higher energy prices could have a major effect on labor productivity by slowing the substitution of energy and capital for labor. It is difficult, however, to find evidence that higher energy prices have contributed in a major way to the post-1973 slowdown. If increased labor inputs were a response to the need to economize on energy, there should have been a comparable drop in energy use within the business sector. Energy represents only about 5 percent of production costs, however, and the decline in energy use is only a small proportion of the rise in labor inputs.[18] If higher energy prices discouraged the substitution of capital for labor, it should have been captured in the measure of the capital-labor ratio.[19] Higher energy prices, however, may have been one

16. Some of the measurement difficulties are discussed more fully in Zvi Griliches, "Issues in Assessing the Contribution of Research and Development to Productivity Growth," *Bell Journal of Economics,* vol. 10 (Spring 1979), pp. 92–116.

17. *Technology and Trade: Some Indicators of the State of U.S. Industrial Innovation,* Committee Print, House Committee on Ways and Means, 96 Cong. 2 sess. (GPO, 1980), p. 34.

18. Ernst R. Berndt, "Energy Price Increases and the Productivity Slowdown in United States Manufacturing," in *The Decline in Productivity Growth,* pp. 60–89. Also see George L. Perry, "Potential Output: Recent Issues and Present Trends," in Center for the Study of American Business, *U.S. Productive Capacity: Estimating the Utilization Gap,* Working Paper 23 (St. Louis: CSAB, 1977), pp. 6–13 (Brookings Reprint No. 336).

19. A different argument is made by Michael Bruno, who attributes much of the productivity growth decline to a rise in petroleum and other raw material prices, which leads to a bias in the calculation of value-added output. See Michael Bruno, "Raw Materials, Profits and the Productivity Slowdown," National Bureau of Economic

34   TAX INCENTIVES AND ECONOMIC GROWTH

among a series of factors that led to more rapid obsolescence of existing capital.

SECTORAL SHIFTS. The story about a shift to a service economy, with its lower average productivity, is about the decline of agriculture and the growth of government, and is not relevant to the nonfarm business sector. Within the private nonfarm economy no shift of output to services has occurred. Moreover, the characterization of the service sector as one of low productivity is inaccurate for such a heterogeneous group of industries. A Bureau of Labor Statistics study concluded that shifts in the nonfarm industrial mix of output had had a trivial effect on the growth of labor productivity.[20] Sectoral shifts between the farm and nonfarm sectors, however, are a very important aspect of the change in labor productivity of the total private economy. In the period from 1948 to 1967, the shift of workers from farms to the industrial sector added 0.6 percentage point to the annual growth rate. After 1973 its contribution was essentially zero.

RESIDUAL. The estimates of the magnitudes of the various factors contributing to the productivity slowdown leave room for controversy. Yet it is clear that under a wide range of possible estimates a substantial proportion of the slowdown of productivity growth remains as an unexplained residual. It is also evident that a slower rate of capital formation cannot account for a major portion of the shortfall. Moreover, the review is useful for highlighting the complexity of the growth process and the large number of contributing factors. Education and R&D, for example, have traditionally been areas of extensive government involvement. If they played a major role in the slowdown, the prescription for future policy would be quite different from recent actions to reduce government financing in those areas and to expand tax incentives for private capital formation.

Research Working Paper 660 (revised) (Cambridge, Mass.: NBER, 1982), forthcoming in *Quarterly Journal of Economics*. His empirical work applies only to manufacturing, however. His argument as it applies to the measurement of productivity is refuted in Martin N. Baily, "Gross Output, Value-Added, and the Effect of Materials Prices on Productivity Growth" (Brookings Institution, April 1983).

20. For an analysis of data through 1976, see Jerome A. Mark, "Productivity Trends and Prospects," in *Special Study on Economic Change,* Hearings before the Joint Economic Committee, 95 Cong. 2 sess. (GPO, 1978), p. 478. A similar conclusion based on more recent data is reported in Baily, "The Productivity Growth Slowdown by Industry," pp. 445–52.

Most of the controversy focuses on the role of capital in the slowdown. The issue is discussed in more detail below.

The Measurement of Capital Services

While most productivity studies have concluded that changes in capital formation did not play a major role in the post-1973 slowdown, the role of capital continues to be at the center of the public policy discussions. Obviously, not everyone agrees. One source of the continuing dispute revolves around measurement issues. Unfortunately, direct information on the flow of capital services comparable to that on the hours worked by labor is not available. As a result, studies of the role of capital in productivity growth have been forced to infer the magnitude of such services by assuming they are related to some measure of the stock of capital. Direct measures of the existing stock of depreciable assets (equipment and structure) are also not available and one must rely upon "perpetual-inventory" estimates that cumulate investment outlays over long time periods and subtract estimated depreciation. This methodology provides two alternative series: a gross stock, which incorporates a unit of capital at its full value until the day it is discarded (sometimes referred to as a "one-hoss-shay" assumption); and a net stock, in which the value of a unit of capital is reduced by the amount of assumed depreciation in each time period.

The net-stock concept is appropriate when the objective is to measure something approximating market value: the income-producing capacity of capital equipment clearly declines as it ages because of the shortening of the remaining period of its useful life. The Department of Commerce produces just such an adjustment by computing the net stock with an assumed straight-line pattern of equal amounts of depreciation in each period of an asset's useful life.

On the other hand, while simple aging and technical obsolescence both provide justifications for declining valuations of the capital stock, they do not imply a decline in the annual flow of services or the output-producing capacity of capital. Disagreements about capital's pattern of decline in efficiency with age have led to a range of alternative estimates of the effective flow of capital services. The use of the net capital stock, based on straight-line depreciation, as an index of capital services implies that the service flow has fallen by one-half at the midpoint of the asset's life. This adjustment strikes a few investigators as too rapid; they advocate use of the gross stock, for which the service flow is constant throughout the asset's life, or some average of the gross and net stocks. On the other hand, others go even further in the other direction and use some assumption of accelerated decline in the efficiency of capital as it ages, such as geometric depreciation.[21]

The flow of capital services is also difficult to measure by reference to the stock of capital when there are variations over time in the mix of investment between short and long-lived assets. A shift toward less durable capital (such as occurred during the 1970s) increases the ratio of capital services to the stock: a $100 machine lasting five years must provide an annual gross service flow substantially above that of a $100 machine lasting ten years. The use of the gross capital stock as an index of the service flow misses this change in durability, and the net capital stock actually declines because of the deduction of a larger estimate of depreciation.[22]

The empirical importance of these measurement issues was examined in an earlier paper.[23] While different assumptions do alter the estimated growth of capital services in various subintervals of the postwar period, they are not sufficient to change the estimates of capital's contribution to the post-1973 productivity slowdown by more than a few tenths of a percentage point.

21. This issue is developed in far more detail in the discussion between Edward F. Denison, Zvi Griliches, and Dale W. Jorgenson, "The Measurement of Productivity," special issue of the *Survey of Current Business*, vol. 52 (May 1972, pt. 2) (Brookings Reprint 244). Although a net capital stock might be combined with a net output measure (exclusive of capital-consumption allowances), it is more difficult to justify the combination of a net capital stock and a gross measure of output. At the same time, some decline of the service flow over time seems appropriate because repair and modernization expenditures are not included in the measure of output. Denison used a 3:1 weighted average of the gross and net capital stocks and combined it with a net output concept.

22. Alternatively, the change in durability of a given capital stock is reflected in the flow of capital-consumption allowances; hence, some investigators have suggested that capital-consumption allowances could be used as an index of the gross service flow. The change in durability is not a problem if the measure of productivity is based on output net of capital-consumption allowances, because the latter is reduced by the shift to less durable capital. Shifts in durability would not alter a measure of net capital services or of net output. Yet only Denison's among the major studies makes use of such an output concept.

23. Bosworth, "Capital Formation and Economic Policy," pp. 277–85. That paper adjusts for changes in the mix of capital between categories with differing service lives. It does not address the possibility that the average life of capital of a given type may have changed over the postwar period.

Other differences in classification and presentation are of greater importance. Several studies subtract pollution abatement equipment from the capital measure.[24] Regulatory effects are classified separately in table 2-4 and there appears to be no strong reason to associate them with capital alone. If such adjustments were made, they should be applied to both capital and labor. Some other studies include farms, nonprofit institutions, and tenant housing. While these sectors seem unrelated to the policy debate over business investment, they account for a large proportion of the slowdown in capital formation.

The importance of these issues of classification is illustrated by a comparison with a study by Baily.[25] He reports a reduction of growth in the net capital-labor ratio from an annual rate of 3.6 percent in 1948–68 to 1.3 percent in 1973–79 for the total private business economy (including farms)—a slowdown of 2.3 percentage points. The comparable estimate in this study of the nonfarm business economy would be a slowdown of 0.5 percentage point.[26] How can these differences be reconciled? First, while the exclusion of the farm sector has little impact on the growth rate of the capital stock, it does change the growth of labor in the 1948–68 period: most of the increased labor demand of the nonfarm sector was met by drawing workers off the farms. This shift off the farms ended during the 1970s and has had little effect on the subsequent data. Thus the growth of labor inputs accelerated for the private sector from 0.4 percent annually in 1948–68 to 1.9 percent in 1973–79, primarily a reflection of the entrance of the postwar baby boom into the labor force. Meanwhile, the growth of labor inputs in the nonfarm business sector rose from 1.2 to 2.1 percent annually. This difference of sector definitions changes the magnitude of the slowdown in the growth of the capital-labor ratio by about 0.6 percentage point even though the growth rates of the two capital stocks are nearly equal.

Second, in the study by Baily nonprofit institutions (private schools, hospitals, and research organizations), whose investment slowed sharply

24. See, for example, Norsworthy, Harper, and Kunze, "The Slowdown in Productivity Growth," pp. 404–05, 416. The deduction of pollution abatement capital reduces the post-1973 annual growth rate of the capital by about 0.5 percentage point.

25. Baily, "Productivity and the Services of Capital and Labor," p. 7. His estimates exclude inventories and land and use the net-stock concept of capital.

26. Table 2-2 reports an even smaller amount of deceleration, but that is based on an average of the gross and net capital stocks. The net stock shows a larger deceleration for reasons reported in Bosworth, "Capital Formation and Economic Policy," pp. 282–84.

38   TAX INCENTIVES AND ECONOMIC GROWTH

in the 1970s, were included in the capital stock data although excluded from the output measure, and the capital stock was not adjusted for changes in its durability. These two factors reduce the magnitude of the overall slowdown by another 0.6 percentage point. The remaining differences can be traced to data revisions and this study's inclusion of inventories and land in the measure of the capital stock.[27]

International Comparisons

International data highlight several interesting facets of the productivity puzzle. First, the slowdown since 1973 is not unique to the United States. As shown in table 2-5, it is a common phenomenon in nine major industrial countries for which data are available. While the United States ranked last among the surveyed countries in growth of productivity between 1960 and 1973, it actually improved its ranking in the post-1973 period because the slowdown was larger in several other countries.

Second, the slowdown of productivity growth in other countries, like that in the United States, cannot be explained by a slower rate of capital formation.[28] The sharp drop in the growth rate after 1973 is as apparent in the measure of multifactor productivity (capital plus labor) as in labor productivity alone; in fact, output per unit of capital actually fell in all nine countries.

In addition, the extent of the productivity decline in other countries casts serious doubt on the notion that the problem in the United States was the outgrowth of a rapid expansion of the labor force (and the associated decline in growth of the capital-labor ratio). The growth of the work force slowed in Europe and Japan after 1973.

A study by Kendrick reached the same conclusion for the international economy as was noted earlier for the United States: only about half of

27. Several analyses have stressed the decline of net investment as a share of GNP or the slower growth of the net capital stock in emphasizing capital as a source of the productivity slowdown. See, for example, the *Economic Report of the President,* February 1983, pp. 78–80. Such measures show a substantial decline because of a shift in the mix of investment to shorter-lived assets. But such measures of the capital input actually increase the problem of explaining the slowdown in productivity as being caused by slower growth in capital services, because the shift to short-lived assets increases the ratio of the annual flow of gross capital services to the stock of capital.

28. Capital-labor substitution—as reported in table 2-5—does make a larger contribution to the productivity slowdown than was reported earlier because the Kendrick study is based on the total business economy (including farms).

Table 2-5. *Annual Average Rates of Change in Gross Product, Factor Inputs, and Productivity in the Business Economies of Nine Countries, 1960–73 and 1973–79*

Country	Gross business product	Factor inputs			Productivity		
		Total	Labor	Capital	Total	Labor	Capital
United States							
1960–73	4.4	2.5	1.3	4.5	1.9	3.1	−0.1
1973–79	2.9	2.3	1.8	3.1	0.6	1.1	−0.2
Canada							
1960–73	5.8	2.9	1.6	4.7	2.9	4.2	1.1
1973–79	3.2	3.3	2.2	4.8	−0.1	1.0	−1.6
Japan							
1960–73	10.8	4.2	0.9	10.9	6.6	9.9	0.1
1973–79	4.2	2.4	0.4	6.4	1.8	3.8	−2.2
United Kingdom							
1960–73	2.9	0.7	−0.9	3.6	2.2	3.8	−0.7
1973–79	0.5	0.2	−1.4	3.1	0.3	1.9	−2.6
France							
1960–73	5.8	1.9	−0.1	5.1	3.9	5.9	0.7
1973–79	3.2	1.1	−1.0	4.3	2.1	4.2	−1.1
West Germany							
1960–73	4.6	1.4	−1.2	6.1	3.2	5.8	−1.5
1973–79	2.2	0.1	−2.1	4.1	2.1	4.2	−1.1
Italy							
1960–73	5.6	−0.2	−2.2	4.3	5.8	7.8	1.3
1973–79	2.6	1.8	1.0	3.4	0.8	1.6	−0.8
Sweden							
1960–73	4.2	0.6	−1.6	4.1	3.6	5.8	0.1
1973–79	0.1	−0.5	−2.3	2.7	2.6	4.4	−0.6
Belgium							
1960–73	5.3	1.1	−0.8	4.4	4.2	6.1	0.9
1973–79	2.1	−0.5	−2.3	2.7	2.6	4.4	−0.6

Source: John W. Kendrick, "International Comparisons of Recent Productivity Trends," in William Fellner, ed., *Essays in Contemporary Economic Problems: Demand, Productivity and Population* (American Enterprise Institute for Public Policy Research, 1981), p. 128.

the growth slowdown can be explained by the enumerated factors of a growth accounting exercise.[29] That is, elsewhere as in the United States, the productivity slowdown remains, in substantial part, a mystery.

Nevertheless, the international data provide the basis for the contention in several studies that capital has a larger impact on output growth

29. Kendrick, "International Comparisons of Recent Productivity Trends," pp. 125–70.

than is allowed for in the growth accounting studies.[30] The assertion is based on statistical correlations of productivity growth with the investment share of output or rates of change in the capital-labor ratio among countries.[31] Such statistical comparisons of growth in capital formation and growth in output per man-hour often yield marginal coefficients of 0.75–1.0: that is, countries with high investment-GNP ratios have high rates of growth in labor productivity.

The effort to infer causation from such correlation studies is fraught with difficulties. There are substantial reasons for believing that the causation runs in the opposite direction (that is, high rates of output growth stimulate investment). In fact, a regression analysis of data for the nine countries listed in table 2-5 indicates a closer correlation of investment shares with the growth in output than with the growth in labor productivity for both 1960–73 and 1973–79. In addition, other favorable factors, such as technological innovation, can contribute to the growth of both output and capital without requiring a causal link from capital to output. Statistical studies that have attempted to take account of lags as a means of identifying the direction of causation generally find that the estimate of capital's contribution to output growth is not greater than that used in the growth accounting studies.[32] The break in productivity growth after 1973 has provided direct evidence of the dangers of inferring causation from simple statistical correlations between growth in productivity and the capital-labor ratio. While the latter has slowed in the United States, it has not in other countries; yet all have experienced a sharp slowing of the former.

It also has been suggested that capital formation is more important than implied in the growth accounting studies because new technology

30. The usual practice in the accounting studies is to multiply an index of growth in the capital stock by capital's share of total income in obtaining an estimate of its contribution to total output. In the United States, the capital-income share implies that a 1 percent increase in the stock of plant and equipment would raise nonfarm business output by about 0.2 percent. In other countries, the marginal contribution varies between 0.2 and 0.3 percent.

31. See, for example, Michael K. Evans, "An Econometric Model Incorporating the Supply-Side Effects of Economic Policy," in Laurence H. Meyer, ed., *The Supply-Side Effects of Economic Policy* (Boston: Kluwer-Nijhoff, 1981), pp. 50–51; and Kendrick, "International Comparisons of Recent Productivity Trends," pp. 139–43. Evans goes so far as to state: "We find almost a perfect correlation between the proportion of GNP spent on fixed investment and the growth in productivity."

32. Richard H. Franke and John A. Miller, "Investment for Economic Growth: Evaluation of Conflicting Evidence" (Loyola College and Bucknell University, 1982).

is embodied in new capital, and higher rates of capital formation speed up the incorporation of technological change. The fallacy of that argument for small changes in the rate of capital formation was effectively pointed out by Denison.[33] He reasoned that capital investments that represent a radical improvement over those previously available will be the first undertaken in any period, and any reasonable amount of gross investment will incorporate the best of such opportunities. As a result, marginal increases in investment levels will involve relatively small quality gains. In addition, the embodiment of technology in new capital implies a faster obsolescence of existing capital. In effect, while the introduction of new technology may require capital investment, it does not follow that an increase in investment at the margin increases technological innovation.

Residual Explanations

At this time, economic studies have not been able to provide a complete account of the causes of the productivity slowdown. Yet there are many potential explanations that have not been explored in detail because of difficulties in quantifying the arguments. Denison has discussed seventeen such candidates.[34]

An argument by Baily is of particular interest. He suggested that the unforeseen economic disruptions of the last decade led to misallocations of capital and accelerated its rate of obsolescence. Those disruptions included changes in energy prices and patterns of international trade and competitiveness and other factors that led to a significant restructuring of relative prices and thus the optimal distribution of capital within the economy.[35] If existing capital was not completely adaptable, it may have been prematurely retired or used less intensively. Yet, because existing estimates of the capital stock are based on a perpetual-inventory cumulation of past investment rather than direct measurement, they cannot

33. Edward F. Denison, "The Unimportance of the Embodied Question," *American Economic Review*, vol. 54 (March 1964, pt. 1), pp. 90–94.

34. Edward F. Denison, "Accounting for Slower Economic Growth: An Update," presented at the Conference on International Comparisons of Productivity and Causes of the Slowdown held at the American Enterprise Institute for Public Policy Research, Washington, D.C., September 30, 1982.

35. This hypothesis is different from the previous story of a simple substitution of labor for energy—an argument that the data refutes.

reflect such changes. The result may have been an overstatement of the effective amount of capital services.[36]

Baily did not have direct evidence of a faster rate of obsolescence, but he pointed to the decline in the market value of corporations relative to the replacement cost of their assets as being consistent with such a hypothesis. If, as is sometimes claimed, the slower growth of productivity resulted from slower technical progress, the market value of firms should have increased, because a slower rate of technical change lowers the rate of depreciation of existing capital and preserves its value. That is, the stock market should rise if there has been a depletion of knowledge and it should fall if there has been a depletion of capital. His interpretation is also consistent with the fact that the sharp fall in the stock market during the 1970s was not reflected in lower investment: he argues that the decline is in the effectiveness of existing capital, not that of new capital.[37]

At the present time it is difficult to assess the importance of the obsolescence hypothesis. There is very little direct information on either retirement or utilization of existing capital. What information does exist points in the direction of somewhat faster obsolescence of capital in the 1970s, but the magnitude appears small. The most striking support for the hypothesis comes from independent surveys of business firms' estimates of their existing capacity. Those surveys report a level of industrial capacity that is significantly lower than that anticipated by an extrapolation of the historical relationship between capacity and the capital stock.[38] In addition, Baily finds some evidence that the magnitude of the productivity slowdown is larger in the more capital-intensive industries.[39]

The obsolescence hypothesis is appealing from a policy perspective. It suggests that the shortfall of productivity growth will correct itself in future years if major disruptions to the economy can be avoided. The

36. Baily, "Productivity and the Services of Capital and Labor."

37. An argument consistent with Baily's is made by Michael Bruno. He argues that the slow growth of demand during the 1970s inhibited the structural adjustments called for by the sharp changes in relative prices during the 1970s. He does not maintain that the adjustment problems are reflected only in capital, however. Michael Bruno, "World Shocks, Macroeconomic Response, and the Productivity Puzzle," in R. C. O. Matthews, ed., *Slower Growth in the Western World* (London: Heinemann Educational Books, 1982), pp. 83–104.

38. Bosworth, "Capital Formation and Economic Policy," pp. 286–90.

39. Baily, "The Productivity Slowdown by Industry," pp. 437–41.

destruction of old capital creates a strong demand for replacement investment.

Alternatively, some economists have been increasingly dissatisfied with the growth accounting framework for the analysis of economic growth, believing that it has reached the stage of diminishing returns and that many interesting phenomena are ignored by the underlying neoclassical theory. The neoclassical model defines an equilibrium, full-employment growth path for the economy. If the forces pushing the actual economy toward an equilibrium are relatively weak, viewing growth as a succession of equilibria may be inadequate. These criticisms are articulated in a recent article by Nelson.[40] He argues for an interpretation of economic growth as an evolutionary process dependent upon the institutional environment.

From a perspective such as Nelson's, the 1970s was a very difficult decade for business firms. The increased instability of the economic environment in which they operated significantly changed the issues of fundamental concern to business managers. In the 1960s they focused on reducing costs and expanding market share; in the 1970s they had to worry about the possible effect of new tax laws, how to comply with an expanding menu of government regulations, how to forecast the next shift in monetary policy, how to provide for an uncertain energy supply, and how to price in a world of high and varying inflation. One explanation for the productivity slowdown may be that, given the competing claims on their time, business managers devoted less effort to efficiency. It does seem that during the 1970s having a lobbyist in Washington, rather than reducing costs and increasing sales volume, was perceived as the key to higher profits. In effect, the increased complexity of the business environment and the competing claims on the scarce time of senior management suggest a slower development and incorporation of new knowledge into production—particularly in the informal area of learning by doing.

Government may have contributed to these problems. There was a substantial expansion of regulatory efforts. And the frequent shifts of

40. Richard R. Nelson, "Research on Productivity Growth and Productivity Differences: Dead Ends and New Departures," *Journal of Economic Literature*, vol. 19 (September 1981), pp. 1029–64. See, in particular, his discussion of the dynamics of technological advance and the role of the economic environment. A further discussion is provided in Richard R. Nelson and Sidney G. Winter, *An Evolutionary Theory of Economic Change* (Harvard University Press, 1982).

emphasis in policy, between stimulating economic activity to reduce unemployment and restraining it to reduce inflation, increased the instability of the economy.

Long-Term Growth and Capital Formation

The preceding discussion was largely concerned with the role of capital formation in the sudden slowing of productivity growth during the 1970s. Much of the current policy discussion, however, has emphasized a longer-term need for additional investment to foster economic growth. In that discussion there has been substantial confusion about the role of the saving rate (or equivalently, the share of output devoted to investment). Many of the participants apparently believe that an increase in the saving (investment) rate provides a means of permanently raising the rate of growth of output and labor productivity. In reality, however, the rate of saving has no effect on the steady-state growth of the economy. Instead, a rise in the saving rate shifts the economy to a higher *level* of output, and once the transition is complete the rate of growth is unaffected. This is a particularly important qualification in international comparisons of national saving rates and rates of GNP growth.

Confusion about the role of saving in the growth process results from misinterpretations of the link between the rate of saving (and investment) and growth in the capital stock. The growth in the capital stock is equal to new investment minus the depreciation that results as capital wears out or becomes obsolete. Initially, a rise in the investment rate will accelerate the growth of the capital stock. But increases in investment today also require that larger amounts of future investment must be set aside simply to maintain that larger stock. Depreciation will ultimately rise to absorb fully the higher investment; and thus there is no sustained effect on the growth of the capital stock. If saving, and thus investment, is assumed to be a constant share of total output, the long-run growth of the capital stock can only be maintained at a rate equal to that of output, regardless of whether the rate of saving is high or low.

The issue is more clearly illustrated by analyzing the effect of an increase in the *net* saving rate (after deducting depreciation). Initially the capital stock will grow more rapidly than output, but a rise in the capital stock implies a less than proportionate increase in output and therefore in the level of saving and investment. That is because there are diminishing returns to additional capital when the other inputs—technical change and the labor force—do not rise in step. At the same time, saving and investment expand at the rate of growth of output. The growth of capital must therefore slow to that of output for any fixed rate of saving.

This result is shown graphically in figure 2-1.There is a whole set of long-term growth paths for output (Y_1, Y_2, . . ., Y_n), parallel to one another, each of which corresponds to a specific saving (investment) rate. A rise in the investment rate will initially increase the stock of capital and raise the economy to a higher output path. During the transition from one output path to another, the period t_1 to t_2, the growth rate is increased. But over time the growth of the capital stock must eventually slow to that of output. In other words, a rise in the saving rate raises the *level* of capital and output, but it does not provide a means by which the economy can permanently grow faster. In the long run the growth rate of output and capital is constrained by the exogenously determined growth in the other inputs, labor, n, and technology, a. The process of adjustment is illustrated in figure 2-1 by the output growth path G_1G_2 that is associated with a change in the saving rate from s_1 to s_2.

The effect of higher rates on investment can also be illustrated numerically by calculating the output gain associated with a permanent increase of 1 percentage point in the net investment share of business output. That share has averaged about 4 percent in the postwar period (see table 2-1). At 1981 output levels the increased investment would amount to about $20 billion annually. If that capital earned the postwar average rate of return of 10 percent, net output would be increased by about $2 billion for each year of its existence. If the investment share is maintained at the new higher level, the benefits in terms of increased output would cumulate over time. The new equilibrium level of output with a 5 percent investment share (a 25 percent increase) would exceed the old output growth path (4 percent investment share) by about 5 to 6 percent.[41] At that point, the rate of growth of the capital stock and output would be the same as under the prior investment program.

The period of the transition to a higher growth path will stretch over

41. This calculation assumes a Cobb-Douglas production function with a capital income share of 0.20. The estimates of capital share of *net* output range from 0.15 to 0.20 for the United States. See Lawrence H. Summers, "Tax Policy on Corporate Investment," in Meyer, ed., *The Supply-Side Effects of Economic Policy*, p. 124.

Figure 2-1. *Illustrative Paths of Output and Its Rate of Growth at Alternative Saving Rates*

Output
(ratio scale)

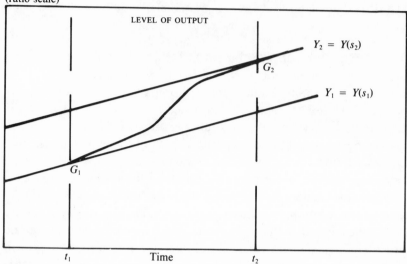

Output
(ratio scale)

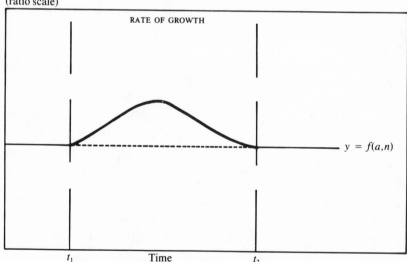

several years. Summers has provided some calculations of the effect on the growth rate of output during that transition.[42] His illustration showed that a doubling of the share of output devoted to net investment (from 4 to 8 percent) would raise the growth of output (and labor productivity) by 0.3 to 0.6 percent over the first decade.

Industrial Capacity

Traditionally, the unemployment rate has served as a summary measure of the overall utilization of resources within the economy. This is particularly true when it is used as an index of demand pressures on inflation. A substantial volume of research has been devoted to measuring the noninflationary unemployment rate—a rate of unemployment at which demand pressures neither add to nor decrease the rate of inflation. In recent years it has been argued that that target rate has increased because of demographic shifts and growing structural problems in the work force.

Far less attention has been given to the potential role of capacity shortages in product markets as a source of inflation. A reserve of the unemployed may be considered necessary to restrain inflation, but a reserve of industrial capacity may accomplish the same objective at less social cost.[43] The importance of this argument depends upon empirical evidence that demand pressures in product markets, independent of labor market conditions, have a significant influence on the rate of price inflation by altering the markup on prices over costs.[44] Certainly capacity restrictions have been important determinants of cyclical variations in

42. Ibid. pp. 124–27.

43. A different argument about the link between capital formation and inflation is made by those who see the reduction in inflation as being achieved through the mechanism of more rapid productivity growth. Higher productivity growth would reduce the increase in unit labor costs associated with any given wage increase. Critics of this argument point out that, while a gain of 1 percentage point in annual productivity growth would be a remarkable accomplishment, it seems small in comparison to annual inflation rates of 5 to 10 percent. It is reasonable to argue, however, that the greater gains in real incomes would substantially moderate pressures for larger nominal wage increases and thereby contribute to moderating inflation pressures by more than the direct effect on unit labor costs.

44. Robert J. Gordon, "The Impact of Aggregate Demand on Prices," *BPEA, 3:1975,* pp. 613–62.

raw material prices, but the markup over costs for finished goods seems to be quite insensitive to cyclical variations in demand.

The 1978 annual report of the Council of Economic Advisers (CEA) argued that the United States was faced with a growing imbalance of capacity utilization between product and labor markets.[45] The failure to expand industrial capacity in line with the growth of the labor force suggested that future efforts to increase job opportunities could be frustrated by the inflationary consequences of widespread capacity bottlenecks in product markets.

The capacity shortfall was illustrated by comparing the past trend of capacity utilization in manufacturing with that of the unemployment rate. By estimating the average relationship between changes in the two indexes, the CEA concluded that the level of unemployment that would be associated with any fixed rate of capacity utilization had increased significantly during the 1970s. On the basis of data extending through 1980, it appears that over the last twenty-five years the unemployment rate associated with any specific utilization of capacity has increased by about 1.5 percentage points, or about 1.5 million workers in 1980.[46] About 0.5 percentage point of this shift might be accounted for by changes in the demographic structure of the labor force, but a significant change remains in the relative balance between the two utilization measures.[47]

While the unemployment rate associated with a fixed rate of capacity utilization drifted up over time, several interesting cycles occurred, as shown in figure 2-2. The early 1950s stand out as a period in which there was a particularly plentiful capacity relative to the labor force and inflation was surprisingly low, given the unemployment rate. Again in the late 1960s the high rates of capital formation significantly shifted the balance between capacity and labor force growth; yet this period is not commonly identified as one of unexpectedly low inflation. Both episodes

45. *Economic Report of the President*, January 1978, pp. 157–61.

46. Such a conclusion follows from a regression that relates the unemployment rate to the index of capacity utilization and a time trend over the period 1955–80. The estimate of 1.5 percentage points of unemployment is the effect of the trend factor between 1955 and 1980. The CEA found that the trade-off had also deteriorated in the early 1960s but that the gradual nature of the subsequent expansion provided time to increase the availability of capacity.

47. The effects of demographic changes in the labor force were recently evaluated in Louise B. Russell, *The Baby Boom Generation and the Economy* (Brookings Institution, 1982), pp. 50–68.

Figure 2-2. *Actual Unemployment Rate and the Unemployment Rate Corresponding to a 90 Percent Utilization of Industrial Capacity, 1950–81*

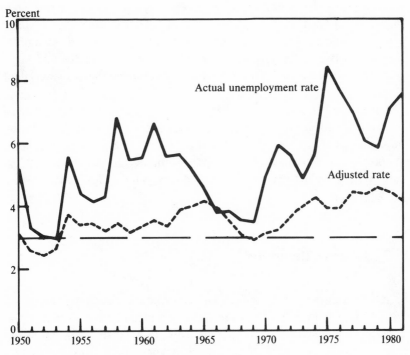

Source: Author's calculations from the following equation:

$$\ln RU = 0.522 - 3.227 \ln CU - 1.254 \ln CU_{-1} + 0.013 \, time$$
$$(5.2) \qquad (7.9) \qquad\qquad (3.0) \qquad\qquad (5.8)$$
$$R^2 = 0.83; \text{ standard error} = 0.1; \text{ period: } 1949-81;$$

where RU is the unemployment rate; CU is manufacturing capacity utilization; and *time* is a trend beginning in 1945. The variables, except the trend, are transformed to logarithms, and numbers in parentheses are *t*-statistics. The adjusted series is computed as:

$$\ln RU + 3.227 \cdot \ln (CU - 0.90) + 1.254 \cdot \ln (CU_{-1} - 0.90).$$

also were periods when the expansion of the armed forces sharply slowed the growth in the civilian labor force. On balance, the aggregate data suggest some shift toward a shortage of capacity relative to the unemployment rate; but that conclusion is very sensitive to changes in the definition of full employment, and it is very difficult to get a meaningful current measure of capacity utilization because of the depth of the 1980–82 recession.

A study of the basic materials industries by de Leeuw and Grimm concluded that there was a shortfall of capacity growth in 1971–75:

the increase in capacity was less than would have been expected on the basis of past relationships with the utilization of existing capacity and output growth.[48] During the last half of the decade the growth of capacity in these industries continued to be abnormally low. The basic materials industries, in turn, have displayed substantial price sensitivity to variations in market conditions over earlier business cycles. For example, these industries experienced significant capacity pressures and large price increases during 1978–79 despite an overall unemployment rate of 6 percent.

Given the magnitude of the 1980–82 recession, capacity limitations may not be an immediate concern. Still, a concern with the inflation implications of capacity shortages would seem to be an added reason for supporting an increased rate of capital formation in future years. New capacity will come forth during the recovery, but the lags in that process are very long.

The Rate of Return on Capital

A third argument in favor of expanded incentives for capital formation can be made without reference to the actual magnitude of growth in the capital stock. The taxation of income from capital causes the before-tax rate of return on capital, as a measure of the benefits to society of an increment of additional capital, to exceed the after-tax rate of return, the private reward to savers for postponing consumption. If both saving and investment are sensitive to the rate of return, the taxation of capital income implies that the amount of capital will be less than is socially optimal.

During the 1970s the failure to adjust for inflation in the definition of taxable income from capital led to a belief that the tax wedge between the social and private returns to capital had increased and had thus become more of a deterrent to capital formation.[49] Hence interest grew

48. Frank de Leeuw and Bruce T. Grimm, "The Growth of Materials Capacity and the Outlook for its Utilization," *Survey of Current Business*, vol. 58 (September 1978), pp. 48–56.

49. See, for example, Martin Feldstein, "Does the United States Save Too Little?" *American Economic Review*, vol. 67 (February 1977, *Papers and Proceedings, 1976*), pp. 116–21.

Table 2-6. *Effective Rates of Taxation on the Capital Income of Nonfinancial Corporations, Selected Periods, 1955–79*

| | Tax rate | | | | |
Tax	1955–59	1960–64	1965–69	1970–74	1975–79
Corporate taxes[a]	56.6	49.4	45.4	50.2	47.2
Personal taxes	12.3	11.6	12.8	19.5	20.5
Dividends	8.6	7.7	6.8	6.6	6.5
Capital gains	2.2	1.8	3.2	6.2	7.0
Interest	1.5	2.1	2.9	6.7	6.9
Total, all taxes	68.9	61.1	58.2	69.7	67.7

Source: Martin Feldstein, James Poterba, and Louis Dicks-Mireaux, "The Effective Tax Rate and the Pretax Rate of Return," National Bureau of Economic Research Working Paper 740 (Cambridge, Mass.: NBER, August 1981), table 3.

a. Includes federal and state corporate income taxes and property taxes.

in proposals to exempt from taxation saving or the income from capital as a means of promoting economic growth.

This argument needs qualification in several respects. First, a proposed change in the tax on capital income relative to other earnings cannot be evaluated in isolation. Work effort, as well as saving and investment decisions, may be sensitive to income and relative price changes.[50] These empirical issues will be examined later in this study.

Second, there is a significant degree of controversy about the measurement of the effective tax on capital income. A study by Feldstein, Poterba, and Dicks-Mireaux (FPD), which focused on the tax on income from nonfinancial corporations, illustrates some of the issues.[51] The analysis included both personal and corporate taxes, and the basic results are shown in table 2-6. The authors concluded that the total effective tax rate on such income was between 65 and 70 percent in the late 1970s, and that, despite a series of rate reductions in the 1960s, inflation had boosted the tax rate during the 1970s to the point that it was again equal to that which existed in the late 1950s.

50. For recent discussions see David F. Bradford, "The Economics of Tax Policy toward Savings," in George M. von Furstenberg, ed., *The Government and Capital Formation* (Ballinger, 1980), pp. 11–71; and Martin Feldstein, "The Welfare Cost of Capital Income Taxation," *Journal of Political Economy*, vol. 86 (April 1978, pt. 2), pp. 29–51.

51. Martin Feldstein, James Poterba, and Louis Dicks-Mireaux, "The Effective Tax Rate and the Pretax Rate of Return," National Bureau of Economic Research Working Paper 740 (Cambridge, Mass.: NBER, August 1981). It is an update of an earlier study by Martin Feldstein and Lawrence Summers, "Inflation and the Taxation of Capital Income in the Corporate Sector," *National Tax Journal*, vol. 32 (December 1979), pp. 445–70.

Inflation affects the tax on capital income in three ways: the failure to adjust depreciation allowances for the rise in the general price level increases the effective tax rate; the deductibility of nominal interest payments as a business expense reduces the effective tax rate; and the taxation of nominal interest, dividend, and capital gains income (inclusive of the inflation premium) within the personal tax system increases the effective tax rate.[52] The FPD study found that the depreciation and interest deduction features of the corporate tax system tended to offset one another and left the corporate tax roughly unchanged despite the acceleration of inflation. But the effect of inflation on the measured capital income of individuals led to a major rise in the effective tax rate during the 1970s.

A contrary view of the burden of capital income taxation is provided in a paper by Steuerle.[53] He points out that less than one-third of the $324 billion of capital income in 1979 was subject to the personal income tax. Much of the income is excluded or deferred from taxation, while offsetting interest expenses are immediately deductible.

In addition, Steuerle finds an average marginal tax rate of about 33 percent on reported income from capital. Thus, he infers that the overall personal tax rate on capital income is about 8 percent. That is about half the rate used in the FPD study for the personal tax on income from corporate business. Steuerle concludes that "the individual income tax can best be characterized as a progressive wage tax, accompanied by a penalty tax on the realization of a modest amount of nominal income from capital and a subsidy for borrowing."[54]

The major source of difference between the two conclusions about capital income taxation is coverage. Steuerle examines total capital income, while the FPD study is concerned only with the income from capital owned by nonfinancial corporations. The FPD study also incorporates several assumptions that may result in an overstatement of the effective tax rate and the extent of its rise.[55] Steuerle did not include

52. Only 40 percent of capital gains income is taxable, and tax payments can be delayed until the gain is realized rather than being paid on an accrued basis. As a result the effective rate of tax on capital gains is quite low.

53. Eugene Steuerle, "Is Income from Capital Subject to Individual Income Taxation?" *Public Finance Quarterly*, vol. 10 (July 1982), pp. 283–303.

54. Ibid., p. 300.

55. Bosworth, "Capital Formation and Economic Policy," pp. 298–99.

corporate taxes. Yet the contrast of the two studies highlights an issue that I examine in a later chapter: it is not that the average tax on capital income is high, but that it varies widely by type of capital, and thus potentially leads to major distortions of investment among sectors of the economy.

As a measure of the social benefit of increased capital formation, the before-tax return on capital in the corporate sector (which the FPD study put at 12 percent) also is probably higher than the average return on all capital. Since one would expect rates of return to equalize on an after-tax basis, the high relative taxation of corporate income probably makes it unrepresentative of other sectors. Most studies find a lower return for farming, noncorporate business, and residential housing.[56]

From a different perspective, however, changes in the rate of return on capital are a highly relevant source of information for the assessment of the adequacy of capital formation in the United States. If increased taxation has discouraged capital formation and if an insufficient stock of capital is responsible for the slower growth of productivity, the "shortage" should be reflected in a rise in the before-tax rate of return on capital. Two alternative measures of the rate of return on business capital are shown in figure 2-3. The first refers to the nonfarm business sector as a whole. The second is limited to nonfarm, nonfinancial corporations. The measure of the return is before tax and includes all returns to capital—interest, rent, and profit; it avoids, therefore, problems of distinguishing between the gains to bondholders and those to stockholders.[57] Both of these measures show a very substantial decline from the peak levels of the mid-1960s.

The return on capital is, however, strongly affected by business cycle conditions and the lower levels of economic activity that prevailed over the late 1970s. It is preferable to focus on trends after adjustment for cyclical factors. Even on this basis, however, the return to capital fell during the 1970s. Within the total business sector the return dropped by about 3 percentage points between 1967 and 1980 (11.2 percent versus 8.2 percent). The decline was slightly smaller for the corporate sector— 2.5 percentage points. These trends in the return to capital are difficult

56. Edward F. Denison, *Accounting for United States Economic Growth, 1929–69* (Brookings Institution, 1974), p. 271.

57. The denominator includes land, inventories, plant, and equipment at replacement cost. It is, thus, a real rate free of inflation effects.

Figure 2-3. *The Rate of Return on Tangible Assets for Nonfarm, Nonresidential Business and Nonfinancial Corporations, Actual and Cyclically Adjusted, 1950–80*

Percent

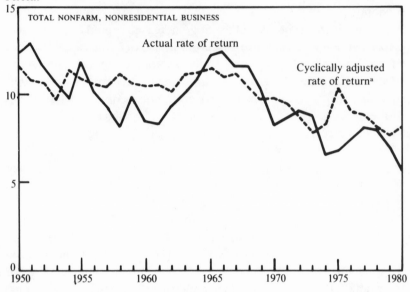

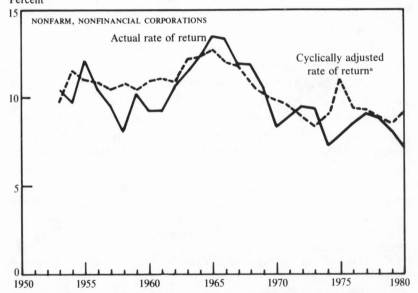

Source: Flow of Funds Division of the Board of Governors of the Federal Reserve System.

a. The cyclical adjustment was made by regressing the actual profit rate on the ratio of actual to potential GNP and the annual percentage change in real GNP. Based on the regression results, an adjusted series was computed that corresponded to full utilization of potential output and a growth of actual GNP equal to that of potential.

to reconcile with the common assertion of growing insufficiency of capital in the United States. If capital is becoming scarce, its relative price should be rising, not falling.

There is less evidence of a major secular decline if the lower rates of return of the 1950s are included in the analysis: the 1960s are atypically high. On the basis of these data one could argue that the reduction of corporate taxes in the early 1960s did lead to an expansion in capital investment relative to the growth of output, and thus a decline in the before-tax return as lower-yielding marginal projects were undertaken. And, in fact, the ratio of tangible assets to output rose substantially after the mid-1960s.

A possible explanation for the decline relates back to the earlier discussion of capital obsolescence. If a large proportion of the existing capital stock has been made obsolete by innovations following the sharp rise in energy and other prices during the 1970s, the true value of that capital stock would be less than is implied by a summation of past investment, and the fall in the measured return on existing capital would not imply a similar decline for the return on new capital.

The 1973 energy price change, however, is an insufficient explanation because capital purchased before 1973 constitutes only a small proportion of the value of today's capital stock: normal depreciation and retirement would have removed much of that capital by 1980. For example, if 25 percent of the stock of equipment became obsolete at the end of 1973, the error in the measurement of total assets, and thus the rate of return, would be less than 2 percent in 1980. One would expect to observe a gradual rise in the average rate of return late in the decade as the capital stock came to be dominated by post-1973 investments. That has not occurred. If the argument is made that the 1979 energy price increase initiated a second wave of obsolescence, one would have to believe that an extremely large proportion of the capital stock was made obsolete by energy price changes, including capital put in place after 1973.

Summary

This review of the knowledge about productivity growth and the causes of the post-1973 slowdown is in some respects very frustrating. From both an economic and social perspective economic growth has been very important. Sustained increases in average standards of living have been a critical means of avoiding divisive conflicts over the distribution of income and wealth. If the focus is simply on the decline in productivity growth since 1973, its importance is highlighted by noting that if the slowdown had never occurred, the real income of the average American worker would today be 20 to 25 percent higher. Such gains would have gone a long way toward meeting the economic and social problems that are of such concern today.

Yet it is not possible to explain convincingly why the slowdown occurred. No single element seems to have played a dominant role. Increases in inputs are one source of growth, but changes in the quality of the inputs, the efficiency with which they are combined, and their interaction with factors that are difficult to quantify, such as technological change, greatly complicate the process.

Several important conclusions do emerge, however. First, a reduced rate of capital formation cannot account for the shortfall. The decline in growth is as evident for multifactor productivity (capital plus labor) as for labor productivity alone. Second, the slower growth of multifactor productivity is pervasive; it is a common phenomenon in all the major industrial countries and in a wide range of individual industries and regions within the United States. That is, it is not the result of shifts of output among sectors of the economy with differing levels or rates of growth of productivity; and it cannot, as is commonly stated, be traced to a shift to a service-based economy.

Third, a large number of more specific factors, such as government regulation, high energy prices, a lower-quality work force, and reduced R&D expenditures, have been investigated as potential sources of the decline. Again, the estimated magnitude of these effects is insufficient to account for the shortfall. By the process of elimination the productivity studies have turned to focus upon changed rates of technical innovation at the level of individual industries.

Equally important, the decline in the before-tax return on capital conflicts with the common assertion that capital formation was insufficient during the decade. Adjusted for changed business cycle conditions and inflation, the rate of return on tangible business capital fell from about 11 percent in 1967 to 8 percent by 1980. At the same time the growth in the ratio of capital to output was substantially greater during the 1970s than the average growth of the earlier postwar period. The reduced before-tax return is particularly puzzling in light of the argument that accelerating inflation was responsible for increasing the effective tax on capital during the 1970s. If that were so, the before-tax return should have increased, and the capital-output ratio should have declined.

The hypothesis that much of the capital stock has become obsolete during a decade of sharp changes in relative prices would reconcile many of the puzzling aspects of the productivity decline and the continuation of high investment in the face of a falling average rate of return. At present, the empirical evidence on that issue is inconclusive, but it appears doubtful that the magnitude of increased obsolescence could fully account for the observed decline in both productivity growth and the average rate of return.

Obsolescence is one factor among several that might have reduced the average rate of return on existing capital (the concept that can be measured), while leaving unchanged or actually increasing the expected marginal return (the relevant concept for new investment). However, the fall in the average rate of return has been in effect for nearly a decade, and the current value of reproducible capital included in the denominator of any measure of the average return is composed primarily of capital purchased within the last decade. Both of these facts make it increasingly difficult to argue that the return on new investments remained high throughout the 1970s. Perhaps business expectations of the return have been consistently more optimistic than realizations, but why the phenomenon should be so large and persistent in the 1970s is not clear.

The inability to account fully for the productivity slowdown should be a sobering influence on the advocacy of specific proposals to reverse it. The uncertainty should not, however, inhibit all discussion of the policy options since it is not necessary to respond to the problem solely by reversing the factors that originally caused the slowdown. Regulation, for example, has reduced the growth of measured productivity; yet the existence of such costs does not argue for the elimination of all regulatory activity. The response to a reduced contribution in one area might involve the offsetting expansion of efforts in others. In such situations, capital formation will be prominent in the discussion because it is one element of the growth process for which government policies are believed to be important.

A better understanding of the causes of the productivity slowdown might, however, lead to a recommendation for no offsetting actions. If the slower growth were a reflection of a diminished rate of technological innovation, for example, it might be rational to reduce the rate of gross capital formation: existing capital would become obsolete at a slower rate, reducing new capital requirements.[58]

An increase in the share of national output devoted to investment cannot permanently increase the rate of productivity growth. But it can raise the *level* of output per worker, and during a transition period it would raise the growth rate. If the net investment share were raised from 4 percent of GNP to 5 percent (a 25 percent increase), net output per worker would be raised in the long run by 5 to 6 percent and the growth rate would be accelerated by 0.1 to 0.2 percent annually in the decade following the change.

The assertion that investment has been too low, rather than declining, because of excessive taxation of capital income is not fully evaluated in this chapter. Such an assessment requires more discussion of the sensitivity to tax rates of saving, investment, and labor supply—the subject of subsequent chapters. An evaluation of the incentive effects of taxes also requires a focus on marginal tax rates, rather than the average rates that have been discussed in this chapter. It is already evident, however, that the taxation of capital income varies sharply among different types of capital, and distortions in its allocation, caused by those differing tax rates, are likely to be as important as the issue of the average tax burden.

58. These general policy considerations are discussed in William Nordhaus, "Policy Responses to the Productivity Slowdown." It is interesting to note the obvious inconsistency in public discussions in which some argue that growth of output has slowed because technical progress has slowed, while others argue that structural unemployment has increased because technical progress has speeded up.

CHAPTER THREE

Saving and Private Capital Formation

IF AN INCREASE in the nation's rate of capital formation is accepted as a major goal of economic policy, significant disagreements remain about how best to achieve that objective. The conflicts in public policy are particularly evident in the tax area, where major new initiatives have been taken to expand incentives for both private saving and investment. The effects of those tax actions on private saving and investment decisions are highly debatable. In addition, the government has encountered severe difficulties in integrating its program for expanding capital formation with other goals of economic policy. For example, the failure during the early 1980s to agree on how to cut expenditures to match previously scheduled tax reductions has created major budget problems, with the result that any induced rise in private saving will almost certainly be offset by increased government dissaving.

Major Issues

Several issues are central to the continuing discussion of policies to expand capital formation. First, should government policies focus on expanded incentives for saving or for investment? In an idealized world of full employment, competitive markets, and no foreign trade, such a distinction would have little relevance. Saving and investment could be viewed as opposite sides (supply and demand) of the same market, with the interest rate serving as the equilibrating price. It would make little difference whether tax incentives were extended to savers or to investors, since the interest rate would adjust to maintain a balance.

In practice, there are many pitfalls in this process. To begin with, the question of an adequate saving rate to support a specific level of investment is relevant only to a fully employed economy in which resources for increased investment must be obtained by forgoing private

59

or public consumption, even though the shares may be unchanged. In an economy in which there is unemployment, an increment to investment can be financed by utilizing idle resources. There the increase in investment raises production and incomes, providing a higher level of both saving and consumption.

Even beginning from a situation of full employment, however, it is paradoxical that an increase in individuals' saving intentions may not lead to an increase in investment—at least in the short run. The increased supply of saving will lower interest rates and serve as a positive inducement to investment; but, at the same time, the decline in consumer spending, which is the counterpart of the rise in saving, will lower current demand and business firms' perceptions of the need for additional capital. The increased planned saving will translate into increased investment only if wages, prices, and interest rates adjust quickly (the world of the neoclassical analysis) to offset the initial decline in demand. Under normal circumstances, lags in the adjustment of prices and wages will result in a period of transition during which increased planned saving will depress total demand and employment. If such a decline is to be avoided, it will be necessary to coordinate changes in saving incentives with direct actions to raise investment.

A second question is, what are the most effective means of increasing national saving? Should government emphasize tax incentives to encourage private saving? Or should it concentrate on reducing its own dissaving (the budget deficit), thereby freeing a larger portion of the existing saving for the financing of private investment?

Government can increase private saving incentives either by reducing taxation of the income from capital or by providing tax benefits tied to current saving. Both of these measures increase the effective after-tax rate of return. But these tax incentives generate both income and substitution effects that pull in opposite directions, and the net effect on the saving behavior of the individual, much less the economy, is indeterminant on a priori grounds. As discussed in chapter 1, a reduction in the tax on the income from capital has an incentive effect of encouraging individuals to reduce their current consumption to take advantage of the higher after-tax return on saving—in effect, lowering the price of future consumption (the substitution effect). On the other hand, the increased lifetime income that will be earned on previously planned saving as a result of lower tax rates encourages higher current as well as future consumption (the income effect). This has not been an easy question for the empirical studies to resolve.

The discussion of saving incentives often ignores the important role played by government fiscal policy. In a fully employed economy, tax reductions to encourage private saving, if not matched by reductions in government expenditures, require the private sector to save the entire tax cut simply to leave the national saving rate unchanged. It is important to note that private saving as a share of national income has remained almost constant over long periods of time and under widely varying economic conditions. Past variations in the national saving rate have been almost entirely due to changes in the government budget balance.

A third issue of controversy is determining the effect of changes in taxes and interest rates on investment behavior. While this has been the subject of more intense research than the impact on saving, important questions still remain in dispute. There is general agreement that the short-run variability of investment is dominated by cyclical fluctuations in expectations of future production requirements. The disagreement concerns the extent to which firms, having decided to build a new plant (the overall capacity decision), will substitute capital for labor (more automated production methods, for example) in response to reductions in the after-tax cost of capital. The issue is simpler for investment than for saving because, whereas saving involves offsetting income and substitution effects, there is only a positive impact on investment— output is assumed to be determined by demand. It is the magnitude of the reponse that is a subject of intense disagreement among the empirical studies.

Finally, although it is often argued that Americans save too little and that the low saving rate is the cause of a low rate of domestic investment, that conclusion ignores the role of the world economy. In a world of international capital movements, domestic saving and domestic investment are not necessarily equal: an increment to private saving could easily flow abroad if the return on foreign investment is above that of domestic investment, and domestic investment can draw on a pool of worldwide saving.

This chapter provides a historical perspective on the pattern of saving and investment in the United States and examines the determinants of private saving behavior and the extent to which government policies can alter those decisions. The role of taxes and interest rates in the investment decision of business firms is the subject of chapter 4. Finally, the transmission mechanism by which changes in private domestic saving are expected to lead to increased domestic investment is examined at the end of chapter 4. This involves four issues: (1) a short-run concern about the speed with which the economy can be expected to adjust to a rise in planned saving so as to avoid a contraction of total demand, (2) the interaction between private saving and government budget policies in determining the total resources available for investment, (3) the allocation of those resources between business investment and home-building, and (4) the extent to which capital can move across national boundaries.

Historical Perspective

Private saving in the United States consists of household saving and saving by business firms (retained earnings plus reserves set aside for income to cover depreciation). Such saving's combined share of the gross national product is shown in figure 3-1. Contrary to many public statements, the private saving rate has actually trended slightly upward since 1948, although a more accurate conclusion would be that it has been surprisingly constant within a range of 16 to 18 percent of GNP since 1951. Second, the composition of that saving has varied. The household saving rate fell during the last half of the 1970s, with an offsetting rise in the business saving rate. The reduction in the household saving rate is the source of most of the assertions that the United States is saving less.

The uses of that private saving can be divided into four major components. The largest share—about two-thirds—goes to nonresidential business investment (plant, equipment, and inventories), which also has been quite stable as a share of GNP apart from business cycle fluctuations. Residential construction has declined as a use of saving from about 5 percent of GNP to less than 4 percent. In part, the low level of homebuilding in the early 1980s is a cyclical reflection of stringent monetary conditions: the secular decline in its share of GNP is more modest. The government budget balance has been the most volatile use of saving, but the largest changes are associated with major shifts in tax policy, and there is an evident tendency in the short run for private

Figure 3-1. *Sources and Uses of Saving as a Percentage of Gross National Product, 1946–82*[a]

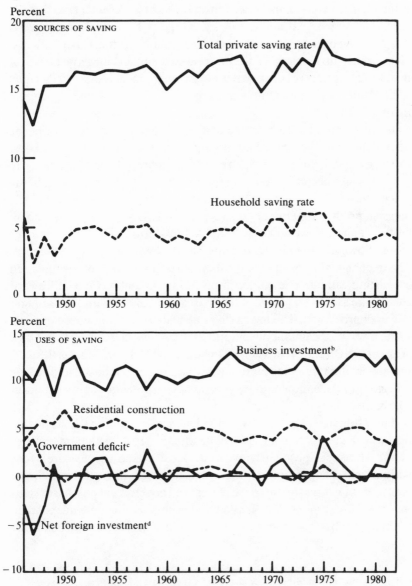

Source: U.S. Department of Commerce, Bureau of Economic Analysis, *The National Income and Product Accounts of the United States, 1929–74 Statistical Tables,* a supplement to the *Survey of Current Business* (Government Printing Office, 1977), and subsequent reports.

a. Private saving includes household saving, business retained earnings, capital-consumption allowances, and the statistical discrepancy.

b. Business investment is nonresidential fixed investment plus inventory accumulation.

c. The government deficit is measured as a positive use of funds.

d. Net foreign investment includes capital grants.

saving to move in a compensatory fashion.[1] The government deficit shown in the figure will strike many observers as surprisingly small. This is the result of combining data from all levels of government, so that the federal deficit is partially offset by the growth in employee pension reserves and other sources of a surplus by state and local governments. Net foreign investment is the current-account balance (inclusive of unilateral transfers) of the balance of payments and it is essentially equal to the outflow of capital funds from the United States minus the capital inflows.

It is also possible to examine aggregate saving rates on a net basis, after deducting the depreciation (capital-consumption allowances) of existing capital. Such a measure is often more relevant to long-term growth issues because it corresponds more closely to the growth in the stock of capital. The net private saving rate averaged 8.4 percent of net national product (compared to 16.5 percent of GNP for gross saving) in 1950–75, and it showed no discernible long-term trend. Since the mid-1970s, however, the net saving rate has declined to about 6.5 percent. The decline is the result of a substantial rise in the rate of depreciation of existing capital. The composition of investment has moved toward shorter life assets—equipment relative to structures—with a consequent rise in depreciation. The net saving rate also has a pronounced cyclical pattern because capital-consumption allowances (a fixed cost) rise as a share of GNP during recessions. On both a net and a gross basis the total private saving rate is far more stable than either the household saving rate alone or the national saving rate (inclusive of the government budget surplus.)[2]

The estimates of saving by individual sectors (such as households, business, and government) should be interpreted with caution because of the statistical problems involved. Most countries measure gross national output (product) as the value of all goods sold for final use (consumption, investment, net exports, and government purchases) plus inventory investment.[3] The United States obtains a second independent estimate of GNP as the sum of all income payments, adjusted for

1. That need not mean that tax cuts have no effect on consumption; but clearly individuals do not immediately adjust their expenditures to changes in income, so initially much of the tax change is reflected in saving.
2. This was pointed out originally in Edward F. Denison, "A Note on Private Saving," *Review of Economics and Statistics,* vol. 40 (August 1958), pp. 261–67.
3. Inventory investment, as a change in stocks, is a particularly tenuous estimate that contributes substantial short-run error to the estimate of GNP and total investment.

payments between the sectors. Because no distinction is made between consumption and investment expenditures of governments, their saving is simply equal to the budget surplus. Business saving is measured on the income side as corporate retained earnings plus depreciation allowances. Household saving is a residual obtained by subtracting an expenditure-side estimate of consumption from household income.

While the discrepancy between the expenditure- and income-side estimates of GNP provides a measure of the accuracy of the aggregate saving data, the measurement errors are concentrated in the residual, household saving. In addition, earnings of unincorporated businesses are included with the household sector. Thus the allocation of private saving between business and households varies with the importance of the corporate form of organization.[4]

Other countries often lack the information to construct reliable estimates of national output from the income side. Their domestic private saving is simply estimated as the sum of domestic and net foreign investment minus the government budget surplus. Thus they often have no independent measures of saving and investment.

Furthermore, the concept of a saving rate for a specific sector of the economy, such as households, becomes even more tenuous in an economy of rapid inflation because of problems of allocating the income from capital. In the national income accounts framework, all interest payments received by the household sector are included in personal income. In addition, interest payments by consumers are recorded as an expenditure and must be deducted from personal income—together with taxes and expenditures on goods and services—in arriving at the measured amount of household saving.[5] Nonprofit institutions, trusteed pension funds, and accounts managed for individuals by insurance companies are included within the household sector, and their earnings represent a significant portion of household interest income.

4. Some analysts have preferred to measure household saving from the flow-of-funds accounts data on net holdings of financial assets by sector. On that basis, the measure of household saving is larger and declines less over the 1970s, but it is offset by a far smaller estimate of business saving, which substantially alters the estimate of total private saving. Difficulties of tracing ownership of financial assets should make the national income accounts estimates preferable to those of the flow-of-funds accounts.

5. Mortgage interest payments are excluded from the household sector of the national income accounts because the purchase and operation of a house is treated as a business activity. A rise in mortgage interest rates does depress household income because it reduces the net profits earned through homeownership, but the higher payments of homeowners are largely offset by the corresponding increase in other households' interest and dividend receipts from financial institutions.

The important point is that these interest payments are recorded in nominal terms. When interest rates rise in anticipation of higher inflation, it is difficult to distinguish between the real and inflation-premium components of interest payments. The inflation premium is that portion of the interest payment that must be set aside to maintain the real value of the initial wealth in the face of expected future inflation. The true interest income—available for consumption—is considerably less than the total payment.[6] If creditors perceive that much of nominal interest income is simply a partial repayment of the principal, they will not increase their consumption in proportion to the rise in reported income, and the inflation premium will pass through into measured saving; indeed, it must, if real wealth is to be maintained. As a result, the measured saving rate for creditors should rise during periods of inflation.

On balance, the household sector occupies a net creditor position because interest receipts exceed interest payments. It is offset by a substantial net borrower position of business and government. Thus the inflation premium in interest payments exaggerates the magnitude of both the saving of households and the dissaving of business and government. For example, much of the rise in the federal budget deficit during the 1970s can be traced to the increase in interest payments. Yet a major portion of those payments represented a repayment of principal, and the real value of the outstanding debt rose far less than implied by the cumulative sum of the annual deficits.[7]

6. This point can be illustrated by starting with a world of no inflation. An individual deposits $100 in a savings account and is credited with $105 at the end of the year. The simple rate of interest is 5 percent and the $5 is all interest income. However, in a world of sustained inflation of 10 percent, the equivalent nominal rate of interest would be 15 percent. While $15 is reported as interest income, $10 must be set aside to maintain the real value of the original investment.

7. The adjustment of balance sheets and income flows for the effects of inflation on asset values has become increasingly popular in recent years. An example of such adjustments for the business sector is provided by John Shoven and Jeremy Bulow, "Inflation Accounting and Nonfinancial Corporate Profits: Financial Assets and Liabilities," *Brookings Papers on Economic Activity, 1:1976,* pp. 15–66. (Hereafter *BPEA.*) Similar adjustments to the federal budget are discussed in Robert Hartman, "The Budget Outlook," in Joseph A. Pechman, ed., *Setting National Priorities: The 1982 Budget* (Brookings Institution, 1981), pp. 204–08; Phillip Cagan, "The Real Federal Deficit and Financial Markets," *The AEI Economist,* November 1981 (American Enterprise Institute for Public Policy Research, 1981), pp. 1–6; and Robert Eisner and Paul J. Pieper, "A New View of the Federal Debt and Budget Deficits," *American Economic Review,* vol. 74 (March 1984), pp. 11–29. In the Eisner and Pieper study the inflation adjustments to the debt shift the budget deficit from an average of $41 billion to a surplus of $5 billion in the 1976–80 period. Finally, a study by Gregory Jump of household saving in the United States and Canada reports a reduction of roughly 50 percent in the measured

While the inflation premium has certainly changed substantially over the postwar period, it cannot be measured precisely because anticipated inflation is not an observable variable and it differs among individuals. These allocation problems are largely absent in measures of national saving, and changes in the rate of inflation do not generate major measurement errors. The problem is also reduced for analysis of the private saving rate because interest payments between business and households cancel each other. In summary, a consideration of the measurement problems—availability of data, the definition of business versus households, and the influence of inflation—suggests that one should be cautious in placing too much emphasis on the trends in saving rates of specific sectors.

At various points below it will be important to distinguish between planned and actual saving and investment. By definition, actual saving and investment—that is, saving and investment realized after the event—must be equal, but that need not be true of planned saving and investment. Individuals may make expenditure decisions on the basis of expected income only to find their actual income has changed. Saving bears the brunt of this adjustment to unanticipated income changes even though major components of saving are contractual in nature. A similar balancing role is evident on the investment side, where inventory accumulation is simply the amount of goods produced but not sold during the period.[8] The government also finds that its budget situation is affected heavily by unforeseen developments in the private sector, since reductions in economic activity reduce revenues and boost expenditures. Changes in short-run economic conditions can, therefore, have major effects on the saving-investment balance that are not indicative of intended saving or investment. As a result of this instability, data on saving and investment rates are primarily useful over longer time periods.

Determinants of Private Saving

The adequacy of national saving has been a major issue in the debate over supply-side economic policies. Attention has focused on the low

saving rate after adjusting for inflation. See Gregory V. Jump, "Recent Behavior of the Personal Saving Rate" (Institute for Policy Analysis, University of Toronto, March 1980).

8. Inventories include goods in process, which simply reflects goods moving through the production and distribution pipeline, but they also fluctuate in response to unanticipated departures of actual from planned sales.

68   TAX INCENTIVES AND ECONOMIC GROWTH

rate of private saving in the United States in comparison with that of other countries, and the tax and transfer system is widely blamed for a weakening of saving incentives. The focus on this aspect of the problem has resulted in the adoption of major new tax incentives to promote saving. The effectiveness of these policies is dependent, in part, on the accuracy of the underlying assumption that saving decisions are influenced by variations in the rate of return.[9] If saving is highly sensitive to the return on capital, the creation of a large and growing wedge between the social (before-tax) and private (after-tax) rates of return is a serious economic problem.[10] On the other hand, if consumption-saving decisions are dominated by other considerations, the taxation of capital income does not have substantial incentive effects, and a reduction in the taxation of capital income can do little to increase the overall rate of capital formation.

Agreement on the major determinants of saving behavior has eluded economists despite several decades of theoretical and empirical research. The disagreement is particularly intense with respect to the effect of changes in interest rates. As already indicated, economic theory is agnostic on the issue. When the rate of return on saving rises, there is both a substitution effect and an income effect, and the sum of the two may be either positive or negative. It is fundamentally an empirical issue. Yet there are serious problems of accurately measuring the response of individuals in the absence of controlled laboratory experiments.

The empirical analyses have used three types of data. First, data on aggregate saving within the United States are available with a fair degree of precision for over forty years. The statistical problems are greater in other countries, however; and estimates of saving by specific sectors of the economy, such as households and businesses, are tenuous. The

9. It is also true that some policies labeled as saving incentives are ineffectual because they do not actually increase the after-tax rate of return to saving. These issues of the design of saving incentives are discussed in David F. Bradford, "Issues in the Design of Saving and Investment Incentives," in Charles R. Hulten, ed., *Depreciation, Inflation, and the Taxation of Income from Capital* (Washington, D.C.: Urban Institute, 1981), pp. 13–47.

10. In addition, any tax imposes a welfare cost in the sense that it distorts individual decisions from what they would be in a no-tax world. But a tax cannot be evaluated from this perspective without assessing the benefits of the expenditures that the tax finances, or the distorting effects of other taxes that would be raised to offset the revenue loss of reduced capital taxation. The problem becomes one of choosing the combination of taxes that minimizes the combined welfare loss. Individual taxes cannot be evaluated in isolation. This study does not attempt to define a comprehensive tax structure.

aggregate data are so dominated by business cycle factors that it is difficult to identify the influence of other determinants.

Second, some studies have relied on survey data collected from a cross section of the household population for a single time period. By definition, the cross-sectional data cannot provide the basis for predicting what would happen if the environment common to all the respondents changed—for example, a change in market interest rates. In addition, much of the variance of behavior within the sample is due to individual peculiarities and errors in survey responses that swamp the economic determinants driving the average.

In principle, panel studies that follow a set of individuals over several periods offer the richest source of information. Such surveys are extremely expensive, however, and the difficulties of obtaining reliable information on saving from individual respondents have limited their use. Thus most studies of saving have been forced to rely on economy-wide aggregates and cross-sectional surveys.

Models of Saving Behavior

During most of the period since World War II empirical studies of saving incentives have been relatively rare. The major studies have focused on the demand-side implications of short-run fluctuations in consumer incomes—such as might be induced by varying business cycle conditions or changes in after-tax incomes. On the other hand, a concern with saving incentives addresses more directly the choice between current and future consumption and the role of the return on saving as the basic cost of forgoing current for future consumption. Ideally, studies of consumer spending should be fully integrated with considerations of current versus future consumption; but, in fact, many of the early studies ignored the potential effects of interest rates—perhaps in the belief that they were small.

Almost all the recent studies of the consumption-saving decision have relied on some variant of the life cycle, or permanent-income, hypothesis to provide a theoretical framework. According to that model, households attempt to maximize the benefits of consumption over a lifetime, subject to the constraint of expected lifetime earnings and initial wealth.[11] The

11. The model is developed and its basic characteristics are explained in Franco Modigliani and Richard Brumberg, "Utility Analysis and the Consumption Function: An Interpretation of Cross-Section Data," in Kenneth K. Kurihara, ed., *Post-Keynesian Economics* (Rutgers University Press, 1954), pp. 388–430; and Albert Ando and Franco

spirit of the life cycle model is that families will smooth out their consumption—possibly dissaving when they are young, repaying debt and saving in their middle years in anticipation of retirement, and then dissaving again during retirement. The model introduces wealth, interest rates, and demographic variables as significant potential sources of changes in aggregate consumer spending.[12]

A general formulation of the aggregate consumption function that encompasses most of the specific empirical studies can be written as:

(1) $$C = F(Yd, W, r, X),$$

where

    C = consumer expenditures,
    Yd = current and expected future labor income (after-tax),
    W = net wealth of households,
    r = the after-tax real rate of interest,
    X = other miscellaneous variables affecting consumption.[13]

The interest of economists in alternative empirical representations of consumer behavior was stimulated during the 1970s by a substantial increase in the variability of the consumption-income ratio and an apparent upward shift of the household saving rate in the late 1960s and early 1970s, neither of which were well explained by the earlier analysis. Initially, the higher saving rate was explained as a response to greater uncertainty occasioned by a more variable inflation. But the decline of the household saving rate in the last half of the 1970s in the face of accelerating inflation weakened that explanation and led to a search for other hypotheses.

INTEREST RATE EFFECTS. The role of the interest rate in the allocation of consumption over time can be illustrated with a simple life cycle model. Consider an individual's lifetime as being divided into two

---

Modigliani, "The Life Cycle Hypothesis of Saving: Aggregate Implications and Tests," *American Economic Review,* vol. 53 (March 1963), pp. 55–84.

12. Although age is a critical determinant of differences in saving behavior among individuals, it has normally been ignored in the aggregate data because of relatively small shifts in the age distribution of the population. That may be an untenable assumption for the future because of the emergence of the postwar baby-boom generation as adults.

13. A derivation of the empirical model from a life cycle perspective is provided by Colin Wright, "Saving and the Rate of Interest," in Arnold C. Harberger and Martin J. Bailey, ed., *The Taxation of Income from Capital* (Brookings Institution, 1969), pp. 275–300.

periods. In the first period the individual works and decides on the allocation of that income between current and future consumption. In the second period he is retired and consumes the first-period saving and any accumulated interest. If his wage income is denoted by W_1, he can, as extremes, either spend the entire amount on first-period consumption (C_1), or achieve a maximum level of consumption in the second period (C_2) of $W(1 + r)$, where r is the rate of return on saving. The price of future consumption, in terms of forgone current consumption, is $1/(1 + r)$; and he faces a budget constraint of

(2) $$C_1 + C_2/(1+r) = W_1.$$

The individual's own preferences for current versus future consumption are reflected in his effort to maximize lifetime utility, U, as a function of consumption in each time period:

(3) $$U = U(C_1, C_2).$$

This consumption-saving decision is illustrated in the upper panel of figure 3-2. The individual's options are represented by the budget line W_1W_2, whose slope is $1/(1 + r)$. W_1 is the amount of current consumption that can be achieved if he forgoes all saving, but C_2 would be zero. His preferences, the utility function, are described by a set of indifference curves, each of which is convex to the origin and represents combinations of current and future consumption at which the individual is indifferent in his choice. Higher curves represent higher levels of satisfaction. The optimal choice is represented by the point A, the highest indifference curve along the line $\bar{W}_1W_2$. In the first period he consumes an amount C_1 and saves ($W_1 - C_1$). The latter is sufficient to finance consumption of C_2 in the retirement period.

Now let the return on saving fall so that the individual faces a new set of possibilities, represented by the budget line W_1W_2'. Utility is maximized at the point B on the lower indifference curve U^1. The rise in the price of future consumption (fall in r) will lead the individual to prefer current relative to future consumption—a substitution effect. But the reduction in r is tantamount to a fall in lifetime income. The individual can cushion the reduction in future income that results from the loss of interest income by shifting some consumption from the present to the future—the income effect. In figure 3-2(a) the substitution effect dominates and the individual responds to a lower interest rate by increasing consumption to C_1'.

Figure 3-2. *The Consumption-Saving Decision*

Retirement period

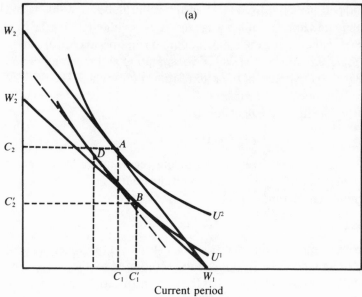

Retirement period

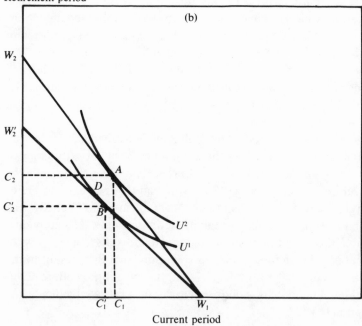

The net change in the consumption-saving allocation can be decomposed into its income and substitution components. This is illustrated in the figure by drawing a new budget line parallel to the old W_1W_2 (thus maintaining the same relative price of current and future consumption) that is tangent to U^1 at D. The distance from the old budget line, W_1W_2, is the reduction in income that is equivalent in lost utility to the decline in the interest rate. The horizontal distance between D and B is the pure substitution effect on current consumption. It is offset by an income effect that is represented by the horizontal distance between A and D.[14]

There is no theoretical basis for determining the relative magnitudes of the income and substitution effects. If current and future consumption are close substitutes for one another, represented by indifference curves with very little curvature in figure 3-2(a), the substitution effect will be large and saving will vary positively with changes in the interest rate. The alternative situation, where current and future consumption are viewed more as complements, is illustrated in figure 3-2(b) with indifference curves that are more convex. In this case the substitution effect will be small and is likely to be dominated by the income effect: saving will vary inversely with changes in the interest rate.

An example of complementarity is provided by some people's desire to maintain a constant relationship between pre- and postretirement consumption. Such individuals may state their saving goals in terms of a desire to prevent a sharp drop in their standard of living after retirement.[15] A high degree of substitutability, on the other hand, implies

14. A mathematical statement of the effects of an interest rate change for the above two-period model is given by the elasticity of current consumption with respect to the interest rate,

$$\eta_{c \cdot r} = \frac{-sr}{1+r}(\sigma - \eta),$$

where
  r = interest rate,
  s = saving rate,
  σ = the elasticity of substitution between current and future consumption (a measure of the curvature of the indifference curve),
  η = elasticity of first-period consumption with respect to wealth.

Since η is likely to be about unity, a substantial elasticity of substitution is required to generate a large interest elasticity of saving. Further details are provided in Anthony B. Atkinson and Joseph E. Stiglitz, *Lectures on Public Economics* (McGraw-Hill, 1980), pp. 62–96.

15. A small substitution effect need not imply, as sometimes stated, that individuals have a fixed goal for retirement consumption, though it is not inconsistent.

that individuals are willing to accept a wide variation in consumption over time in order to increase the total: they are relatively indifferent with respect to the timing of their consumption.

A full evaluation of the effect taxation of capital income has on saving requires knowledge of the empirical magnitude of both the substitution and income effects. Within a proportionate tax rate system, where average and marginal tax rates are equal, a tax on capital income can be represented, as in figure 3-2, by a simple reduction in the after-tax return, $(1-t)r$. The United States, however, relies on a graduated tax rate system. The incentive effects (substitution) are identified with the return on an additional dollar of saving—in effect, the marginal tax rate. The income effect is more closely identified with the average return—and thus the average tax rate. It is possible to raise a given amount of revenue with tax systems of widely varying marginal tax rates. Thus a concern with saving incentives in the design of a tax system implies a need to know the magnitude of both effects.

STATISTICAL PROBLEMS. The statistical estimation of the consumption-saving decision by using aggregate data presents several problems. First, the theory requires a measure of after-tax labor income, but under a graduated tax-rate system the allocation of an individual's taxes between labor and property income involves several arbitrary assumptions. Many empirical studies resort to the use of total disposable income (including capital income); but that creates problems of double-counting because wealth and the income from wealth are both included in the same equation.

Second, the after-tax real rate of interest, r, depends on expected inflation (an unobservable variable) and the marginal tax rate. They are related according to $r = (1-t)i - \pi$, where i equals the nominal interest rate, t equals the marginal tax rate, and π equals the expected rate of inflation. Several studies have used a moving average of past rates of inflation as a proxy for the expected inflation rate and have ignored the marginal tax rate. There are also differences among the studies in their choice of an interest rate that is most representative of the options available to savers.

Econometric studies that use aggregate data to infer the influence of interest rate changes are also affected by another major complication. Interest rate changes can be expected to have sharply different effects on the behavior of different age cohorts of the population. For the young worker who has not accumulated assets, the interest rate change will induce offsetting income and substitution effects, as discussed earlier. But for workers who have completed much of their lifetime saving and are approaching retirement (and therefore tend to have higher wealth-income ratios), a change in the interest rate also implies a change in the amount of future income that they will receive from their existing wealth. Higher interest rates will create a surprise income gain from existing wealth that will tend to augment the normal income effect and increase the possibility of a positive association between interest rate changes and current consumption.[16] Thus the average short-run response to interest rate changes for a group of households of different ages may differ dramatically from the long-run response as exemplified by the behavior of the youngest cohorts who are less affected by changes in the value of existing wealth.

Finally, statistical attempts to relate consumption, income, and interest rates are plagued by the fact that all of these variables are mutually interdependent. Changes in consumption have significant effects on income and interest rates. Thus the measured variables include, to an unknown degree, two-way causation. This simultaneous-equations bias may seriously affect the estimated coefficients from any statistical regression; yet all the techniques for handling this problem introduce equally serious measurement problems of their own.

MARGINAL TAX RATES. Average tax rates are relatively easy to compute, but it is the marginal rate on an additional dollar of income that is most relevant to the saving decision, and in a progressive tax system, such as that of the United States, the two measures can differ by substantial amounts. The Treasury Department has prepared estimates of the marginal tax rates applicable to hypothetical families at specific points in the income distribution. Those rates are reproduced for 1954–80 in figure 3-3.

After remaining constant for nearly a decade, the marginal tax rate faced by the median-income family was reduced from 20 to 17 percent by the 1964 tax act. The rate increased with the enactment of the 1968–70 tax surcharge, but is estimated to have been about 19 percent in 1971. During the subsequent decade, the marginal rate steadily drifted up to about 24 percent in 1980, as inflation pushed taxpayers into higher marginal tax brackets. A more dramatic increase occurred in the marginal

16. This assumes that households are net creditors. In practice, unanticipated changes in real interest will generate large capital gains and losses that greatly complicate any estimate of the *average* response to an interest rate change.

Figure 3-3. *Alternative Estimates of Marginal Income Tax Rates, 1954–80*

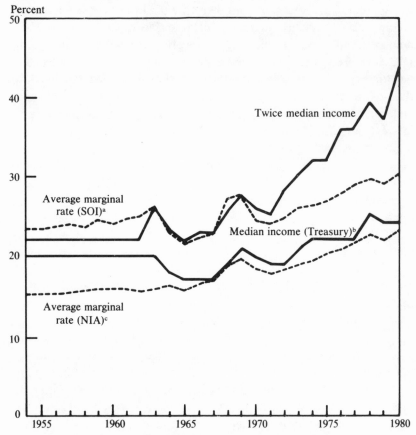

a. Marginal tax rates weighted by adjusted gross income in tax brackets. Obtained from U.S. Internal Revenue Service, *Statistics of Income*, selected years, 1962–77; estimated from Brookings tax file, 1978–80; and author's estimates, 1954–61.

b. Family of four, one earner. Itemized deductions are 23 percent of income. Obtained from U.S. Department of Treasury, Office of Tax Analysis.

c. Marginal tax rate derived from regressions linking tax revenue to personal income eligible for tax use as reported in Department of Commerce, *National Income and Product Accounts*.

rate applicable to families with twice the median income, rising from 25 percent in 1971 to 43 percent in 1980.

Alternatively, an average marginal tax rate (weighted by the percentage of total adjusted gross income earned by taxpayers in each marginal tax bracket) that reflects the full range of the income distribution of tax filers is available from the *Statistics of Income* (SOI), published by the Internal Revenue Service. It captures many of the aspects of the general rise in marginal rates, but excludes unreported income and the portion of capital gains that is not included in the tax base.[17] That measure also shows an increase during the 1970s, but the magnitude of the rise is closer to that for the median income family.

A final perspective on the trend in marginal tax rates was derived from the statistical models used to predict government tax revenues from changes in total income of individuals, as reported in the national income accounts (NIA).[18] On this basis marginal tax rates have increased in step with the rise in the average rate—rising from about 18 percent in 1971 to 23 percent in 1980—but the marginal rate in any given year is considerably lower than the SOI estimate.[19] The major difference between the NIA and SOI estimates of marginal tax rates is that the latter ignores all the income that is exempt from taxation.

These measures of the marginal tax on an additional dollar of income are seriously deficient as measures of the effective tax on saving, however. They assume that incomes from different sources are all taxed at the same rate: the tax on an additional dollar of wage income is the same as that on a dollar of income earned from capital. That is clearly not the case. Instead, the tax on income from saving is dependent upon the uses to which the saving is put. Income from state and local securities is completely exempt from federal taxes, pension fund contributions are fully deductible from taxable income, investments in homeownership not only generate untaxed income in kind but they also give rise to a large stream of interest deductions, long-term capital gains are taxed at 40 percent of the rate on wage income, and large wealth holders can often create special investment situations that are sheltered from taxation. On the other hand, the returns to capital (interest, dividends, rent, and capital gains) are not adjusted for erosion of the value of the original investment as a result of inflation.[20]

17. There are also changes over time in the proportion of income earners who were required to file tax returns (joint versus separate returns, for example).

18. Those models estimate the elasticity of tax revenues with respect to personal income. Since the elasticity is itself the ratio of the marginal to the average tax rate, and the average is known, the marginal rate can be computed. I used for this purpose a tax model prepared by Frederick Ribe, "Bracket Creep and the Elasticity of the Individual Income Tax" (Congressional Budget Office, December 1981).

19. If marginal tax rates were rising faster than the average rate, the elasticity of taxes with respect to income would increase. The available statistical studies find only a weak upward trend in the elasticity. See, for example, ibid.

20. An approach to measuring the expected after-tax return on capital that reflects this diversity is provided in a study by George M. von Furstenberg, "Saving," in Henry

There is a large tax wedge between the private and social returns on some forms of saving, but for others it is actually negative. On average, as Steuerle demonstrated,[21] the marginal individual income tax rate on returns from all forms of savings is not high. Whether it is above or below that of labor income depends upon the inclusion or exclusion of corporate income taxes and social security.

Some studies of saving behavior have used the tax on individuals' dividend and interest income, but that seems even less appropriate. It is the tax rate of high-income individuals living off property income and does not measure the effect of taxes on the incentive to save out of current income.

The analysis calls for the effective tax rate on the most attractive saving option in each tax bracket, weighted by the percentage of total income earned by individuals in that tax bracket. Because of the differential tax treatment of capital incomes and because the before-tax return may change in response to a change in the tax, none of the available measures of the tax rate approach such a concept.

Some doubts about the truth of the common assertion of a rising marginal tax rate on nominal capital income are illustrated by a comparison of the yields on taxable and tax-exempt securities. If investors exploit all alternative investment options to equalize the after-tax return, the interest differential between taxable and tax-exempt bonds provides an estimate of the effective marginal tax rate. The effective marginal tax rate implied by this comparison has been relatively constant within the range of 30 to 33 percent since the mid-1950s, with a rise to 37 percent in 1978–80 and a fall to 28 percent in 1981.[22] Those interest receipts are not adjusted for inflation, however. Thus, even if the tax rate on nominal

---

J. Aaron and Joseph A. Pechman, eds., *How Taxes Affect Economic Activity* (Brookings Institution, 1981), pp. 327–90, especially app. B. He adjusts actual capital income from different sources to an after-tax basis rather than using a single market interest rate as an estimate of the expected return. Von Furstenberg is skeptical that the after-tax return could be measured with enough precision to determine its effect on saving behavior.

21. Eugene Steuerle, "Is Income from Capital Subject to Individual Income Taxation?" *Public Finance Quarterly*, vol. 10 (July 1982), pp. 283–303.

22. Specifically, the marginal tax rate, t, is given by: $t = (1 - R_{te})/R_t$, where R_{te} = the yield on tax-exempt securities and R_t = the yield on taxable securities. The estimate of the level of the tax rate is affected by the choice of an alternative asset of comparable risk and liquidity, but it has little effect on the trend. I used Aa-rated corporate and Aa-rated state and local bonds for the comparison. The relative yield is also influenced by the volume of tax-exempt bonds as they become attractive to individuals with lower marginal tax rates.

interest income remained relatively constant, the effective personal tax on real income from capital increased.

EXISTING EMPIRICAL STUDIES. It is readily apparent from a review of existing empirical studies that no consensus has emerged with respect to the effect of interest rates on saving.[23] Many of these studies, however, were designed with a focus on other issues and some did not adjust interest rates for inflation or ignored tax rates. The interest rate issue was addressed most directly in the three recent studies by Boskin, Howry and Hymans, and Gylfason.[24] The Boskin and Gylfason studies both found significant interest rate effects, but that conclusion was disputed by Howry and Hymans.

In his study, Boskin objected to the notion that the previously noted constancy of the private saving rate implied that saving decisions were insensitive to the rate of return. He argued that such a situation could be the result of offsetting changes in other determinants of saving. Boskin found a significant interest rate effect in a regression equation relating consumption to total disposable (after-tax) private income, wealth, the unemployment rate, and the real after-tax rate of interest over 1934–69 (excluding 1941–46). His work implied that a 1-percentage-point rise in the real after-tax rate of interest would reduce the ratio of consumption (raise the ratio of saving) to income by about 1 percentage point.[25]

The Boskin study was criticized by Howry and Hymans because the results were very sensitive to relatively minor changes in the period of estimation and the specification. When they restricted the analysis to the postwar period and experimented with alternative interest rates, the interest rate coefficients were invariably positive (a rise in the interest rate increased consumption—the opposite of what might be expected).

23. For a summation of the results of these studies, see Organization for Economic Cooperation and Development, "International Differences and Trend Changes in Saving Ratios," prepared for Working Party No. 1 of the Economic Policy Committee (Paris: OECD, October 1981), pp. 65–66.

24. Michael J. Boskin, "Taxation, Saving, and the Rate of Interest," *Journal of Political Economy*, vol. 86 (April 1978, pt. 2), pp. S3–S27; E. Philip Howry and Saul H. Hymans, "The Measurement and Determination of Loanable Funds Savings," *BPEA*, 3:1978, pp. 655–705; and Thorvaldur Gylfason, "Interest Rates, Inflation, and the Aggregate Consumption Function," *Review of Economics and Statistics*, vol. 63 (May 1981), pp. 233–45.

25. Boskin's measure of private after-tax income included corporate retained earnings and an estimate of the rental income on consumer durables in addition to the national income accounts definition of personal disposable income. With a real rate of interest of 4 to 5 percent, the interest elasticity of consumption was estimated at about 0.4.

It has not been possible to reproduce Boskin's subjective method of constructing the after-tax interest rate in order to extend his study into the 1970s. In addition, Boskin's estimated relationship included as separate variables wealth, the income from wealth, and the interest rate. It is difficult to infer from such a model the net effect of a rise in the interest rate because it increases income but reduces the market value of existing wealth. The elasticity of consumption with respect to changes in wealth, 0.3, is also low in comparison with other studies.

Howry and Hymans preferred to focus on a concept of personal cash saving that they believed to be more appropriate for understanding discretionary saving decisions. Within this framework they were unable to find a significant interest rate effect. On the other hand, critics of this study felt that it was misleading to infer the overall effects of interest rates on saving from the response of such a small component.

The study by Gylfason is the most recent addition to the debate. He found a significant interest rate effect, comparable to that of Boskin, using data that extended through the 1970s. At the same time, his results for various subperiods are supportive of the point made by Howry and Hymans that the results are sensitive to changes in the data period and specification. Gylfason used the nominal rate of interest with a separate inflation rate measure, but he did not attempt to adjust for tax rate changes. The specific equation estimated by Gylfason also did not allow for a lagged response of consumption to income changes—perhaps the most important conclusion of earlier empirical studies of the consumption function. A modification of the statistical equation to include lagged income effects eliminates the significance of the interest rate variable.[26]

A STATISTICAL UPDATE. A set of statistical estimates of the consumption function, based on the newly revised national income accounts, is shown in table 3-1. The equations are estimated for the 1952–80 period using annual observations.[27] The results are presented simply to illustrate

26. Gylfason fit an equation with the consumption-income ratio on the left-hand side and the wealth-income ratio on the right together with the interest rate, inflation rate, and the lagged consumption-income ratio. While the interest rate term was statistically significant, the equation produced much larger errors in predicting consumption than other studies. I simply added the ratio of current to lagged income in order to introduce some dynamics of income change. The term was highly significant and sharply improved the overall statistical fit of the equation, but eliminated the significance of the interest rate term.

27. Annual data were used because some investigators have argued that the dominating influence of short-term fluctuations and measurement errors in the quarterly data may unduly bias the studies against detecting the influence of variables, such as interest rates, that operate with long lags. The criticism seems particularly relevant to

Table 3-1. *Alternative Regression Equations for Consumer Spending, 1952–80*[a]

Variable and summary statistic	Total consumption		Nondurables and services		Durable purchases	
	Disposable income (1)	Labor income (2)	Disposable income (3)	Labor income (4)	Disposable income (5)	Labor income (6)
Variable						
Current income	0.35	0.33	0.33	0.31	0.39	0.41
	(3.2)	(3.8)	(4.0)	(3.9)	(8.5)	(11.4)
Prior income	0.69	0.43	0.20	0.29	−0.21	−0.13
	(3.6)	(5.6)	(2.6)	(4.1)	(3.9)	(3.2)
Wealth (lagged)	0.06	0.06	0.05	0.05	0.01	0.01
	(5.2)	(5.5)	(5.8)	(5.4)	(1.6)	(1.4)
Interest rate (lagged)	−0.002	−0.001	−0.001	−0.001	−0.086[b]	−0.080[b]
	(3.7)	(2.2)	(1.9)	(0.6)	(3.7)	(4.3)
Transfer income	. . .	0.66	. . .	0.41	. . .	. . .
		(5.4)		(3.7)		
Stock of durables	. . .	. . .	. . .	. . .	−0.23	−0.23
(lagged)					(5.4)	(7.7)
Constant	−0.19	0.0	0.10	0.17	−0.10	−0.20
	(4.0)	(0.1)	(2.8)	(2.0)	(2.5)	(6.2)
Summary statistic						
R^2	0.998	0.999	0.998	0.998	0.92	0.95
Durbin-Watson	1.3	1.6	1.6	1.8	1.7	2.2
Standard error (dollars per capita)	29	23	22	21	12	10

Sources: The measure of labor income was provided by Charles Steindel and updated by the author. The method of construction is described in Franco Modigliani and Charles Steindel, "Is a Tax Rebate an Effective Tool for Stabilization Policy?" *Brookings Papers on Economic Activity, 1:1977,* pp. 175–203. The measure of total consumption is one that replaces durable expenditures with their service flow equivalent. The disposable income measure is from the MIT-Penn-Social Science Research Council (MPS) model and incorporates interest income on a net basis. The household wealth data were obtained from the MPS model data bank.

a. All variables are deflated by prices and population, and they are measured in thousands of 1972 dollars. The numbers in parentheses are t-statistics. Wealth and the stock of durable goods are beginning of period values. The interest rate is an after-tax real rate and it is scaled by wealth: $C = a + b \cdot Y + c \cdot W + d \cdot rW$.

b. The interest rate term is replaced by the current rental price, which represents the interest and depreciation costs of holding durable goods for one period. The specific formulation is: (Pd/Pc) $(r + d)$, where Pd and Pc are the price indexes for durables and total consumption, respectively. The annual rental cost is measured by the real after-tax rate of interest, r, and the rate of depreciation, d.

that it is possible to obtain significant statistical results for the addition of an interest rate term with a minimum of data manipulation. The basic equation formulation is the same as that used for many years in the MIT-Penn-Social Science Research Council (MPS) model of the U.S. economy with two specific additions. A measure of the after-tax real interest rate was constructed from the Baa bond rate, the estimated marginal tax rate for a median-income family as shown in figure 3-3, and an expected

those studies that undertake autoregressive transformations that effectively convert the data to first differences.

inflation rate measure obtained as a four-year weighted average of the actual inflation rate. In addition, a constructed series on after-tax labor income made it possible to abstract from the problems caused by including interest earnings in the definition of disposable income.

The statistical results are interesting in several respects. First, there is a significant negative interest rate effect on consumption, but only if it is adjusted for inflation and taxes, and only if it is lagged one year. The current year's interest rate was never significant and was eliminated from the reported equations. The estimated equation for total consumption (an interest rate coefficient of -0.002) implies that an increase of 1 percentage point in the real rate of return will reduce consumption by about 0.9 percent—very close to the lower range of the estimates obtained by Boskin.[28] When the data period was restricted to 1953–70, however, the interest rate coefficient was not significant and diminished sharply in magnitude.

Second, the inclusion of data for the 1970s substantially increased the average prediction error of the equations for total consumption expenditures and nondurables and services. Apparently it is much more difficult to explain consumer behavior during the 1970s than during prior decades. In addition, none of the equations succeeds in explaining fully the rise in the ratio of consumption to income at the very end of the decade. While the real after-tax rate of interest did decline, its influence on consumption was partially offset by a fall in the ratio of household wealth to income, due primarily to a fall in stock market values.

The equations for durable-goods purchases also support the notion of a significant interest rate effect. In this case, however, it was not necessary to lag the interest rate and it is included as part of a rental price term. Initially, the effect of an interest rate change is very substantial as it alters the desired stock of durables. A 1-percentage-point rise in the interest rate reduces the current year's gross expenditures on durables by about 3 percent. But once the stock adjustment is complete, the effect on new purchases is limited to replacement demand.

28. Boskin's elasticity of saving of 0.4 corresponds to a 1 percent change in consumption per percentage-point change in the interest rate. The effort to replicate Boskin's results by including the unemployment rate and defining income to include corporate retained earnings did not improve the results. In the equations that used labor income and wealth, the implication is that households do see through the "corporate veil" because variations in corporate payout rates do not affect private consumption. In addition, there appeared to be no additional role for the inflation rate or various estimates of consumer attitudes.

In contrast to the consumption equation estimates, the results were not sensitive to changes in the data period, and surprisingly, there is no tendency toward larger prediction errors during the 1970s.

If the empirical results for durables are combined with those for consumer outlays on nondurables and services, a 1-percentage-point increase in the after-tax real interest rate could be expected to reduce consumer expenditures in the subsequent year by about 1.5 percent, or in 1980 by about $25 billion. These equations make no effort to distinguish the effects of interest rate changes on expected future capital income. Thus, the coefficient on the interest rate should reflect the net effect of an interest rate change—income plus compensated substitution effects. Since the income effect on consumption is positive, the implied substitution effect is quite substantial.

One difficulty with the use of historical U.S. data to resolve the issue of the relationship between saving and its rate of return is that the latter has until recently varied within a narrow range and with a predictable cyclical pattern that was highly correlated with the other factors. Since 1980 that has not been the case. The unprecedented increase in nominal interest rates, a slowing of inflation, and a sharp reduction in marginal tax rates, all in the midst of a severe recession, have raised the real after-tax return. Thus one should expect substantial increases in the private saving rate during the early 1980s. It is useful to use the equations of table 3-1 to determine whether any such change is evident in the data for 1981–82.

All of the equations of table 3-1 underestimate consumption in 1981–82, and the errors for 1982 are generally far greater than the standard error of the estimation period. For total consumption (equation 1), for example, the 1982 error is $3\frac{1}{2}$ times the standard error of estimate. The forecasts are most accurate for durable purchases, where the 1982 residual is within one standard error. In addition, while the equations using labor income fit better than those based on total income during the period of estimation, their forecast errors are substantially larger in both 1981 and 1982—six times the standard error of estimate in the case of equation 2.

According to these regressions, consumer spending was unusually strong in 1982. Real interest rates rose back to the levels of the early 1970s and the wealth-income ratio declined; yet both total consumption and spending on nondurables plus services rose sharply as a share of income. The reported saving rate rose only because of the decline in durable purchases, but that decline was actually less than would have been expected on the basis of historical experience.

The reasons for the larger forecast error for the equations based on labor income can be traced to the sharp shift in the distribution of income between 1979 and 1982. After adjusting for inflation and population growth, labor income fell by 2.6 percent, while property income grew by 6.7 percent. Given that the growth in total income was inadequate to explain the strength of consumer spending, it is not suprising that labor and transfer income alone perform even worse.

Overall, these statistical results provide a good example of the ambiguity of the evidence from aggregate time series data as to the role of interest rates in consumption-saving decisions. In addition, empirical equations that distinguish between labor and property income failed to account for the pattern of consumption during 1981-82; this raises questions about the adequacy of the basic analytical framework—the life cycle model.[29] Indeed, the consumption-income relationship has become increasingly unstable throughout the 1970s and early 1980s. Assertions that an increase in the return to capital will or will not raise the overall private saving rate must be based on personal beliefs, because the existing empirical evidence must be judged as inconclusive.

NUMERICAL ANALYSIS OF THEORETICAL MODELS. Frustration with the econometric problem has led some investigators to analyze and draw conclusions about empirical magnitudes through the simulation of theoretical life cycle models that incorporate specific numerical assumptions about the parameters. They postulate a specific mathematical form of a consumer's utility function and determine the optimal lifetime pattern of saving in response to a change in the interest rate. There have been several recent examples in the research on consumer saving behavior.[30] These studies have been useful in highlighting some of the complex

29. For a discussion of some criticisms of the life cycle model, see Henry J. Aaron, *Economic Effects of Social Security* (Brookings Institution, 1982), pp. 45–50, and the studies referenced therein.

30. See, for example, James Tobin and Walter Dolde, "Wealth, Liquidity and Consumption," in *Consumer Spending and Monetary Policy: The Linkages*, conference series no. 5 (Federal Reserve Bank of Boston, 1971), pp. 99–146; Betsy B. White, "Empirical Tests of the Life Cycle Hypothesis," *American Economic Review*, vol. 68 (September 1978), pp. 547–60; and Lawrence H. Summers, "Capital Taxation and Accumulation in a Life Cycle Growth Model," *American Economic Review*, vol. 71 (September 1981), pp. 533–44.

interactions in the models of consumer behavior and in identifying, through sensitivity analysis, the critical parameters for future empirical work. But to interpret these studies as providing evidence on the empirical magnitudes is wrong.[31] In particular, such studies cannot be used to determine the magnitude of parameters that depend upon the preferences of individuals, such as the interest elasticity of saving. It is precisely those preferences that are at issue and they cannot be assumed away by selection of some specific form of the consumer's utility function.

THE DISTRIBUTION OF INCOME. The distribution of income has played an important role in the debate over policies to increase private saving. Many of the arguments for reducing the rate of taxation on upper-income groups reflect, at least implicitly, the view that the rich do most of the saving and that saving rates increase as relative incomes rise. Certainly the common view is that the rich save a larger share of their income than the poor. That view, however, may confuse saving, the increment to wealth, with savings, the stock of wealth. By definition the rich have most of the latter, but if they had higher propensities to save, other things being equal, the distribution of income and wealth would become more unequal over time, unless there were offsetting changes in other determinants.

Surveys of households have shown that higher income groups have higher average saving rates, but, as Friedman pointed out, this result is predominantly a reflection of transitory changes in income. Consumers do not alter their consumption in response to temporary income changes; thus individuals with a transitory income gain will report a high saving rate. In fact, modern theories of consumer behavior are specifically

---

31. Summers, "Capital Taxation and Accumulation," p. 543, seems to imply that such exercises can provide evidence of the magnitude of the saving elasticity, and the values that he obtained are cited as though they were empirical estimates in Jared Enzler, William E. Conrad, and Lewis Johnson, "Introduction and Summary," in Board of Governors of the Federal Reserve System, *Public Policy and Capital Formation* (Washington, D.C., April 1981), p. 16, note 22. This specific issue is evaluated in some detail in Owen J. Evans, "Tax Policy, the Interest Elasticity of Saving, and Capital Accumulation: Numerical Analysis of Theoretical Models," *American Economic Review*, vol. 73 (June 1983), pp. 398–410; and David A. Starrett, "Long-Run Saving Elasticities in the Life Cycle Model," Research Paper No. 24, Workshop on Factor Markets, Department of Economics, Stanford University, August 1982. The latter two papers show that the life cycle model is consistent with any saving elasticity and the result is dependent upon the nature of consumer preferences.

based on the assertion that the saving rate is independent of the level of lifetime income unless bequests to future generations are a luxury good.[32]

The issue was tested empirically by Blinder.[33] He investigated the role of the distribution of income in an aggregate consumption equation similar to those of table 3-1. Blinder found that a more equal distribution of income would either have little influence on the average saving rate or slightly increase it.[34] Similar results were generally found in international studies that compared countries with differing distributions of income.[35]

Interdependence of Sectoral Saving

The difficulties of measuring the saving of individual sectors of the economy were discussed earlier. In addition, there are good behavioral reasons to suppose that the saving of households, business, and governments is interrelated. The observed constancy of the overall private saving rate in the face of substantial variation in the household and business components has already been noted. One explanation would be that households "pierce the corporate veil" and perceive corporate decisions to retain earnings as essentially the actions of an agent acting on their behalf. The effect of decisions to retain earnings would be reflected indirectly through the change in the value of corporate stock. It is difficult to reach any conclusion from the statistical data about whether aggregate consumption is explained more accurately by total disposable income or by labor and transfer income alone because the dividend component changes so slowly over time. This is reflected in the empirical equations reported in table 3-1, where both income measures performed about equally well. The equations using wealth, labor

32. This independence is asserted in models other than the life cycle hypothesis. See, for example, James S. Duesenberry, *Income, Saving, and the Theory of Consumer Behavior* (Harvard University Press, 1949); and Milton Friedman, *A Theory of the Consumption Function* (Princeton University Press for the National Bureau of Economic Research, 1957).

33. Alan S. Blinder, "Distribution Effects and the Aggregate Consumption Function," *Journal of Political Economy*, vol. 83 (June 1975), pp. 447–75.

34. This does not rule out the possibility that a proportionate change in tax rates might have a larger effect on the savings incentives of high-tax-rate groups because it implies a larger change in their after-tax rate of return.

35. George Kopits and Padma Gotur, "The Influence of Social Security on Household Saving: A Cross-Country Investigation," *International Monetary Fund Staff Papers*, vol. 27 (March 1980), pp. 161–90.

income, and transfers were consistent with the hypothesis because the results were not improved by the addition of dividends or retained earnings, but the results are hardly conclusive.

A study by von Furstenberg did find a strong negative correlation between household and corporate saving rates.[36] From this he concluded that shifts in income between the household and corporate sectors, such as might result from offsetting changes in relative taxation, would have little or no effect on the total amount of saving.

The above argument about the interrelation between the business and household sectors is sometimes extended to private and public saving: that individuals also view the government as an agent making consumption and investment decisions on their behalf. One view of this ultrarational behavior was put forth by David and Scadding when they argued that the private sector regards tax-financed expenditures as equivalent to their own consumption and bond-financed public outlays as equivalent to private investment.[37]

The David and Scadding article was motivated by the previously noted constancy of the ratio of private saving to GNP. They pointed out that, if this ratio had been constant during a period in which government purchases had grown as a share of GNP, it must be that private saving increased as a share of private after-tax income in an offsetting fashion. They interpret this to mean that the relevant income measure is before-tax income (GNP), and public consumption is offset on a one-to-one basis by private consumption, thus explaining the stability of the ratio of private saving to GNP.

They define net taxes as taxes minus government transfers and divide government purchases into consumption (net taxes) and investment (the deficit). This division is necessary because David and Scadding agree that the private saving rate is more stable than national saving (private saving plus government saving). They view public investment (the deficit) as substituting for private investment: changes in the deficit change investment, not saving. They also argue that this displacement

36. Von Furstenberg, "Saving." His results were questioned in the subsequent discussion as reflecting offsetting cyclical factors rather than implying any caused response. Similar conclusions were also reported, however, in Howry and Hymans, "The Measurement and Determination of Loanable Funds Saving," p. 681.

37. Paul A. David and John L. Scadding, "Private Saving: Ultrarationality, Aggregation, and 'Denison's Law,'" *Journal of Political Economy*, vol. 82 (March–April 1974), pp. 225–49.

occurs without the need for a rise in interest rates to crowd out private investment (so-called ex ante crowding out).[38]

Certainly there is a degree of truth in their hypothesis, and it is a point often overlooked in analyses of tax policy that implicitly assume that the expenditures financed by taxes are pure waste and have no value to consumers. If the government took over all private health insurance plans and reclassified the insurance premiums as taxes, private consumption expenditures would decline in an offsetting fashion, and one might expect little or no effect on private saving. Many user taxes would also be expected to have this characteristic of substituting for private consumption.

But the association of net taxes with consumption and deficits with investment is a stronger and more controversial statement, as is the argument that private investment offsets changes in the deficit directly without the need for a change in interest rates. In many cases private and public investments might be seen as complements, rather than substitutes.[39]

A slightly different version of the ultrarationality hypothesis was proposed by Barro in a model where the relevant time horizon for planning consumption extends over generations, rather than an individual's lifetime, because of the desire to leave bequests. The current generation perceives the government debt as a negative bequest to future generations and thus adjusts its own saving and bequests to offset this effect.[40] This type of model has played a significant role in the discussion of the effects of social security on saving.[41] It is also relevant to government fiscal policy because it implies that real economic outcomes are unaffected by methods of financing government expenditures— whether by taxes, debt issues, or the printing of money. The hypothesis

38. One implication of the David and Scadding hypothesis is that fiscal policy has no effect on aggregate demand and is therefore useless as a stabilization device. That does not apply to its effect on private capital formation, however, as a shift toward a budget surplus would directly increase private investment—even without the need to operate through the mechanism of increased funds to the capital markets and thus lower interest rates.

39. In practice, government taxes may exceed or fall short of those expenditures that might reasonably be classified as consumption; yet, if the actual deficit cannot be associated with investment, David and Scadding do not have an explanation for the greater stability of the private saving rate, as opposed to the national rate.

40. Robert J. Barro, "Are Government Bonds Net Wealth?" *Journal of Political Economy*, vol. 82 (November–December 1974), pp. 1095–1117.

41. For a summary, see Aaron, *Economic Effects of Social Security*.

differs from that of David and Scadding because the relevant concept of the public debt is the excess of the public liabilities, minus assets, that is passed on to future generations.[42] That is, the Barro analysis is specifically concerned with debt financing that is used to support current consumption.

These issues of public versus private saving have been examined by several authors, and the empirical evidence was reviewed by Buiter and Tobin.[43] They found that the debt neutrality view was not supported in empirical studies of short-run consumer spending behavior, but that "further empirical work is urgently needed, however, before any conclusion can be more than tentative." A second study by von Furstenberg found asymmetric effects of changes in government saving on private saving, depending on whether the change in the budget originated on the tax or expenditure side.[44] Finally, a study by Feldstein found that the empirical data contradicted the more extreme versions of the ultra-rationality argument, which argues that fiscal policy has no impact on the economy.[45]

Perhaps a reasonable tentative conclusion would be that the empirical evidence and theoretical arguments provide considerable support for the notion that individuals do in large part pierce the veil between corporate and household saving and are aware of the future benefits of corporate retentions, as reflected in the market value of their corporate stock. The veil between private and government saving is more opaque, however. The assumptions required to derive the notion that the public is indifferent between tax and debt financing are very restrictive. And while the empirical analysis is not conclusive, it is not supportive of the ultrarationality hypothesis. Instead, the arguments are of primary value in pointing to the ambiguity of the long-term effects of debt finance on saving and the importance of examining the purposes for which tax revenues are used before one can evaluate the effect on private behavior.

42. At the end of 1980, public ownership of tangible capital was valued at $2.4 trillion and net financial liabilities totaled $0.5 trillion for a positive net worth of $1.9 trillion. Eisner and Pieper, "A New View of the Federal Debt and Budget Deficits," p. 30.
43. William H. Buiter and James Tobin, "Debt Neutrality: A Brief Review of Doctrine and Evidence," in George M. von Furstenberg, ed., *Social Security Versus Private Saving* (Ballinger, 1979), pp. 39–63.
44. Von Furstenberg, "Saving." Also note the critique of the study in the subsequent discussion.
45. Martin Feldstein, "Government Deficits and Aggregate Demand," *Journal of Monetary Economics*, vol. 9 (January 1982), pp. 1–20.

90 TAX INCENTIVES AND ECONOMIC GROWTH

SOCIAL SECURITY. The above statistical analysis has ignored the influence of social security on saving behavior. While that issue has been among the most active areas of theoretical and empirical research in recent years, no consensus has emerged. There is a better understanding of the basic issues in the debate, but the empirical studies have been controversial and ambiguous in their conclusions.

The most straightforward view would be that social security, by shifting income from an individual's working years to retirement, reduces the need to accumulate private assets for retirement. Since the social security system does not accumulate a reserve equal to the present value of the future benefits, the net effect is to reduce national saving. It can be argued, however, that the availability of social security induces earlier retirement. A longer period of retirement, in turn, requires a higher rate of saving during the working years; and from that perspective social security may serve as a stimulus to saving. The net effect on individuals' saving depends on the relative strength of these two offsetting forces—hence the controversy.

Conflicting views of the effect of social security on private saving can also be highlighted in terms of alternative theories of consumer behavior. From the perspective of the life cycle model, the individual optimizes his consumption over his lifetime (including, perhaps, a bequest). Thus a rise in the present value of future social security benefits would be expected to reduce private saving or encourage earlier retirement. Since the system is financed on a "pay-as-you-go" basis, the result would be a decline in national saving. On the other hand, the intergenerational model (discussed earlier) argues that the social security tax and transfer system simply replaces a private system of transfers between generations. The major effect of social security has been to reduce those private transfers with no significant effect on private saving.

No attempt will be made in this chapter to summarize the voluminous literature on this subject. Several comprehensive reviews have recently been published.[46] At present, the fairest conclusion would seem to be that the evidence that social security either increases or reduces saving

46. For a discussion of the major issues see Aaron, *Economic Effects of Social Security*. The footnotes of that study provide citations to the major contributions and review articles. In addition, a useful discussion of the issues is provided by Mordecai Kurz, "Analyzing Social Security and Intergenerational Capital Formation and Transmission," paper presented at the Center for Economic Policy Research Conference on Social Security, Stanford University, May 6–7, 1983.

is not convincing. The theoretical articles have clarified the issues, but they have raised more questions than the empirical studies have been able to answer.

One problem is that the system itself is very complex. In addition to retirement, it provides benefits for disabled workers and surviving dependents. It also incorporates significant elements of income redistribution. There are severe problems of interpreting the data because few retired individuals have been covered over their full working life, and the net return (benefits in excess of payments) to future retirees will be much different from the returns realized by past retirees. Thus the aggregate data is primarily a reflection of a system in transition. At the same time, very limited information is available on the behavior of individual households that would allow for an analysis of the program's effect on their saving decisions. Furthermore, the system has become so comprehensive that it is difficult to find a significant noneligible subpopulation that can be used as a control group.

INTERNATIONAL COMPARISONS. Saving rates do vary substantially among countries. Potentially these differences offer an additional opportunity to resolve some of the issues. Unfortunately, any analysis is complicated by major differences in economic institutions and social values. As shown in table 3-2, the United States, Great Britain, and Sweden stand out as countries with relatively low saving rates, while the rate for Japan is extraordinarily high.

Previous studies have accounted for a large proportion of the observed variation by reference to differences in income growth, the ratio of retired persons and children to the working population, the labor force participation of persons over age sixty-five, and the ratio of social security benefits to average wage rates.[47] Japan, for example, has had a very high rate of income growth, a small retired population, a high labor force participation rate for those aged sixty-five and over, a limited social security system, and a small population under twenty years of age. These are all factors that should contribute to higher saving rates.

The assignment of a major role to income growth, when the causation may run in the opposite direction (higher saving accelerates the growth of capital and thus income), and the lack of a significant role for interest

47. See, for example, Martin Feldstein, "International Differences in Social Security and Saving," *Journal of Public Economics*, vol. 14 (October 1980), pp 225–44. Other studies have stressed similar factors although there are differences of view about the importance of social security.

Table 3-2. *Private Saving and Its Uses in Major Industrial Countries, Five-Year Averages, 1970–79*
Percent of gross domestic product

Country	Private saving	Uses of private saving					
		Business investment	Government deficit	Net foreign investment	Residential construction	Inventory change	Statistical discrepancy
Canada							
1970–74	17.8	13.0	−0.8	−0.2	5.3	0.9	−0.4
1975–79	19.6	13.9	2.0	−2.4	5.8	0.5	−0.2
United States							
1970–74	16.4	10.5	0.6	0.1	4.6	0.9	−0.2
1975–79	17.3	10.9	1.3	0.0	4.6	0.7	−0.1
Japan							
1970–74	31.5	22.3	−1.8	1.0	7.6	2.1	0.3
1975–79	29.3	18.1	3.0	0.6	7.5	0.6	−0.6
France							
1970–74	20.9	13.1	−1.2	−0.3	7.0	2.2	...
1975–79	20.4	12.4	0.7	−0.3	6.7	0.9	...
Germany							
1970–74	21.1	13.6	−1.7	1.1	7.3	0.9	...
1975–79	21.0	11.9	1.5	0.7	6.0	1.0	...
Italy							
1970–74	26.8	12.4	7.0	−0.4	5.7	2.1	...
1975–79	27.2	11.1	8.5	0.7	5.2	1.8	...
Netherlands							
1970–74	22.3	13.8	−0.9	1.7	5.8	1.9	...
1975–79	19.9	11.7	1.2	0.8	5.5	0.6	...
Sweden							
1970–74	14.2	11.1	−4.0	0.7	5.1	1.2	...
1975–79	14.0	11.6	−1.2	−1.5	4.3	0.8	...
United Kingdom							
1970–74	14.8	10.7	−0.1	−0.8	3.5	0.9	0.5
1975–79	17.3	11.4	3.2	−0.9	3.5	0.5	−0.4
Australia							
1970–74	20.5	15.3	−1.2	−0.5	4.9	1.0	0.9
1975–79	19.5	13.9	1.8	−1.8	4.8	0.5	0.4

Source: Computed by the author from Organization of Economic Cooperation and Development, *National Income Accounts of OECD Countries, 1962–1979*, vol. 2 (Paris: OECD, 1981).

rates are controversial aspects of these studies. In addition, the retirement decisions of older workers may be a reflection rather than a cause of high national saving rates. In effect, the international comparisons suggest that rapid aggregate demand growth, rather than increased after-tax rates of interest, is the most effective means of increasing the national saving rate.

The problems are highlighted in the study of international differences in saving rates by Feldstein.[48] He found that a 1-percentage-point change in a nation's growth rate raised its private saving rate by 5 percentage points. His analysis excluded Japan. Using data estimated by the staff of the Organization for Economic Cooperation and Development (OECD), however, the Feldstein equation can be applied to Japan, for which it overestimates the saving rate by a factor of two.[49] An error of that magnitude illustrates the difficulties of inferring conclusions from the existing studies.

The comparison in table 3-2 of national saving rates between the first half and last half of the 1970s reinforces the view that the existing studies overemphasize the causal role of aggregate income growth in determining saving rates. Private saving rates remained surprisingly constant despite a very sharp worldwide slowing of income growth after 1974.

A recent OECD study examined the international differences in saving rates. The authors of that study stressed restrictions on consumer borrowing and statistical differences caused by differences in national income accounting conventions as important factors, in addition to income growth and demographic variables.[50] Financial markets for consumer borrowing are more developed in the United States and Canada than in most other countries and may reduce the saving rate of young households, which typically have limited income and high expenditure needs. Most significantly, they concluded that differences in rates of return earned by savers appeared to play a minor role.

The strongest international evidence that rates of return may affect saving emerges from the comparison of Canada and the United States— two countries with similar economic institutions and social values— during the 1970s. In the United States household saving as a percentage of after-tax income declined from about 8 percent at the beginning of the decade to 5.5 percent at the end. The comparable rate for Canada rose from 6 to 10 percent.

48. Ibid.
49. If the causal interpretation of the relationship were reversed, it would imply that a rise of 1 percentage point in the saving and investment rate increases a country's annual growth rate by 0.2 percentage point, but even that is a little high compared to the effect estimated from the growth accounting studies. The data on the saving rate and the explanatory variables are published in OECD, "International Differences and Trend Changes in Saving Ratios," pp. 92–93.
50. Ibid. Among the accounting conventions they examined were the classification of durable purchases as consumption versus investment, indirect business taxes, and social security fund balances.

Some of this difference can be explained by the difficulties, discussed earlier, of measuring interest income in an inflationary environment.[51] If comparable adjustments are made for both countries, however, a growing divergence is evident after 1975 that cannot be attributed to income growth or inflation. Instead, several investigators have pointed out that in Canada: (a) consumer interest payments are not deductible from taxable income, (b) there have been more substantial exclusions from taxation of income placed in special saving accounts, and (c) interest rates for small savers are not constrained by regulations as severely as in the United States.

On the other hand, a study by Jump has argued that the Canadian tax treatment of saving accounts will influence the composition rather than the total amount of saving, and that Canadian studies have not normally found significant interest rate effects on consumer spending.[52] He points out that most of the tax benefits can be achieved by shifting existing wealth into the tax-exempt deposit accounts rather than through an increase in the saving rate. It would appear, however, that this option would be exhausted after a few years; the financial wealth of most savers is equal to only a few years of such saving. The question of whether individuals would continue to pay into these accounts over long periods remains. In effect, after adjusting for inflation, Jump concludes that the divergence of household saving rates between Canada and the United States is due to a decline in household saving in the United States rather than a rise within Canada. The decline within the United States may be due to reductions in corporate taxes that shifted the pattern of private saving.

Summary

If the United States is to achieve a higher rate of capital formation at sustained levels of full employment, it will be necessary to increase the nation's rate of saving. Government can achieve that goal directly by increasing its own saving through budget surpluses, or it can seek to .

51. Jump, "Recent Behavior of the Personal Saving Rate."
52. Gregory V. Jump, "Tax Incentives to Promote Personal Saving: Recent Canadian Experience," *Saving and Government Policy*, conference series no. 25 (Federal Reserve Bank of Boston, 1982), pp. 46–64. See also the subsequent discussion as a criticism of his view.

increase the private sector's saving. At the beginning of this chapter it was noted that the share of GNP saved by the private sector has been very constant since the early 1950s. While it is possible that it is the net result of several offsetting forces, the stability of the rate should give pause to those who argue that it can be significantly altered by marginal adjustments in government policies.

The sensitivity of consumer expenditure decisions to variations in the after-tax rate of return on savings plays a vital role in the discussion of programs to promote a higher rate of national saving. That is an empirical issue that cannot be resolved by a priori reasoning. Obviously, a change in the rate of return increases the gain from an additional dollar of current saving; but at the same time it increases the amount of future income that will be earned on past and previously planned future saving. That rise in expected lifetime income has an offsetting positive effect on current consumption. Thus the net effect of a change in the rate of return cannot be resolved except by empirical analysis of consumer decisions.

As has been shown, the existing empirical evidence is ambiguous. In part this is the result of limitations in the available data. Nearly all the empirical studies have had to rely on aggregate time-series data, where interest rate changes are heavily entangled with other aspects of the business cycle, and the heterogeneous nature of the population being examined greatly complicates the analysis. It is not difficult to obtain statistically significant coefficients on the interest rate variable for several different empirical formulations of the consumption decision, but the results are very sensitive to changes in the period of estimation. The basic model also performs poorly in explaining the actual path of consumer spending in 1981–82—a period of seemingly ideal circumstances in which to observe a rise in private saving rates.

The evidence of a significant negative effect of higher interest rates is strongest for expenditures on consumer durables. The role of interest rates was significant in the statistical equations and the forecasts for 1981–82 were reasonably accurate.

The results were less convincing for the broad category of expenditures on nondurables and services. A statistical equation estimated over 1953–80 implied that a 1-percentage-point increase in the after-tax real interest rate would reduce such expenditures by about 1 percent. But the equation drastically underpredicts consumption in 1981–82, when the rate of return rose sharply.

While a finding of a small net effect of changes in the rate of return on consumer spending suggests that variations in market interest rates are of limited importance, it does not imply that changes in tax policy cannot affect saving decisions. In the long run, consumption responds proportionately to any change in income and wealth—a unitary income elasticity. Thus a finding that the net effect of an interest rate change is close to zero, in combination with an income elasticity near unity, still implies a substantial substitution effect. The distinction between the income and substitution effects is important because it is possible to change the tax system so as to collect the same amount of revenue (no income effect), but to reduce the taxation of capital income. Such a policy should unambiguously increase saving. That is an issue of substantial importance to a later discussion of proposals that the United States shift from an income tax to a consumption tax.

Given the uncertainties about the effectiveness of government policies to alter private saving, direct actions to increase the nation's saving by reducing the government budget deficit would seem to be a more certain prescription. Here too, however, there is controversy. Some economists have argued that variations in the government deficit have no effect on the overall saving rate because the private sector adjusts its own saving and investment to offset variations in the government budget balance.

One version of the argument, by David and Scadding, argues that expenditures financed by taxes are equivalent to private consumption, while deficit financing substitutes for private investment. A second argument, emphasized by Barro, argues that the private sector perceives the government debt as a negative bequest to future generations and undertakes offsetting adjustments. Both of the arguments would imply that government budget deficits have no effect on the aggregate economy.

At present, the empirical evidence conflicts with the extreme versions of the argument that government deficits do not matter for the overall economy. However, most of the research is too tentative to conclude that there is no offsetting private-sector saving response. A reasonable interim view would be that increased government saving can augment national saving, but the relationship should not be assumed to be one-to-one. Certainly, in the short run a rise in the budget surplus achieved by an increase in taxes will not be immediately reflected in a equal reduction in private consumption. Consumers will only gradually adjust their spending to a lower level of after-tax income. Thus there is a tendency in the short run for private and public saving rates to move in an offsetting fashion; but the lags in consumer responses are of much less importance over a period of several years.

CHAPTER FOUR

Investment Demand and Its Relation to Saving

THE EFFORT to discover the basic determinants of investment demand has been one of the most active areas of economic research and debate. From a theoretical perspective, current investment should be a function of expected future sales (a scale factor) and the cost of substituting capital for labor. The cost of capital is a composite measure of the cost of hiring a unit of capital, including depreciation, financing, any capital gain or loss because of price changes, and taxes. A controversy arises, however, from conflicting views about the importance of the cost of capital in investment decisions.

The primary issue is an empirical one, involving the technological constraints on the substitution of capital for labor in production. If firms can choose from a range of production processes using different combinations of capital and labor, they should be sensitive to the relative costs of the two factors in their investment decisions. If the opportunities for substitution are limited, the components of the cost of capital—inflation, interest rates, and taxes—are largely irrelevant to investment decisions; and the government's ability to affect investment is limited largely to altering expectations about the future growth of sales.

The neoclassical model of investment behavior is based on the assumption that substitution among the factors of production in response to variations in their relative costs is an important element of firms' decisions. The opposing hypothesis is identified with the pure accelerator model of investment. The accelerator model does not require fixed proportions of capital and labor over time (it acknowledges that technology does change); but it does assume that these proportions are not influenced by changes in relative prices. That may be because the potential for substitution at any point in time is limited or because firms do not accurately perceive the full range of possibilities in making their investment decisions.

Models of Investment Behavior

The analytical framework for empirical research on business investment behavior is based on extensions of the neoclassical theory of
optimal capital accumulation.[1]

The Neoclassical Model

The neoclassical model assumes that firms seek to maximize profits
(or minimize costs) over time, operate in competitive markets, and are
subject to a set of technological constraints summarized by a production
function that describes the relation between capital and labor inputs on
the one hand and the level of output on the other. The assumption of
profit maximization implies that the firm will add capital up to the point
where the marginal revenue product of the last unit is equal to the cost
of using it for one period. That is,

(1) $$P_q \cdot MPP_k = c,$$

where P_q is the price of output and MPP_k is the output gain attributed to
the last increment of capital (its marginal physical product as given by
the technological parameters of the production function). In the absence
of taxes, the cost of using capital for one period (its rental price), c, is a
straightforward concept. It is the acquisition price of capital (P_k) multiplied by a fraction equal to the rate of interest (i), plus depreciation of
the asset during the period (d), minus any capital gain resulting from a
change in the asset's price $(\dot{P}_k)$:

(2) $$c = P_k(i + d - \dot{P}_k).$$

For example, for an asset with an annual rate of depreciation of 15
percent, a 5 percent rate of interest, and no inflation, the annual rental
price is 20 percent of its acquisition cost. The rental price can also be
thought of as the minimum, or hurdle, rate that an investment must earn
to justify its cost.

This formulation is particularly useful when the analysis is extended
to include taxes because nearly all aspects of the tax code can be
represented in terms of specific changes in the rental price of the capital

1. Dale W. Jorgenson, "Capital Theory and Investment Behavior," *American
Economic Review*, vol. 53 (May 1963, *Papers and Proceedings, 1962*), pp. 247–59.

variable, c. Thus, in empirical work, instead of having to deal with separate evaluations of the effect of interest rates, price changes, and a host of different tax measures, all these factors are combined into a single composite price variable. The critical issue for giving the neoclassical investment model empirical content is in the choice of the specific production function, which determines the marginal physical product of capital (MPP_k).

The analytical framework is similar to that used earlier to illustrate the choice between current and future consumption (saving). In this case, a technological relationship describing the ability to substitute between capital and labor at various levels of output replaces the concept of utility of current and future consumption. Because the level of expected future output is held constant, there is no income effect, and the issue is the magnitude of the substitution effect. For a wide range of representative production functions, the potential for substitution can be summarized in terms of the elasticity of substitution, σ: the percentage change in the ratio of capital to labor (at a given level of output) corresponding to a 1 percent change in the ratio of their prices.[2] In the case of constant returns to scale, the desired capital stock, K^*, implied by the maximizing condition of equation 1, is proportionate to the expected level of output, Q, and inversely related to the rental price of capital,

$$(3) \qquad\qquad K^* = A\left(\frac{P_q}{c}\right)^{\sigma} Q,$$

where A is a parameter that shifts over time to represent technological change. If the elasticity of substitution equals unity, a 1 percent rise in output and a 1 percent decline in the price of capital both raise the demand for capital by an equal amount—1 percent. If it is equal to zero, the desired stock of capital is a function only of output and technical change.

The empirical models of investment are made more complex by the need to explain the process by which firms adjust their investment spending to changes in the desired stock of capital. Given the observed

2. It may be helpful to refer back to the graphical analysis of figure 3-2. The elasticity of substitution is a measure of the curvature of the isoquants. If they are right-angled, σ equal to zero, variations in the slope of the budget line will cause no change in the proportions in which the inputs are used—a single dominant production process. As the isoquants approach straight lines, large values of σ (the distance between B and D), the substitution effect increases.

fact that variations in the growth of the capital stock are far less than the variations in output, this adjustment process must stretch over several years. Most empirical studies have modeled it as a partial adjustment process where gross investment, I, is equal to the replacement (or depreciation) of existing capital, K, plus a weighted average (with weights of w_i) of past changes, Δ, in the desired stock,

(4)
$$I_t = \sum_{i=0}^{n} w_i \cdot \Delta K_{t-1}^* + d \cdot K_{t-1}.$$

Tax policy enters into the investment decision through its effect on the rental price term and thus the desired stock of capital. If the elasticity of substitution were as large as unity, the model would imply a very powerful role for government policy in the capital-formation process because monetary and tax policy could be used directly to alter the desired capital-output ratio through changes in the after-tax rental price of capital.

The Accelerator Model

The neoclassical formulation is not the only interpretation of the investment process. Other investigators have objected to the rigidity of the underlying assumptions about profit maximization and the existence of a full resale market for capital, which makes it possible to ignore any sunk-cost aspect of capital and makes its purchase (rent) comparable to short-run employment decisions. The greatest disagreement, however, has focused on the magnitude of the elasticity of substitution. If no factor substitution is possible ($\sigma = 0$), the investment relationship simplifies to a weighted average of past rates of growth in output, replacement of existing capital, and perhaps a trend term to reflect any tendency for technical change to increase the capital-output ratio:

(5)
$$I_t = \sum_{i=0}^{n} w_i \cdot \Delta Q_{t-i} + d \cdot K_{t-1}.$$

This is commonly referred to as the pure accelerator model because of the link between the *level* of investment and the *change* in output. The neoclassical model has the same relationship between the level of investment and the change in output, but the pure accelerator model includes no role for relative prices. Thus, if the accelerator model is correct, government can affect business investment only by altering the growth of aggregate demand: not by varying taxes, interest rates, or other determinants of the rental price of capital.

The analytical formulation of the model has been refined in several respects since Jorgenson's original contribution.[3] The basic framework, however, has dominated empirical studies of investment and the discussion of business tax policy for the past two decades. One major benefit has been the ability to evaluate a wide range of complex tax measures within the confines of business firms' response to changes in a single composite price variable—the rental price.

Measures of the Rental Price of Capital

The expression for the rental price of capital, c, given in equation 2, becomes more complex once taxes are introduced into the analysis. The essential features of the U.S. corporate tax system are captured in the following formulation for the rental price term:

$$(6) \qquad c = P_k (i + d - \dot{P}_k) \left[\frac{1 - \rho z - k}{1 - \rho} \right],$$

where

$i =$ the after-tax cost of funds to the firm,

$\rho =$ the corporate tax rate,

$k =$ the investment tax credit as a percentage of the purchase price,

$z =$ the present value of the depreciation allowances that are allowed for tax purposes.

For the corporate investor the after-tax nominal cost of funds is a weighted average of the cost of debts, i_d, and equity finance, i_e:

3. For example, some studies include the after-tax cash flow of business to reflect the reluctance of firms to seek external funds to finance their investments. This provides a secondary mechanism, other than relative prices, by which taxes and interest rates may directly alter investment. The specification of the after-tax discount rate (i) also has been expanded to incorporate the combination of debt and equity in firms' financial structures. Different lags on output and relative prices have been introduced to allow for some rigidity of the capital-labor mix in production processes that use existing capital, while allowing for input substitution in new investment (putty-clay models). A good survey of these issues is provided by the individual papers and the discussion in Gary Fromm, ed., *Tax Incentives and Capital Spending* (Brookings Institution, 1971).

(7) $i = f(1 - \rho)i_d + (1 - f)i_e,$

where f is the proportion of debt in the liability structure, and the market rate of interest is multiplied by $(1 - \rho)$ to reflect the deductibility of interest payments in computing tax liabilities. The cost of equity finance includes dividends and any expected rate of capital gain on corporate stock.

On a historical basis, difficulties of measuring the rental price of capital arise because the expected rate of capital gain on equity is not an observable variable, and because there are uncertainties about the extent to which firms have taken advantage of the various tax law changes that have liberalized the treatment of depreciation allowances over the last three decades.[4] In addition, the corporate tax system is not indexed for inflation; therefore, the present value of the depreciation allowances varies inversely with the nominal interest rate.

Several different methods have been used to measure the cost of funds. One approach is to assume that the after-tax return to capital (adjusted for inflation) has been relatively constant.[5] A smoothed average of past rates of price inflation is added in order to obtain a measure of the expected nominal rate of interest. Alternatively, some investigators begin with the market rate of interest on corporate bonds and subtract an estimate of expected inflation in computing a changing implicit real rate of return. That approach ignores the return for risk taking that is included in the equity return—measuring, in effect, the cost of riskless debt finance. Because nominal interest rates do not appear to adjust quickly to changes in the rate of inflation, the estimate of the rental price of capital can vary substantially depending upon whether one begins with a nominal or a real interest rate measure. Uncertainty about the true value of the cost of funds introduces a significant element of measurement error into the empirical studies of investment behavior; and it is probably one cause of the conflicting nature of the conclusions.

The importance of changes in the tax law—principally depreciation and the investment tax credit—is illustrated by the measure of the

4. The required equity return, i_e, will also vary with changes in the proportion of debt in the liability structure because the risk of the project is assumed by the equity owners.

5. Barbara M. Fraumeni and Dale W. Jorgenson, "The Role of Capital in U.S. Economic Growth, 1948–1976," in George M. von Furstenberg, ed., *Capital, Efficiency, and Growth* (Ballinger, 1980), pp. 73–92.

effective tax rate on corporate business investment shown in figure 4-1.[6] Throughout most of the 1950s the effective tax rate was slightly above the statutory rate, as tax depreciation was less than economic depreciation. But liberalization of depreciation allowances and the introduction of an investment tax credit substantially reduced the effective tax rate in 1962. Low rates of inflation also contributed to a high present value of the depreciation allowances in the early 1960s. Suspension of the investment tax credit, a higher statutory rate, and more rapid inflation all acted to raise the tax rate during the late 1960s. In 1971 a more generous investment tax credit was reintroduced and depreciation allowances were again liberalized. During the remainder of the 1970s the effective tax rate remained relatively constant as periodic reductions in tax rates were offset by an accelerating rate of inflation, which raised nominal interest rates.

The Economic Recovery Tax Act of 1981 dramatically cut the effective tax on corporate capital. The period over which capital assets could be written off for tax purposes was sharply reduced (the accelerated cost recovery system) and the investment tax credit was increased.[7] Under the 1981 act the effective tax rate on corporate capital would have become negative after 1984 and many categories of investment would have received a subsidy. In 1982, however, the Congress acted through the Tax Equity and Fiscal Responsibility Act to scale back the 1981 tax reduction. As a result, the effective tax rate will rise from 5 percent in 1982 to 16 percent in later years.

Most studies that employ the rental price concept to explain investment behavior conclude that the rental price of capital, deflated by the price of output, has declined since the end of World War II. The decline is primarily due to sharp reductions in the effective rate of taxation of corporate investments, as shown in figure 4-1. An offsetting influence is introduced by a secular tendency for capital goods prices to rise more rapidly than the price of output in general. That is primarily a reflection of the poor productivity performance in the construction industry.

6. The effective tax rate is the difference between the before- and after-tax rates of return on a marginal new investment expressed as a ratio to the before-tax return. It incorporates all the tax parameters of equation 6.

7. The effective tax rate continues to be sensitive to the expected rate of inflation, however. A lower assumed rate of inflation would increase the effective tax rate because it lowers the discount rate used to evaluate the present value of the depreciation allowances.

Figure 4-1. *The Effective Tax Rate on Corporate Investment and the Rental Price of Capital, 1952–86*[a]

Percent

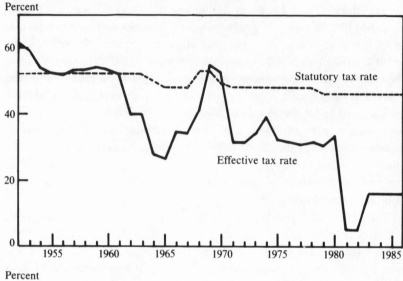

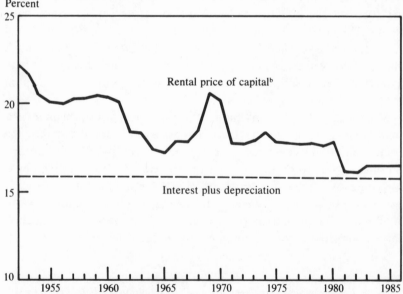

Sources: Charles R. Hulten and James W. Robertson, "Corporate Tax Policy and Economic Growth: An Analysis of the 1981 and 1982 Tax Acts" (Washington, D.C.: Urban Institute, December 1982), table 3-1; and calculations by the author.

a. The estimates are based on a 4 percent after-tax real cost of funds, and a depreciation rate that averages 11.6 percent. Their measure of expected inflation, and thus the nominal interest rate, is basically an average of actual inflation rates. For the years after 1981 expected inflation was assumed equal to 6 percent.

b. The rental price of capital excludes the effect of changes in the relative price of capital goods.

The estimated relative rental price of capital is shown in the bottom panel of figure 4-1. The dotted line, as a reference base, is a measure of the rental price in the absence of taxes and changes in the relative price of capital—the sum of the real interest cost and depreciation. The decline in the relative cost of capital is consistent with the observation in chapter 2 that the stock of capital has grown more rapidly than output since the mid-1960s and that the average after-tax return on tangible capital in the business sector has declined.

The above analysis, however, implies a greater certainty about the knowledge of past trends in the cost of capital than actually exists. It ignores the problem of measuring the cost of funds by assuming a constant after-tax real return of 4 percent. The expected nominal interest rate is simply the real return plus an estimate of expected inflation. In reality the cost of funds is a weighted average of the returns on debt and equity finance. The real cost of debt finance appears to have declined substantially throughout the 1970s, as the market rate of interest did not rise in step with any available measure of expected inflation of capital goods prices. That situation appeared to undergo a dramatic reversal in the early 1980s as interest rates rose and inflation declined.

On the other hand, the equity market has been depressed since the late 1960s, when the price-earnings ratio fell sharply. That implies a sharp increase in the cost of equity finance during the 1970s. But under some interpretations the decline in market value reflected unexpected obsolescence of existing capital and did not indicate an increased cost of financing new investment.[8] That is, the present value of the future income from existing capital really had declined, and existing stockholders were not surrendering large amounts of future income by agreeing to the issuance of new equity financing.

Others have interpreted the decline in share values as reflecting confusion by investors in valuing future earnings in an inflationary environment.[9] According to this view, the 1970s was a period of high financing costs that offset much of the incentives for investment that were extended through reductions in the effective tax rate.

8. Martin N. Baily, "Productivity and the Services of Capital and Labor," *Brookings Papers on Economic Activity, 1:1981,* pp. 1–50. (Hereafter *BPEA.*)

9. Franco Modigliani and Robert Cohn, "Inflation, Rational Valuation and the Market," *Financial Analysts Journal,* vol. 35 (March–April 1979), pp. 24–44. See also Roger E. Brinner and Stephen H. Brooks, "Stock Prices," in Henry J. Aaron and Joseph A. Pechman, eds., *How Taxes Affect Economic Behavior* (Brookings Institution, 1981), pp. 199–238.

Empirical Verification

The elasticity of substitution continues to be central to the debate over the effect of government tax policy on investment. It is perhaps best illustrated by the ongoing exchange between Dale Jorgenson and Robert Eisner. For twenty years Jorgenson has argued that the elasticity of substitution is close to unity (changes in relative prices strongly affect the demand for capital), and Eisner has argued for a value closer to zero (relative prices have no effect). Today, despite an enormous proliferation of empirical studies, neither of these two scholars has convinced the other.

In part, the lack of progress in resolving this issue reflects a tendency for many of the studies to assume a specific value for the elasticity of substitution between capital and labor rather than to estimate it directly as part of the investment equation. Jorgenson and his associates, in particular, have preferred to rely on evidence from studies of the production process as supporting a Cobb-Douglas specification (a unitary value of σ) of the aggregate production function.[10] By postulating a specific value for the elasticity of substitution in the investment equation, they have reduced the empirical issue to the determination of the lags in the adjustment of investment to changes in the desired capital stock. The long-run effect of tax policy on the capital stock is determined fully by prior specification. Eisner, in particular, has objected to this procedure and argued in favor of models that allow for direct tests of the role of relative prices.

In any case, the existing studies of the production function do not yield a specific value of the elasticity of substitution for the aggregate economy. There are serious data problems, and several of the tests allow for only a narrow range of alternative specifications. On balance, they provide substantial evidence in favor of some substitutability ($\sigma > 0$) without concluding that it is as high as unity.[11]

Furthermore, evidence from production function studies of a specific

10. Dale W. Jorgenson, "Econometric Studies of Investment Behavior: A Survey," *Journal of Economic Literature*, vol. 9 (December 1971), pp. 1111–47.

11. See, for example, Marc Nerlove, "Recent Empirical Studies of the CES and Related Production Functions," in Murray Brown, ed., *The Theory and Empirical Analysis of Production* (Columbia University Press for the National Bureau of Economic Research, 1967), pp. 55–122; and Lawrence R. Klein, "Issues in Econometric Studies of Investment Behavior," *Journal of Economic Literature*, vol. 12 (March 1974), pp. 43–49.

value for the elasticity of substitution cannot be applied to the investment decision without additional restrictive assumptions: firms must aim to maximize profits, and they must be aware of the full potential for substitution between capital and labor in their initial decisionmaking. In practice, firms may rely on "rules of thumb" in determining required returns on payback periods for investment projects, rather than the precise marginal conditions implied by the neoclassical model.

Over the last decade the efforts to resolve the issue by comparing the predictive performance of alternative investment models have been inconclusive. Both the neoclassical and accelerator models fit the data about equally well.[12] The historical data on investment spending is dominated by business cycle variations in output. Changes in the after-tax price of capital have been smaller in magnitude. As a result, the simpler model, the accelerator, can account for most of the variation in investment; and it is difficult to achieve significant statistical improvements through the addition of the relative price variable. The lack of major fluctuations in relative prices is a problem that is exacerbated by the difficulty of measuring some of the price variable's components—particularly expected inflation and the cost of funds—with precision.[13] The results are very sensitive to the choice of statistical methods and other issues such as the inclusion or exclusion of a constant term in the regression.

Alternatively, some studies have attempted to estimate the elasticity of substitution directly within the investment model: that is, they allow for a more intermediate situation in which the elasticity of substitution lies between the extremes of zero and unity.[14] The various models have sharply differing values for the substitution term, and their predictive performance is not impressive.[15]

---

12. Charles W. Bischoff, "Business Investment in the 1970s: A Comparison of Models," *BPEA, 1:1971*, pp. 13–58; and Peter K. Clark, "Investment in the 1970s: Theory, Performance and Prediction," *BPEA, 1:1979*, pp. 73–113.

13. Even a parameter such as the expected depreciation rate (d) of equation 6 is not a known value because of the need to anticipate the pace of future technological change that might make the current investment obsolete.

14. Clark, "Investment in the 1970s," pp. 110–11; and Charles W. Bischoff, "Hypothesis Testing and the Demand for Capital Goods," *Review of Economics and Statistics*, vol. 51 (August 1969), pp. 354–68.

15. See, in particular, the review by Chirinko and Eisner of the investment equations of six major econometric models: Robert S. Chirinko and Robert Eisner, "The Effects of Tax Policies on Investment in Macroeconometric Models: Full Model Simulations," Office of Tax Analysis paper 46 (U.S. Treasury Department, January 1981); and Robert

108   TAX INCENTIVES AND ECONOMIC GROWTH

The relative performance of the neoclassical and accelerator models was reexamined in a recent study by Hendershott and Hu.[16] Their study incorporated several refinements in the measurement of the rental price term. They found that the neoclassical model was unsatisfactory as an explanation of investment in structures, but that the inclusion of the rental price term (with the elasticity of substitution assumed equal to unity) in the neoclassical model significantly improved its explanation of equipment purchases, compared with the pure accelerator model. However, the further addition of the rate of capacity utilization eliminated the statistical significance of the rental price variable in their equations. It was also not possible to obtain an estimate of the role of interest rates, because an alternative equation based on a constant after-tax return performed as well as an equation using a market interest rate.

The ambiguity about the role of relative prices can be exaggerated, however, by focusing exclusively upon the variation in estimates of the elasticity of substitution. The empirical models also differ in the length of time required to adjust to changes in the desired capital stock. Some studies suggest there is a trade-off between the length of the adjustment lag and the magnitude of the estimated elasticity of substitution. Statistically, a high value of the substitution parameter is most compatible with a long lag structure.

In their initial empirical estimates of the neoclassical model, Hall and Jorgenson combined a high assumed value for the elasticity of substitution with a short lag structure—a mean lag of less than two years.[17] This combination led to the conclusion that dramatic increases in investment could be achieved through changes in tax policy.

Subsequent studies often retained the assumption of a unitary elasticity of substitution in the long run, but they significantly altered the method of estimating the lag structure. In two major econometric models relying on the neoclassical formulation as a central feature of the investment equation, the period of adjustment to a change in the price of capital stretches over fifteen years and it requires five years after the

S. Chirinko and Robert Eisner, "The Effects of Tax Parameters on the Investment Equations in Macroeconomic Econometric Models," OTA paper 47 (U.S. Treasury Department, January 1981). They also provide an extensive bibliography of other empirical studies.

16. Patric H. Hendershott and Sheng-Cheng Hu, "Investment in Producers' Equipment," in Aaron and Pechman, eds., How Taxes Affect Economic Behavior, pp. 85–126.

17. Robert E. Hall and Dale W. Jorgenson, "Application of the Theory of Optimal Capital Accumulation," in Fromm, ed., Tax Incentives and Capital Spending, pp. 9–60.

change in prices to achieve half of the increase in the capital stock.[18] In effect, at the end of five years the elasticity of substitution is 0.5, and the lengthening of the lag is equivalent to assuming a lower value of the elasticity term. Over a period of time relevant for most policy issues, therefore, it would be reasonable to assume an effective elasticity of substitution of about 0.5.

The average of the results obtained in a survey of the major econometric models by Chirinko and Eisner suggests that the above values should be reduced by about one-half—an elasticity of substitution, based on cumulating investment, over the first five years, of about 0.3.[19] Their survey of the major econometric models would seem to represent a lower bound on the range of reasonable values.

The model of Data Resources Incorporated was used to obtain some rough estimates of the effect of changes in relative prices on investment. According to this model, a 10 percent change in the rental price of capital would increase gross investment (inclusive of replacement demand) as a share of GNP by 0.5 percentage point during the five-year period following the change.[20] That implies that the increase in annual investment is approximately equal in value to the loss in tax revenues that results from a change in the investment tax credit or tax depreciation on future investment. If the government is limited in the amount of revenue that it can forgo in order to stimulate investment, this simulation implies

18. The business equipment equation of the Data Resources model achieves an elasticity of substitution of 0.2 after two years, 0.58 after five years, and 0.91 after eleven years. The FMP model maintained by the Federal Reserve Board staff has an elasticity of 0.5 after five years. Both models assume a long-run elasticity of substitution of unity, but they incorporate a lag structure on the price variable that is much longer than that attributed to cyclical variables such as output. The formulation implies that existing capital is used in fixed proportions with labor, and factor substitution is limited to new investments.

19. Chirinko and Eisner, "The Effects of Tax Policies on Investment."

20. Based on a simulation of the model of Data Resources Inc. The actual simulation was done for equipment only over the period of 1981–85 with no allowance for feedback effects from other parts of the economy. The net stock of equipment would rise by $30 billion (1972 prices) at the end of 1985, and the time path of investment would be quite flat after the first year at an average of $8 billion annually. The results are derived from Allen Sinai and Otto Eckstein, "Tax Policy and Fixed Investment Revisited," OTA paper 50 (U.S. Department of the Treasury, December 1981), table 8, p. 21. The effects of policy changes are also investigated by simulation of econometric models in R. Jeffery Green, "Investment Determinants and Tax Factors in Major Macroeconometric Models," in George M. von Furstenberg, ed., *The Government and Capital Formation* (Ballinger, 1980), pp. 337–81.

110   TAX INCENTIVES AND ECONOMIC GROWTH

a "bang for the buck" of about unity. On the other hand, it is near zero for a change in the corporate tax rate because most of the revenue loss is associated with existing capital.

On balance, the results of the empirical studies support at least a modest role for relative prices. This is particularly true given that substantial difficulties in measuring the rental price terms are likely to bias the estimated coefficient toward zero. There is considerable uncertainty, however, about the precise magnitude of the effect, and the response lags extend over many years. An elasticity of substitution in the neighborhood of 0.5 may be a reasonable compromise for the purposes of evaluating alternative policy actions.

Housing Investment

Public policy toward housing plays an important role in current discussions of capital formation because of the assertion by many economists that the nation has overinvested in housing at the expense of other investments. This overinvestment is seen as the result of a highly favorable tax treatment of homeownership. The investment is viewed as excessive in the sense that two equal before-tax investments will not yield equal after-tax returns if one investment is in housing and the other is not. Thus households will allocate an excessive portion of their assets to housing because of the attractive tax preferences. Elimination of the tax preferences for housing, or at least equalization of its treatment relative to other investments, is seen as a means of increasing national income, even without an increase in total saving, by improving the allocation of investment.

The importance of such proposals for shifting the allocation of investment between residential and nonresidential uses depends upon the answers to three questions. First, how does the current tax treatment affect the user cost of residential capital? Second, how sensitive is the demand for housing to changes in its relative cost? Certainly the current tax system encourages ownership relative to renting, but from the perspective of freeing resources for nonresidential investment, it is the elasticity of net housing demand that matters. Third, how responsive is the supply of housing to price changes? If supply is unresponsive, the tax preferences raise the price of existing housing and land, but they do not absorb real resources. In the case of nonresidential capital, it is common to undertake the analysis under the assumption that supply is perfectly elastic with respect to price. But it is suggested that there is a special problem in the case of housing because of the importance of location. Factors such as zoning restrictions may limit the response of supply and translate the rise in demand into higher prices rather than higher output.[21]

Taxes and the Price of Housing

The fundamental source of the favorable tax treatment of housing is the exclusion from tax of the income earned on such investments. The income from housing consists of an implicit flow of net services (rent minus maintenance and depreciation costs) plus the capital gain or loss.[22] The income in kind is not reported as taxable income by homeowners. In contrast, individuals who invest their wealth in other assets and use the proceeds to pay rent on their housing are subject to full taxation of that income and cannot deduct their rent payments from taxable income. It is important to note that this basic tax preference is not the result of allowing interest costs to be deducted from taxable income. The interest deduction simply extends to all taxpayers a benefit that otherwise would be restricted to those taxpayers with sufficient wealth to be able to finance their homes entirely with their own equity.[23] It is, of course, very important to take account of the interest deduction in evaluating the

21. There is a fourth issue that affects all of the prior analysis of saving and investment behavior. The analysis has been a partial one: it has examined the effect on saving and investment of a change in prices without allowing for any feedback effect of the change in saving or investment on the economy and thus prices. This more complete full-equilibrium analysis is taken up later.

22. In principle, the capital gain on homeownership is taxed at time of sale. But the tax can be avoided by reinvesting in another residence, and the first $125,000 of such gain is exempt from taxation for taxpayers above age fifty-five. In combination with the deferral of the gain until the time of sale, these factors reduce the effective tax rate to approximately zero.

23. The interest deduction creates no incentive to borrow on a home in order to invest in other taxable assets. While individuals might borrow against their home, take an interest deduction, and invest in tax-exempt securities, this type of activity is supposed to be prohibited by IRS regulations. That provision is difficult to enforce, however. Concern that taxpayers in high marginal tax brackets may borrow to invest in the expanding list of other assets with tax preference (capital gains or individual retirement accounts) seems to be the motivation for some proposals to limit the magnitude of the tax deduction for mortgage interest.

aggregate effect of the tax treatment because its elimination would limit
the tax benefit to the wealthy.

Homeownership is actually subsidized under current tax law because
the interest rate relevant to discounting the expected future stream of
implicit income is the after-tax return on alternative investments—the
opportunity cost. As long as other capital is taxed, the user cost (rental
price) of capital (comparable to equation 6 for nonresidential capital) is:

$$(8) \qquad\qquad c = P_k[(1 - t)i + d - \dot{P}_k],$$

where

i = the before-tax nominal interest rate,

$\dot{P}_k$ = expected rate of housing price change,

t = the marginal tax rate.[24]

One implication is that a higher tax rate actually encourages homeownership because the rise in taxes on other capital income reduces the
relative cost of homeownership. A rise in the general inflation rate also
raises the incentive for homeownership because it raises current nominal
interest expense while converting the associated income to a capital gain
at time of sale.[25]

The user cost of homeownership for taxpayers in all tax brackets is
believed to have fallen significantly during the 1960s and 1970s.[26] This

---

24. The above equation should probably include the property tax rate. Even though
such taxes go for services, such as schools, the amount of tax is related to the value of
the home as well as the amount of services. It was not included in the equation for
business investment and is excluded here for simplicity. On the other hand, the formula
may overstate the effect of taxes: the appropriate marginal tax rate on alternative
investments may be very low for some taxpayers because they have not fully exploited
investments in assets taxed at a low rate, such as IRA accounts. This issue of the
appropriate after-tax discount rate is discussed in Harvey Galper and Eric Toder,
"Transfer Elements in the Taxation of Income From Capital," presented at Conference
on Research in Income and Wealth: Social Accounting for Transfers, sponsored by the
National Bureau of Economic Research, May 1982, pp. 27–28.

25. This effect is also not dependent on actually having a mortgage because interest
income on other assets is not indexed for inflation in computing the tax. The effect is
ameliorated, however, because capital gains on other assets also are taxed at a low
effective rate.

26. Patric H. Hendershott and Sheng-Cheng Hu, "Inflation and Extraordinary
Returns on Owner-Occupied Housing: Some Implications for Capital Allocation and
Productivity Growth," *Journal of Macroeconomics*, vol. 3 (Spring 1981), pp. 177–203.
This article also provides a detailed survey of the tax treatment of homeownership. In
defining the real user cost, they deflated the nominal cost by a measure of consumer
prices that excluded shelter.

resulted because the inflation rate for housing rose and because the tax rate limited the effect of the rise in nominal interest rates: the real after-tax rate of interest, $(1 - t)i - \dot{P}_k$, fell. By 1978 the user cost for homeowners in the higher tax brackets was close to zero. Since then the cost has risen significantly with lower inflation and higher nominal interest rates. The corresponding cost measure for investments in rental housing shows no discernible trend between 1960 and 1978.

Prices and Housing Demand

The major consequence of the current tax treatment of housing is to encourage a shift between renting and homeownership. If that were the extent of the effect, it would have no implication for the distribution of total investment between residential and nonresidential users.

The shift to owner-occupied housing can be expected to increase total housing demand, however, for three reasons. First, a low price of owner-occupied housing encourages the formation of more separate households (single-person households, for example), with a loss of economies of scale—large families require proportionately less space than small families. Second, the switch from renting to owning often involves a move to a larger housing unit. Third, if households act to equalize the after-tax return on alternative investments, they will purchase larger and more expensive housing than if the income were taxed.

On the other hand, the cash-flow constraint of rising monthly mortgage payments in an inflationary environment acts as a powerful offset, limiting households' ability to exploit fully the tax advantages. Inflation shifts income forward into capital gains and increases those current expenses that are tax deductible, but the increased financing costs impinge on the buyer immediately. Because homebuyers cannot change the pattern of their mortgage payments to correspond more closely to the timing of the income gains, increased inflation may reduce housing demand.

A recent study by Hendershott measured separately the magnitude of the price incentive and monthly payment constraints on housing demand.[27] He found that both factors exerted strong offsetting effects

---

27. Patric H. Hendershott, "Real User Costs and the Demand for Single-Family Housing," *BPEA, 2:1980*, pp. 401–44. The study measures the net price effect because no effort is made to separate out the income and substitution terms.

on housing demand, but that the price effect dominated. Thus inflation is a net stimulus to housing. On the basis of a simulation of the 1964–79 period, Hendershott estimated that the decline of about 50 percent in the user cost raised the stock of housing by about 15 percent. Of this total increase, about one-third was reflected in increased quality (larger units) and the rest came from the switch from rental to owner units. On average, this represented a net annual increment to homebuilding of about 0.5 percent of GNP.

There are several reasons for believing that this represents the upper bound of the effect of inflation and the tax system. First, Hendershott attributed all the decline in the real user cost of housing since 1965 to inflation. In effect, his analysis began with the observed nominal mortgage interest rate and deducted an estimate of the expected inflation of home values in arriving at a measure of the real interest rate.[28] He found that, because the rise in housing prices greatly exceeded the overall inflation rate over the last two decades, real interest costs had declined even more than for other types of capital. If real interest rates declined for other reasons or if actual home price increases were not fully reflected in expectations of future increases, the Hendershott study overstated the contribution of inflation in reducing the user cost.

Second, the shift from renting to ownership was treated as a rise in demand for units housing one to four families, without allowing for the growth of condominiums and cooperatives, which have a smaller cost differential than rentals. This maximizes the magnitude of the resource cost associated with the shift to homeownership. Finally, the Hendershott study assumed that supply was infinitely elastic with respect to increased purchase prices.[29] If supply was limited, some of the rise in demand would have been reflected in higher prices rather than additional production of housing.

In summary, the Hendershott study provides the most specific estimate of the stimulus to housing demand and the extra resource cost that resulted from the fall in the user cost; but it is not clear that all of that stimulus should be attributed to higher inflation. The study does document the powerful effect that interest rates exert on housing demand. In

28. This is the reverse of the procedure used in the studies of business taxation discussed in the prior section. They assumed a constant real return and added the expected inflation rate to obtain an expected nominal interest rate.

29. A highly elastic supply implies that a small increase in price is sufficient to increase greatly the resources available for homebuilding.

the historical simulation discussed previously, a rise in inflation increased monthly interest payments as an offset to the decline in the real user cost of homeownership. But in the case of a simple reduction in interest rates, with no change in inflation expectations, the two effects reinforce one another. In fact, the existing empirical evidence argues that the magnitude of the response of homebuilding to a change in interest rates is greater than that for business investment in plant and equipment even though it is a much smaller component of total demand.

The Price Elasticity of Housing Supply

The issue of the supply elasticity of housing is critical to evaluating the magnitude of distortion in resource use introduced by the current tax treatment. Some studies have attempted to answer the question by examining cyclical fluctuations in the supply of labor, materials, and entrepreneurial skills to the building industry. Generally they have concluded that the supply is very responsive to changes in prices.[30]

On the other hand, the supply of land may not be so elastic, and local communities can exert strong control over this supply through zoning regulations. If homebuyers have a preference for location (such as distance from central city), the supply of equivalent-quality land can be expanded only with a rise in price. Furthermore, mortgage capital may be supplied only at rising costs because of imperfections in capital markets that limit the substitutability of mortgages for other financial assets.[31] The rise in the price of housing relative to other goods during the 1970s creates at least a presumption that the supply has been less than perfectly elastic. In 1970–80 new home prices (including land) rose by 163 percent, compared with 95 percent for the general price level. Variations in local zoning laws suggest that it is virtually impossible to obtain a meaningful estimate of the average national price elasticity of supply. It would seem to be very low in a state such as California, but high in one such as Texas.

Finally, one should not conclude that the tax incentives for housing

30. Richard F. Muth, "The Demand for Non-Farm Housing," in Arnold C. Harberger, ed., *The Demand For Durable Goods* (University of Chicago Press, 1960), pp. 29–96.

31. These arguments for a limited supply response are made in Michelle J. White and Lawrence J. White, "The Tax Subsidy to Owner-Occupied Housing: Who Benefits?" *Journal of Public Economics*, vol. 7 (February 1977), pp. 113–14.

are undesirable. They reflect a national decision to promote homeownership as a public goal. However, to the extent that the decline in the
user cost of homeownership during the 1960s and 1970s was the product
of an unforeseen interaction between inflation and the tax system, there
was an unintended increase in the size of the incentive relative to that
for other investments. The Hendershott study concluded that a halving
of the real user costs between 1965 and 1980 shifted about 0.5 percent of
GNP into housing. Even if the rigidity of supply limited the amount of
resources diverted into housing, the high level of demand raised prices
on existing homes and increased consumer net worth. Some economists
have suggested that the higher net worth encouraged consumption. Thus
the effect on resource allocation is not represented exclusively by
analyzing the direct effects on homebuilding.[32]

An Overview of Taxation and Capital Formation

Much of the confusion over past trends in capital income taxation and
its effect on capital formation results from a failure to distinguish
adequately between average tax rates on capital income and the marginal
tax rate relevant to investment decisions. First, the *average* tax rate on
all capital income within the personal tax system alone is quite low—
about 10 percent—because so much income is exempt from taxation
(residential housing, state and local securities) or deferred (pensions and
capital gains). (See chapter 2.) On the other hand, the *average* tax rate
on the income from corporate capital is high both because of the corporate
tax itself and because most of the income paid out by corporations—
interest and dividends—is subject to the personal income tax.

For investment, however, it is more relevant to examine trends in the
effective *marginal* tax rates on an additional unit of capital. The tax on
income from new capital differs significantly from that on old capital.
That issue has been examined in several studies of the corporate tax,
which were reviewed earlier in this chapter. The general conclusion is
that effective rates of taxation on new investments fell throughout the
1970s because of liberalization of depreciation allowances for those

---

32. The analysis of consumer spending in chapter 3 implied, however, that inflation-
induced increases in total household wealth did not have a major effect on spending in
the 1970s because the rise in the value of the housing stock was offset by a decline in
the value of corporate equities.

investments, the expansion of the investment tax credit, and the deductibility of nominal interest payments during a period of rising inflation. The study by Hulten and Robertson reported a decline in the effective corporate tax rate from 53 percent in 1960 to a low of 26 percent in 1965, a rise to 55 percent in 1969, and a subsequent decline to 33 percent by 1980 (see figure 4-1).[33] As a result of the 1981 and 1982 tax acts, that rate will continue to fall to about 15 percent in the 1983–86 period, and some individual categories of investment will be subsidized (negative tax rates) by the corporate tax system.

It is useful to examine the total tax (corporate, individual, and property) on a new investment financed by domestic private saving because some of the decline in the corporate tax—particularly the deduction of nominal interest cost—is offset by increased taxation at the personal level. Such a summary is provided in a recently completed comparative study of capital income taxation in four countries, edited by King and Fullerton.[34] They found that within the United States the overall marginal tax rate on income from investments in the corporate sector was about 32 percent in 1983, a decline from 48 percent in 1960 and 47 percent in 1970. The study also concluded that elimination of the corporate tax in its present configuration would have very little net effect on the expected total tax rate on the average new investment.[35]

One interesting result of the study was the finding that the marginal tax rate on capital income is lower in the United States than in Germany, about the same as in Sweden, and far higher than in the United Kingdom.[36] The differences in capital taxation certainly do not correlate well with differences in rates of capital formation among these countries.

The conclusion that emerges from the most recent studies, such as that of King and Fullerton, is in sharp contrast to the earlier studies that argued that inflation had sharply increased the taxation of capital income.

33. Charles R. Hulten and James W. Robertson, "Corporate Tax Policy and Economic Growth: An Analysis of the 1981 and 1982 Tax Acts" (Washington, D.C.: Urban Institute, 1982).

34. Mervyn A. King and Don Fullerton, eds., *The Taxation of Income from Capital: A Comparative Study of the United States, United Kingdom, Sweden, and West Germany* (University of Chicago Press, 1984).

35. That is because the elimination of the corporate tax also eliminates the advantage of deducting interest expenses and property taxes from taxable income.

36. The major reason for the low tax rate in the United Kingdom is immediate expensing of depreciation combined with the full deductibility of nominal interest payments.

118 TAX INCENTIVES AND ECONOMIC GROWTH

The major source of the difference is an improved understanding of the interaction between the corporate and personal tax systems in their treatment of interest income. Inflation lowers the tax on business income by raising the value of the interest deduction. That deduction is supposed to be offset by taxation of the interest receipts within the personal tax. However, because the marginal tax rate at which the interest is deducted (corporate) is substantially above the tax rate on the interest receipts (personal), the net tax on interest is actually negative. In addition, a very large proportion of interest income is not taxed. One study estimated that if interest income were taxed at the same rate as it is deducted, say 30 percent, net tax revenues on interest income would be $32 billion in 1981. In fact, net tax collections were a negative $29 billion—a difference of $61 billion.[37]

The major problem that is highlighted by these studies is not so much that the effective tax on investment has increased, but that tax rates are highly variable by type of capital asset, method of financing, and owner. That issue was examined in detail in a study by Fullerton and Henderson that extended the previous results for the corporate sector to investments in noncorporate businesses and housing.[38] They also estimated effective tax rates on twenty categories of equipment, fifteen types of structures, inventories, and land. The basic results are summarized in table 4-1. The combined effect of corporate, personal, and property taxes resulted in an overall tax on private investment of 29 percent under 1980 tax laws and 26 percent under 1982 tax laws.[39] More important, they found that the tax rate varies substantially across different classes of assets. Many categories of equipment have negative effective taxes while structures, land, and inventories are taxed at rates between 30 and 40 percent.

The variability of tax rates is the result of several factors. Owner-occupied housing is subject only to the property tax, and a portion of

37. Eugene Steuerle, "Tax Arbitrage, Inflation, and the Taxation of Interest Payments and Receipts," presented at conference of Wayne State University Law School, September 30, 1983.
38. Don Fullerton and Yolanda K. Henderson, "Incentive Effects of Taxes on Income from Capital: Alternative Policies in the 1980s," presented at the Urban Institute Conference on Reagan's Economic Policies and Long-Term Growth, Washington, D.C., September 1983.
39. Fullerton and Henderson assumed that investors earned an average after-tax real return of 5 percent and inflation was set at 7 percent annually. Since the effective tax rate is the difference between the pre- and posttax returns as a percentage of the pretax return, the choice of a lower return would raise the estimated tax rate. The results are not fully comparable with the Fullerton and King study because of different assumptions about the rate of return.

Table 4-1. *Effective Marginal Tax Rates on Capital Investments,
1980–82*[a]

Type of investment	1980	1982
Corporate capital		
Equipment	5.4	-4.0
Structures	49.6	37.7
Public utilities	33.2	32.6
Inventories	35.6	35.6
Land	39.9	39.9
Weighted average	34.5	30.0
Noncorporate capital		
Equipment	-2.0	-5.6
Structures	38.8	29.3
Public utilities	24.5	24.1
Residential structures	39.5	33.4
Inventories	32.8	32.8
Land	35.8	35.8
Residential land	40.9	40.9
Weighted average	35.8	32.7
Owner-occupied housing	18.6	18.6
Overall tax rate	28.8	26.4

Source: Don Fullerton and Yolanda K. Henderson, "Incentive Effects of Taxes on Income from Capital: Alternative Policies in the 1980s," presented at the Urban Institute Conference on Reagan's Economic Policies and Long-Term Growth, Washington, D.C., September 1983, table 4.

a. Calculations are based on an assumed 5 percent real after-tax return to investors and a 7 percent inflation rate.

those taxes and interest costs are deductible expenses under the income tax. In addition, firms are allowed to depreciate equipment and structures at a rate higher than that suggested by studies of the actual rate of economic depreciation. However, because those depreciation allowances are based on the original cost of the asset, their value to the firm declines rapidly at higher rates of inflation. Equipment also receives a tax credit. In contrast, inventories and land receive no such special tax treatment.

Furthermore, the effective tax rate on an asset is heavily influenced by its method of financing. Fullerton and Henderson estimate that the effective personal tax is 6 percent for retained earnings (capital gains), 36 percent for dividends, and 24 percent for debt. Because corporations can deduct interest payments at a 46 percent rate while individuals pay 24 percent on the receipts, debt-financed investment receives a substantial tax subsidy. Since the noncorporate tax on business income is about 36 percent, a smaller subsidy is implied for debt-financed investment of that sector.

Fullerton and Henderson report that the overall tax rate on new investments does not change substantially with inflation, but inflation does cause sharp changes in relative taxation of different assets. As inflation rises, the tax on owner-occupied housing changes very little, the tax on equipment rises very rapidly, and that on land and inventories declines. The magnitude of the subsidy to debt-financed investments increases with inflation because inflation raises the nominal interest rate and thus increases the importance of the tax rate differential between interest payments and receipts.

In recent years increased attention has been directed to the economic implications of such diverse rates of taxation. Tax differentials tend to distort the allocation of capital. Some investments are undertaken that would not be justified on the basis of their social return alone, and others with a potentially high social return are not undertaken. The economic importance of these distortions depends upon the degree of possible substitution between different types of capital—both directly through substituting one type of machine for another and indirectly through altering the relative prices and thus the demand for the products they produce. If units of capital are used in fixed proportion to one another within an industry, the tax rate differentials would have little overall significance for the mix of inputs used in that industry. They would not distort the choice of a production process beyond the previously dis-cussed concern with substitution between labor and capital as a whole. But these differences in tax rates extend across industries that use different combinations of capital in production. By changing the relative costs and prices of the goods these industries produce, the variation in tax rates would still distort the pattern of resource use. Unfortunately, very little is known about substitution among types of capital assets.[40] There has been considerable discussion of the tax differential between residential and nonresidential capital, and the empirical studies discussed earlier do suggest that it shifts investment between short- and long-lived assets (equipment and structures).

The Linkage between Saving and Investment

The earlier discussion of the determinants of private saving and investment has been a partial analysis in the sense that no consideration

40. The effort to evaluate the economic cost of variable tax rates with various assumed rates of substitution among assets is illustrated in Jane Gravelle, "The Social Costs of Nonneutral Taxation: Estimates for Nonresidential Capital," in Charles R. Hulten, ed., *Depreciation, Inflation, and the Taxation of Income from Capital* (Wash-ington, D.C.: Urban Institute, 1981), pp. 239–50.

has been given to the relationship between domestic saving and domestic investment. As mentioned in chapter 3, that linkage raises both short- and long-run issues.

Short-Run Responses to Higher Saving

In the short run the counterpart of a rise in planned saving is a fall in consumer spending. While the rise in saving may be seen as a spur to investment through lower interest rates, the associated drop in consumer spending also sets in motion a series of contractionary income effects that may swamp the interest rate effect and lead to a lower level of investment spending as business firms reduce their estimates of future output growth. At the same time, the unexpected contraction of production and consumers' income will lead to an actual level of saving below that which was initially planned. The perverse result may be a new balance of actual saving and investment at lower levels of both.

It is argued that this period of reduced economic activity should be transitory, however, because over a longer time period competitive market forces will push production back toward the full-employment level. This process of recovery is most easily illustrated by considering a rise in saving in a situation where the money supply is fixed. Initially, the decline in consumer spending will reduce output. In addition, unemployment will rise, reducing wages and prices. Thus the nominal level of spending is lower both because of the initial fall in real demand and the decline in the price level. At the lower level of total demand the public has less need for money to finance transactions, and it can be induced to hold the fixed supply of money only through a fall in the rate of interest. The lower interest rate stimulates, in turn, a rise in investment spending and therefore a recovery of total output. As long as real output remains below the full-employment level, wages and prices will continue to fall, lowering the demand for money and thus the rate of interest. The fall in the rate of interest will persist until the rise in investment fully offsets the original decline in consumption and total output and employment have returned to their full-employment levels. In the new equilibrium, saving and investment will be higher than in the initial situation, and interest rates will be lower. The only permanent effect is to shift the allocation of output between consumption and investment.

Disagreements about the magnitude and duration of this transition, however, are central to the debate about the use of saving incentives as a means of increasing capital formation. Economists who are concerned

about the potential for a substantial disruption of economic activity
emphasize several factors. First, if total demand (including investment)
is highly sensitive to short-term fluctuations in income, the initial decline
in consumer spending may be greatly magnified by the secondary income
effects. Second, if the demand for money is highly sensitive to interest
rates, the excess money balances (occasioned by the fall in nominal
GNP) will be absorbed with only a minor decline in the rate of interest.
Third, if investment is relatively insensitive to interest rates, a very large
change in the interest rate may be required to restore the economy to
full employment.

There are also significant differences regarding the behavior of wages
and prices. If the neoclassical perspective of highly flexible wages and
prices is accepted, the initial decline in output will be rapidly reversed
by a reduction in the price level and, through its effect on the nominal
demand for money, a fall in the rate of interest. The transition to an
economy of higher rates of capital formation can be made at the cost of
a mild and very temporary rise in unemployment. On the other hand,
the Keynesian analysis, with its assumption of inflexible wages and
prices that respond very slowly to the rise in unemployment, implies a
large initial contraction of production and a long period of unemployment.

This emphasis on the problems of adjustment does not justify the
criticism that Keynes was opposed to saving.[41] Instead, the analysis
suggests that any actions to increase saving should be combined with a
simultaneous expansion of direct incentives for investment, rather than
leaving the adjustment to be achieved through reductions in wages and
prices.

The Keynesian preoccupation with the consequences for income
flows is sometimes characterized as a short-run analysis, while the
neoclassical emphasis on price or incentive effects is of greater relevance
for the long term. Yet it is important in making policy decisions to know
how long the adjustment period would be. One means of evaluating that
issue is to examine the results of simulating the policy change by using

41. See, for an example of that view, Martin Feldstein, "The Retreat from Keynesian
Economics," *The Public Interest,* no. 64 (Summer 1981), pp. 92–105. The fact is that
Keynes frequently and forcefully stressed the desirability of investment and its impor-
tance for economic progress. See, for example, Joseph A. Schumpeter, "Keynes, the
Economist," in Seymour E. Harris, ed., *The New Economics: Keynes' Influence on
Theory and Public Policy* (Knopf, 1947), pp. 73–101.

Table 4-2. *Simulation of the Economic Effects of an Autonomous Increase in Saving Rates*[a]
Billions of dollars unless otherwise indicated

Item	Year following change			
	1	2	3	4
Gross national product (1972 dollars)	−14.0	−12.0	1.3	16.8
Consumption	−11.6	−13.0	−6.4	2.3
Investment	−4.1	−2.5	3.9	10.4
Residential construction	0.6	1.9	1.7	1.4
Net exports	1.4	1.5	1.5	1.5
Government purchases	−0.1	0.0	0.6	1.2
Gross national product (current dollars)	−25.2	−30.5	−21.6	−4.0
Price level (percent)	0.1	−0.1	−0.6	−1.1
Unemployment rate (percent)	0.3	0.3	0.1	−0.2
Real money supply	−0.3	0.2	1.5	2.6
Corporate bond rate (percent)	−0.2	−0.5	−0.7	−0.6
Government budget surplus	−8.2	−5.6	2.2	11.0
Corporate retained earnings	−3.2	1.2	8.1	12.1

Source: Simulation of the econometric model of the Federal Reserve for 1983–86 by Eileen Mauskopf of the Federal Reserve Board staff.

a. Consumer spending was reduced by $10 billion (1972 dollars) throughout the simulation period, about 1 percent of disposable income.

econometric models that embody the adjustment mechanism outlined above.

An illustration of the consequences of a rise in planned saving is shown in table 4-2, as derived from the econometric model of the Federal Reserve Board. In the simulation the level of consumer expenditures is reduced exogenously by $10 billion. The money supply is unchanged throughout the simulation period. As would be expected, the initial impact on GNP is larger than the simple decline in consumption because lower demand reduces investment. The drop in GNP quickly translates into a reduced money demand and a fall in interest rates (corporate bond rates). Thus there is an immediate offsetting rise in residential construction; and after a few years the stimulus from lower interest rates offsets the depressive effects of lower output, and business investment begins to increase.[42] Although real output has recovered fully by the third year and is significantly higher in the fourth, the nominal value of GNP is

42. Most of the output gain by the fourth year is concentrated in business investment because, in contrast to the model of housing formulated by Hendershott ("Real User Costs"), the FRB model attributes much of the volatility of housing demand to credit rationing rather than interest rates.

reduced throughout because of a lower price level (the cumulative effect of lower prior rates of inflation).

In the FRB model private expenditures are highly sensitive to interest rates, which are in turn very responsive to variations in economic activity. The combination implies that capital markets can offset the depressing effect of a drop in consumer spending by the end of the second year. In fact, because the price level adjusts with a long lag, a fixed-money-stock rule actually implies that total output and employment will overshoot and go above prior levels in the fourth year. If the simulation had continued over a longer period, output would have fluctuated about the initial level, but the price level and interest rates would have remained, on average, at lower levels to maintain a rise in investment equal to the fall in consumption.[43]

The FRB model was constructed with the objective of emphasizing the influence of financial markets on the economy. Other models imply that the transitional period would be substantially longer. A similar experiment with a model constructed by Fair implies that only half of the adjustment back to prior output levels is completed by the fourth year.[44] Interest rates do not decline as much and they have a smaller effect on total expenditures. Simulations of other models yield a wide range of results: it is not possible to obtain a very specific answer to the question about the length of the adjustment period.[45] However, all the

43. The FRB model has some features that complicate the adjustment process, however. First, consumption is responsive to changes in wealth. Because the decline in interest rates initiates a capital gain on existing wealth, a recovery of consumption is an important element of the expansion. In fact, the stimulus to consumption through wealth is so strong that there is little ex post rise in personal saving. Instead, the higher levels of investment are financed by a rise in corporate retained earnings (business saving) and the government budget surplus. In both cases, the rise in saving of these sectors is primarily the result of lower interest payments to households. Second, because the adjustment of prices lags behind the changes in wages, there is a large shift of income away from households to business, which has a higher marginal saving propensity. Thus, although nominal GNP is above its initial value by the end of the fourth year, personal income is still reduced by $30 billion. Such changes in the distribution of income and saving that emerge from the model seem a little peculiar.

44. Ray C. Fair, "Specification, Estimation, and Analysis of Macroeconometric Models" (Yale University, November 1982), table 9.4, p. 424.

45. A model constructed by Coen and Hickman is of particular interest because it was designed to address some of the long-term growth issues. The transition period in that model is comparable to that of the FRB; but the composition of the investment gain is completely different. Most of it flows into residential construction. See Robert M. Coen and Bert G. Hickman, "Tax Policy, Federal Deficits, and U.S. Growth in the 1980s," Discussion Paper 6 (Center for Economic Policy Research, Stanford University, April 1983).

models imply a period of output loss extending over at least two years. A shift in the composition of output between consumption and investment is common to the simulations, but little confidence can be placed in the estimates of the time required to restore output and employment to prior levels.

The Long-Run Response to Higher Saving

In the long term, sufficient price flexibility to maintain full employment is often assumed in order to justify abstracting from the issue of resource utilization. Nevertheless, it is still uncertain whether a rise in domestic saving is sufficient to ensure a higher rate of business capital formation. Business must compete in capital markets with other potential claimants, and the increment to saving will flow to those uses that promise the highest rate of return. To the extent that returns may be greater for homebuilding and consumer durables, the diversion of some saving to these uses is appropriate; if the goal of policy is an increase in business capital, however, it is important to recognize that the rise in business investment may be significantly less than the rise in saving.

A more significant issue arises when the analysis takes account of the international aspects of capital markets. If capital is free to move across national boundaries, domestic saving does not constrain domestic investment: saving is allocated according to worldwide opportunities for investment, while domestic investment draws from a worldwide pool of saving. In such a situation, increases in domestic saving may be an ineffectual means of encouraging higher rates of capital formation.[46]

The role of international capital flows has been examined by several studies. Harberger examined the relationship between the rate of return on capital and the capital-output ratio in different countries.[47] Because he found no association, Harberger concluded that capital must move across national boundaries to equate the rate of return. On the other hand, he did find that there was a strong positive correlation between

46. This does not imply that the tax treatment of the income to savers is unimportant. Such taxes may still impose a loss of national wealth by promoting current consumption over saving. From the perspective of the welfare of the savers, capital should be free to move to those uses of maximum return.

47. Arnold Harberger, "Perspectives on Capital and Technology in Less Developed Countries," in Martin J. Artis and A. R. Nobay, eds., *Contemporary Economics Analysis: Papers Presented at the Conference of the Association of University Teachers of Economics* (London: Croom Helm, 1977), pp. 15–40.

the capital-labor ratio and variations in wage rates. That result would be expected if labor could not move as freely as capital.

In contrast, Feldstein and Horioka found a very strong correlation between national saving and national investment rates.[48] They averaged domestic saving (including government) and investment shares of total output over 1960–79 for a sample of seventeen countries. They then estimated a regression of the form $I/Y = a + b\, S/Y$, and obtained an estimate of the coefficient b that was very close to unity. Since in a world capital market shifts in domestic saving and investment rates should be uncorrelated with one another, they interpreted their results as evidence of significant national barriers to capital flows. Feldstein and Horioka concluded that nearly all of any rise in domestic saving will flow through into domestic investment.

There are a number of statistical problems in the Feldstein-Horioka study that affect their conclusions. One problem results from the potential for a common correlation of saving and investment with third factors. As discussed earlier, both saving and investment rates are strongly related to the growth of GNP. This common influence is present both in the time-series data for an individual country and in the cross-sectional data for countries with different rates of output growth. The averaging of annual observations does not remove it. Second, previous mention was made of the serious difficulties of measuring saving and the consequent practice in many countries of estimating saving from data on investment. Thus common measurement errors impart a degree of spurious correlation. Both factors would lead to a positive correlation between domestic saving and investment rates, yet a causal relationship could not be inferred.

The issue has been examined in two other studies that avoided some of the statistical problems. First, a study by Sachs focused on the relationship between domestic investment and net foreign investment— two data series that are estimated by independent statistical procedures.[49] For an average of fourteen industrial countries over 1968–79,

48. Martin Feldstein and Charles Horioka, "Domestic Saving and International Capital Flows," *The Economic Journal*, vol. 90 (June 1980), pp. 314–29. Also see Martin Feldstein, "Domestic Saving and International Capital Flows in the Long-Run and the Short-Run," presented at the National Bureau of Economic Research Conference, Fifth Annual International Seminar on Macroeconomics, University of Mannheim, Germany, June 1982.

49. Jeffrey D. Sachs, "The Current Account and Macroeconomic Adjustment in the 1970s," *BPEA, 1:1981*, pp. 201–68, especially table 14, p. 250.

he found that between 30 and 60 percent of the change in domestic investment was reflected in compensatory changes in the current-account balance.

Second, von Furstenberg constructed a small model for the United States of the basic income flows involved in the saving-investment relationship.[50] He concluded that domestic factors relating to saving and investment explain as much as 80 percent of the variation in the net foreign investment balance. His study implies that a major effect of a policy-induced increase in the national saving rate would be to shift the foreign account toward a surplus.

The Sachs and von Furstenberg studies suggest that the international aspects cannot be ignored in the discussion of alternative measures to expand capital formation. While many investigators would agree with the Feldstein-Horioka view that there are significant barriers to the free movement of capital among countries in the short run, it is in the short run that the Keynesian income effects are most important. In the long run the income effects may be of less concern, but it is more difficult to argue that capital will not flow to the country where the returns are greatest.[51] It seems unreasonable to combine for analytical purposes a long-run model of flexible prices and full employment with a short-run assumption that capital will not move among nations to equalize rates of return. It is more reasonable to take the view that incentives to expand saving must be matched by concurrent actions on the investment side if there is to be an effective increase in domestic capital formation.

Summary

Economists have achieved a greater consensus about the effect of interest rates and tax policy on investment than about their effect on private saving. In part, this is because there is less uncertainty from a

50. George M. von Furstenberg, "Domestic Determinants of Net U.S. Foreign Investment," *International Monetary Fund Staff Papers,* vol. 27 (December 1980), pp. 637–78.

51. It must also be admitted that the full range of response of the foreign account is not easily predicted. A rise in national saving may initially lead to an outflow of capital, but if the resulting rise in the demand for foreign currencies leads to a fall in the nation's exchange rate, there will be an improvement in the expected rate of return on domestic investment because of the decline in the relative cost of domestic labor and materials.

theoretical perspective about the direction of the effect. Whereas the response of saving to an increased rate of return involves an evaluation of offsetting income and substitution effects, lower interest rates and taxes unambiguously increase investment. The disagreements are limited to the magnitude of the response. In addition, the investment response has been a subject of more intensive empirical research.

For business investment in plant and equipment, the primary issue involves the technological constraints on the substitution of capital for labor. If firms can choose from a range of production processes that incorporate different combinations of capital and labor, a reduction in the relative after-tax cost of capital leads to the use of more capital-intensive methods of production. If no such substitution is possible, government can affect the demand for capital only by altering expectations of the future growth in demand: taxes and interest rates are relevant only through their indirect effects on aggregate demand. Empirical estimates of the elasticity of substitution between capital and labor for the overall economy have ranged between zero and unity (a 1 percent reduction in the required rate of return raised the desired stock of capital by 1 percent). There is less disagreement about the effect on investment in the first few years following the change in the required return, however, because those studies that find a large potential for substitution typically incorporate long lags in the adjustment of the actual stock to its desired level. On average, the studies imply that a tax reduction limited to new investment will generate a rise in business spending over a five-year period following the change that is about equal to the loss of tax revenue—a "bang for the buck" of about unity.

Government policies do have a substantial effect on investment in residential buildings. Those policies are relevant to the discussion of overall capital formation because of the assertion by some economists that the favored tax treatment of homeownership has led to overinvestment in housing at the expense of other capital projects. They argue that the nation would benefit from a reallocation of existing saving away from housing and toward business plant and equipment.

Certainly the real user cost of homeownership declined substantially compared to other investments during the 1960s and 1970s. The tax system offset much of the cost of higher mortgage interest rates, while the accelerating rise in housing prices created substantial opportunities for capital gains. The stimulus to housing demand of a lower user cost was limited by the rise in monthly mortgage payments relative to incomes, but the empirical evidence indicates that the price effect dominated. One study found that the net effect was to raise the share of GNP devoted to homebuilding by an average of 0.5 percentage point in the 1965–80 period. In the early 1980s the situation was reversed as market interest rates rose sharply, home price inflation declined, and the preferential tax treatment was extended to include other types of capital.

The estimates of a large diversion of resources to housing may be overstated, however, because the supply of housing may be constrained by zoning restrictions and other factors. If that is the case, the high level of demand was partially absorbed by a rise in the price of existing homes instead of leading to new construction.

At times, the public discussion of proposals to expand capital formation has appeared to imply that increased saving would automatically translate into an increase in domestic investment through adjustments of interest rates in capital markets. But there are problems with this interpretation in both the short and long run. Instead, incentives to expand saving must be matched by concurrent actions on the investment side if there is to be an effective increase in domestic capital formation.

CHAPTER FIVE

Labor Supply

THE DETERMINANTS of labor supply are frequently overlooked in discussions of the supply side of the economy. Yet the quantity and quality of work effort are critical to any program to expand aggregate supply, and the behavior of workers can be expected to be sensitive to their evaluation of the economic incentives for choosing between work and leisure. Because labor represents about 75 percent of the value of the inputs into production, even relatively small marginal responses can have substantial aggregate implications.

It is sometimes alleged that the tax and transfer systems have contributed in a major way to the slowing of economic growth in the United States. High marginal tax rates are seen as a major disincentive to work effort, and the availability of unemployment insurance and welfare programs leads some economists to conclude that the unemployed are unwilling to work. In many respects the supply response is fundamental to current disputes over the nature of today's unemployment problem. Some agree with Keynes's view of unemployment as a reflection of inadequate total demand for labor; others see a supply-side problem created by legislation that holds wages too high and transfer programs that create disincentives to work. The first group views unemployment as involuntary and supports an expansion of aggregate demand to increase job opportunities. The other interprets unemployment as a voluntary decision and urges structural reforms to reduce transfer programs and intensify competition for existing job openings.

The responsiveness of labor supply to price incentives is also important to the debate on capital formation because many of the proposals to reduce the taxation of capital income are implicitly proposals to increase the tax on wages.[1] The supply-side gains in higher rates of capital

1. This is true of proposals to shift the income tax structure toward a consumption-based tax. But some supply-side advocates would object to the need for an increase in labor taxes of an equal offsetting magnitude because they foresee such a large increase in aggregate income that the rate of taxation is permanently reduced.

formation may be offset by some losses of labor if a lower after-tax wage rate induces workers to withdraw from the labor force or reduce their hours worked.

Once again, economic theory by itself can say little about the net incentive effect of the tax system on labor supply because the income and substitution effects are offsetting. On the one hand, the imposition of a tax will reduce work since the reward for an additional hour is less—the substitution effect. On the other hand, individuals must work harder if they wish to restore their pretax purchasing power—the income effect. As with so many supply-side issues, the net effect must be determined empirically.

Even then, other economic and social factors have been operating to change labor supply decisions, and those changes are entangled with the hypothesis that the expansion of tax rates and the social welfare programs may have significantly reduced labor supply. Moreover, while most of the empirical studies have emphasized hours of work, there are other dimensions to labor supply—the timing of retirement, intensity of work effort, the quality of work, and investment in education and job training—that are also influenced by economic policy decisions.[2] Research in these areas is still in the early stages.

Over the last decade substantial advances have been made in the empirical research on labor supply. There is more agreement on the size of the incentive effects of changes in the rate of return for labor than there is for saving and investment behavior. In part, this is the result of the fact that it is easier to obtain meaningful data on hours of work than on individual saving. Thus, while most of the research on saving has emphasized time-series data for the economy as a whole or international comparisons, labor force studies have been able to make greater use of survey data from individual households, both cross-sectional studies at a given point in time and panel studies of individuals over time. Significant quantitative differences do remain, however, particularly with regard to the effects of transfer programs.

This chapter is devoted to a review and evaluation of previous studies of labor supply. The first section is directed to the issue of the effect of taxes on the supply of broad groups of the labor force. These studies have mainly examined the labor force behavior of individuals faced with different after-tax wage rates. But it is also one of the few areas where

2. This point is made effectively by Harvey S. Rosen, "What Is Labor Supply and Do Taxes Affect It?" *American Economic Review*, vol. 70 (May 1980, *Papers and Proceedings, December 1979*), pp. 171–76.

Table 5-1. *Civilian Labor Force Participation Rates, by Age and Sex, Selected Years, 1950–80*

Category	Participation rate			
	1950	*1960*	*1970*	*1980*
Total	59.9	60.2	61.3	63.8
Male	86.8	84.0	80.6	78.0
16–19	68.7	62.4	60.5	62.0
20–24	89.1	90.2	86.6	87.0
25–44	96.9	97.7	96.8	95.5
45–54	95.8	95.8	94.3	91.2
55–64	86.9	86.8	83.0	72.3
65 and over	45.8	33.1	36.8	19.1
Female	33.9	37.8	43.4	51.7
16–19	43.7	42.5	46.0	53.3
20–24	46.1	46.2	57.8	69.2
25–44	36.6	40.2	48.1	65.5
45–54	38.0	49.8	54.4	59.9
55–64	27.0	37.2	43.0	41.5
65 and over	9.7	10.8	9.7	8.1

Source: U.S. Department of Labor, Bureau of Labor Statistics, *Employment and Earnings*, vol. 27 (January 1981), pp. 164–67, and prior issues.

specific experiments have been undertaken by the government to observe the response to different marginal wage rates. The second section examines the effect of the major transfer programs on specific groups. These include the unemployment insurance program, social security, disability insurance, and the low-income welfare programs. The concluding section focuses on education and job training (human capital) and examines the tax treatment of these investments relative to physical capital formation.

The basic trends in labor supply by age and sex are shown in table 5-1. The total labor force participation rate has risen at an accelerating pace since the end of World War II. The increase in the total, however, is the result of offsetting changes in the participation rates of women and men. The male participation rate has declined both because a growing proportion of the population is represented by teenagers and older workers who have low participation rates and because there has been a drop in the participation rate of adult male workers—particularly for the age brackets of forty-five to sixty-five. Meanwhile the female participation rate increased from 34 percent in 1950 to 52 percent in 1980. The rise in the participation rate for females has been large in all the age cohorts up to retirement.

Table 5-2. *Marginal Federal Income Tax Rates at Alternative Levels of Family Income, Selected Years, 1955–85*

		Marginal tax rate at:		
Year	Median income (dollars)	One-half median income	Median income	Twice median income
1955	4,847	0	20	22
1965	7,800	14	17	22
1975	15,848	11	22	32
1980	24,332	18	24	43
1985[a]	32,684	14	22	38

Source: U.S. Treasury Department, Office of Tax Analysis. Tax calculations are based on a family of four members.
a. Scheduled under Economic Recovery Tax Act of 1981. Income is estimated.

Taxes and Hours of Work

The potential effect of taxes on work effort takes on particular importance today because of recent major changes in marginal tax rates. In a previous chapter trends in marginal income tax rates applying to saving decisions were examined. From a labor supply perspective, however, it is also important to take account of the sharp increase in employment taxes—social security and unemployment insurance.

Trends in Tax Rates

For purposes of evaluating the effects of taxes on work incentives it is important to distinguish between average and marginal (the tax on an additional dollar of earnings) tax rates. Also, the interpretation of the effect of employment taxes on labor supply depends on whether workers view such payments as a tax or as part of a saving program with future benefits. The measurement of effective tax rates is affected further by the growth in the proportion of families with two incomes.

Estimates of the marginal federal income tax rate faced by families at various points in the income distribution are shown in table 5-2.[3] For example, the marginal income tax rate paid by the median-income family rose from 17 to 24 percent between 1965 and 1980. An even more

3. These are the same data that underlie the estimates of marginal tax rates on saving shown in figure 3-3.

dramatic increase is evident for the family earning twice the median income, whose marginal income tax rate rose from 22 to 43 percent between 1965 and 1980.

It is also interesting to examine the historical change in the distribution of taxpayers by marginal tax rate bracket. In 1961, 70 percent of all taxpayers were subject to marginal tax rates of 20 to 22 percent, 21 percent paid no tax, and only 9 percent faced a tax rate of 25 percent or above. By 1980 the tax rate structure had become much more progressive at both ends of the distribution: 46 percent of taxpayers faced marginal rates of 19 percent or less, and 31 percent paid 25 percent or above.[4] This rise in marginal tax rates stands in sharp contrast to the fall in the average tax rate from 23.2 percent of taxable income in 1961 to 19.6 percent in 1980.

The changing pattern of marginal and average tax rates reflects several modifications that have been made in the personal tax system. First, the rate structure has changed. The number of brackets was increased at the bottom with a minimum rate of 14 percent replacing one of 20 percent, while the inflation-augmented growth of incomes pushed a larger percentage of taxpayers into the higher marginal tax brackets. Second, there was a sharp curtailment of personal exemptions, making a larger percentage of income subject to a positive tax rate. And third, there was an increase in the use of tax credits aimed primarily at low-wage workers. The shift toward a more progressive income tax structure is most evident in a comparison of marginal tax rates and much less evident in the average tax rates at various income levels.[5]

Changes in tax legislation, however, were not the major cause of the rise in marginal tax rates, shown in table 5-3. Instead, the large shift toward two-earner families pushed families who file joint returns into higher tax brackets. The importance of this phenomenon is illustrated by the fourfold increase in family income between 1955 and 1980, compared to a tripling of average wage rates. The above computations also ignored the role of employment taxes.

In table 5-3 the marginal tax rates are reported for families with a fixed number of earners where earnings are tied to the average economywide

4. U.S. Treasury Department, Internal Revenue Service, *Statistics of Income*, 1961, p. 172; and *SOI Bulletin*, vol. 2 (Winter 1982–83), p. 22.

5. For a more detailed discussion see Eugene Steuerle and Michael Hartzmark, "Individual Income Taxation, 1947–79," *National Tax Journal*, vol. 34 (June 1981), pp. 145–66.

Table 5-3. *Marginal and Average Tax Rates for a Family of Four at Alternative Wage Income Levels, Selected Years, 1955–84*[a]

Item	1955	1965	1975	1980	1984
Single earner, earning ⅔ of average wage					
Income (dollars)	2,622	3,894	7,260	10,452	13,131
Average tax rate	0.0	3.2	2.1	4.3	5.3
Marginal tax rate	0	14	26[b]	16	14
FICA[c]	4.0	7.2	11.7	12.3	13.4
Combined marginal rate[d]	3.9	20.5	36.2	26.7	25.7
Single earner, earning average wage					
Income (dollars)	3,914	5,812	10,836	15,600	19,598
Average tax rate	5.7	7.2	8.3	8.7	8.6
Marginal tax rate	20	16	19	18	16
FICA[c]	4	0	11.7	12.3	13.4
Combined marginal rate[d]	23.5	16	29.0	28.5	27.6
Single earner, earning twice average wage					
Income (dollars)	7,828	11,624	21,672	31,200	39,196
Average tax rate	11.2	10.9	12.1	13.7	12.3
Marginal tax rate	22	19	25	28	28
FICA[c]	0	0	0	0	0
Combined marginal rate[d]	22	19	25	28	28
Second earner, earning ⅔ average wage; primary worker earning average wage					
Average tax rate[e]	17.2	15.2	16.1	13.4	8.9
Marginal tax rate	20	19	22	24	22
FICA[c]	4	7.2	11.7	12.3	13.4
Combined marginal rate[d]	23.5	25.3	31.8	34.2	33.2
Second earner, earning ⅔ average wage; primary worker earning twice average wage					
Average tax rate[e]	18.9	18.2	21.0	21.7	17.2
Marginal tax rate	22	22	28	37	33
FICA[c]	4	7.2	11.7	12.3	13.4
Combined marginal rate[d]	25.5	28.2	37.5	46.4	43.5

Sources: Author's calculations based on relevant tax return forms for each year. Income is the average wage per full-time employee as reported in table 6.9B of U.S. Department of Commerce, Bureau of Economic Analysis, *The National Income and Product Accounts of the United States, 1929–74 Statistical Tables*, a supplement to the *Survey of Current Business* (Government Printing Office, 1977), and subsequent reports.
a. Itemizing of deductions is assumed for those families with income in excess of the average. The rate of deductions for each year beginning with 1955 is: 14, 15.5, 22, 22, and 22 percent.
b. Includes effect of the earned-income credit on the marginal rate.
c. Combined social insurance tax rate when wage income is below the ceiling.
d. Income is defined to include employer contribution to social insurance.
e. Applies to income earned by secondary worker rather than that of the family.

wage rate. By controlling for the number of earners per family, it is possible to distinguish between the effects of changes in legislation and social patterns on marginal tax rates.

An interesting case is shown for the worker earning only two-thirds the average wage. Such families have experienced a sharp increase in both marginal and average income tax rates.[6] The high marginal tax rate reported for 1975 is a perverse effect of the introduction of the earned-income credit. Under this provision, workers who earn less than $5,000 and have dependents receive a 10 percent tax credit; but as incomes rise within the range of $6,000 to $10,000, the taxpayer must refund the credit at an effective marginal tax rate of 12.5 percent.[7] Thus there is a 22.5-percentage-point upward shift in the marginal tax rate faced by workers as their earnings rise from $5,000 to $6,000. If employment taxes are included, these workers face marginal tax rates comparable to workers in much higher income brackets.

The marginal income tax rate for a family supported by a single wage earner, earning an average wage, has actually declined slightly since 1955 (from 20 to 16 percent), while the average income tax rate has increased. There is a significant rise in marginal tax rates only if the large increase in social insurance taxes is included.

The result for a family with a single worker earning twice the average wage is also much different from the earlier emphasis on a family with twice the median income. The marginal federal income tax rate in 1980 is 28 percent rather than the previously reported 43 percent and earned income is above the FICA ceiling. The marginal tax rate did rise, however, from 19 percent in 1965 to 28 percent in 1980. Unlike that of workers in lower tax brackets, these workers' average income tax burden increased very little.

What emerges from table 5-3 is a general pattern of rising marginal tax rates on labor income, but it is a pattern common to workers throughout the wage distribution and not just high-wage workers. For low- and average-wage earners it is the result of social security taxes. If employment taxes are included, marginal tax rates are surprisingly even across a broad range of wage rates.

The situation is much different for the second income earner in the family. If the wage is treated as an increment to the income earned by the primary worker, both average and marginal tax rates are very high. And, at least at the top of the income distribution, marginal income tax rates have increased. The introduction of a special deduction for two-

6. The high levels of the personal exemption and the standard deduction in the 1950s allowed them to exempt all income from taxation.
7. In 1975 the effective income limits were $4,000 and $8,000. In 1980 and 1984 two-thirds of the average wage was above the ceiling of the earned-income credit and thus the credit had no effect on marginal tax rates at the income level shown in the table.

earner families in the 1981 tax act sharply reduces the average tax rate of the second earner, but it has less effect on the marginal tax.

The table excludes state and local income taxes, which rose from 0.3 to 2.2 percent of income between 1953 and 1980 for the average one-income family. Very little is known about overall trends in marginal tax rates under state income tax systems.[8] Unemployment insurance taxes, which are also excluded, rose from 1.2 percent of the first $3,000 of earnings in 1955 to 2.5 percent of the first $6,000 of earnings in 1980. Thus in real terms the taxable income limit has declined, while the rate has risen. The limit is so low relative to the typical wage that this tax is like a lump-sum tax on employment, and it should have little effect on hours worked by the employed.

In summary, marginal income tax rates on labor income have increased over time for all levels of income (a more progressive tax structure), but the major cause has been the shift toward two-earner families rather than new tax legislation. The increased importance of two-earner families has also sharpened concern about an old tax issue— the definition of the taxpaying unit. If ability to pay is a major justification for a progressive tax system, should the definition of taxable income be based on the family or the individual? The United States has traditionally used the family as the basis for comparison, but that does imply a high marginal tax on the income of the second earner. Recent legislation has moved the U.S. tax system in the direction of equal treatment of individuals rather than families. On the other hand, the average income tax burden has increased for low-income families, while for high-income families it has remained unchanged (single earners) or declined (two earners).

Conclusions about average and marginal tax rates on labor income are also strongly influenced by the treatment of employment taxes. The appropriate treatment is controversial because it depends upon workers' perceptions of the link between current taxes and the value of future benefits. If social insurance contributions are considered a tax, marginal tax rates have risen most dramatically for low-wage workers regardless of family status.

Finally, it is also important to remember that a substantial portion of labor income, in the form of medical insurance, pensions, and other

8. Advisory Commission on Intergovernmental Relations, *Significant Features of Fiscal Federalism, 1980–81 Edition* (Washington, D.C.: ACIR, December 1981), p. 49.

fringe benefits, escapes taxation. This form of income has been growing far more rapidly than wages and salaries and is a larger portion of the earnings of upper-income wage earners.

Theoretical Considerations of Labor Supply Incentives

The labor supply decision has long been of special interest to economists because of the historical observation that increases in wage rates have been associated with a reduction in the average hours of work. This suggests, contrary to convention, that the supply curve for labor is backward-bending: higher wage rates reduce supply. The obvious explanation is that the higher income that accompanies a wage rate increase generates a higher demand for both purchased goods and leisure, and the rise in income will normally be split between the two.[9]

Thus, to make any sense of the labor supply decision, it is especially important to distinguish between the substitution and income effects of wage rate changes. By making leisure more expensive in terms of forgone income, the substitution effect must operate to increase labor supply when wages rise. The income effect, however, will reduce supply as long as individuals desire more leisure as income rises. The distinction is particularly important for tax policy. With simultaneous manipulation of marginal tax rates and deductions, it is possible to achieve a whole range of combinations of income and substitution effects. An evaluation of the labor supply effects of tax changes, therefore, requires knowledge of both the income and substitution effects, and not just the net impact.

In a simple context the issue can be illustrated graphically as in figure 5-1. Income is measured on the vertical axis, and the consumption of leisure is measured horizontally where H_0 represents the point of zero work—all leisure. Increasing hours of work are measured right to left. The individual's preferences can then be described in terms of a set of indifference curves, each of which is convex to the origin and represents combinations of income and leisure that yield comparable levels of satisfaction. Higher curves represent increased levels of satisfaction. The individual's options can be represented in terms of the budget line H_0W_0, whose slope is equal to the wage rate. Thus W_0 is the amount of

9. On the other hand, the labor force participation rate of women has increased, while that of men has declined, despite little or no change in relative wage rates by sex. These divergent trends highlight the difficulty of differentiating between economic and noneconomic factors in interpreting the historical record.

Figure 5-1. *The Work-Leisure Decision*

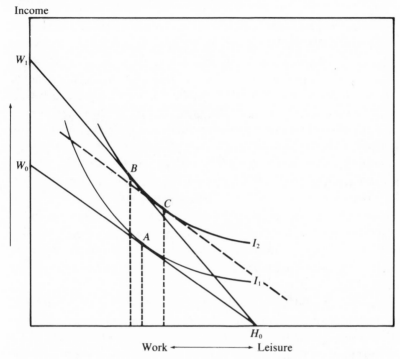

Work ←—————————→ Leisure

income that can be earned if he forgoes all leisure. The rational individual will then maximize his welfare at A, tangent to the highest indifference curve along the line H_0W_0.

Now assume that the wage rate rises so that the individual faces the new set of possibilities represented by the line H_0W_1, with a potential maximum income of W_1. In the example, satisfaction is maximized at the point B, tangent to the higher indifference curve I_2, where both income and hours of work are increased.

The decomposition of the net change in hours into income and substitution effects can be illustrated by drawing a new budget line parallel to H_0W_0 that is tangent to the indifference curve I_2 at C. The vertical distance between the two lines is the lump-sum income payment that would make the individual just as well off as receiving the new wage rate. The horizontal distance from A to C measures the change in work that results solely from the change in income—the income effect. The horizontal distance between C and B is the change in work due to the change in the marginal return, and it is the pure substitution effect of that wage rate change.[10]

There is no necessary relationship between the positions B or C relative to A. We know that B must be to the left of C, a positive substitution effect on labor supply, because H_0W_1 is steeper than H_0W_0. Furthermore, C will normally lie to the right of A, a negative income effect, on the plausible assumption that the demand for leisure rises with income. This would be shown by a progressive shift to the right with higher indifference curves. The position of B relative to A depends on whether the substitution effect exceeds the income effect in absolute value. In the figure the income effect offsets about two-thirds of the substitution effect. There is no theoretical basis, however, for determining which effect is larger. The historical trend toward a shorter workweek suggests that the income effect is dominant, but this spans a period in which many of the other factors affecting the work-leisure decision also changed. For example, from the perspective of trends in female participation in the work force, the evidence suggests that the substitution effect dominates.

In practice the situation is made complex by difficulty in distinguishing the effect of incentives from that of differences in preferences between work and leisure and by the need to extend the analysis to families where husbands and wives make joint decisions. Nor do all workers have the option of varying their hours above or below a standard workweek. In addition, when the concept of labor supply is expanded to include the intensity of work, retirement decisions, and educational investments, the potential effects of tax policy become even more involved.[11] The budget lines H_0W_0 and H_0W_1 in figure 5-1 can be used to represent the effects of a change in a simple proportionate tax, and other graphical modifications can be made to illustrate the effects of nonlabor income and a lump-sum tax (such as a simple head tax). But when a progressive tax schedule is included, the budget line itself is nonlinear and concave to the origin, greatly complicating the analysis.[12]

10. The pure substitution effect is sometimes referred to in the literature as the income-compensated substitution effect to distinguish it from the net effect on hours of work (income plus substitution).

11. Rosen, "What Is Labor Supply?"

12. The role of a progressive tax system is considered by Robert E. Hall, "Wages, Income, and Hours of Work in the U.S. Labor Force," in Glen G. Cain and Harold W. Watts, eds., *Income Maintenance and Labor Supply* (Rand McNally for the Institute for Research on Poverty of the University of Wisconsin, 1973), pp. 102–62; and Gary

Furthermore, the normal treatment of the income effect of a tax increase as an offset to the substitution effect ignores the value of public expenditures that those taxes finance. That is, when taxes rise it is assumed that the lower after-tax income encourages work effort as an offset to the disincentive (substitution) effect of the higher tax rate. However, if individuals place a high value on public expenditures, the positive income effect of a tax increase on labor supply will be mitigated, increasing the likelihood that labor supply will fall. Nearly all the empirical studies reviewed below implicitly attach no value to public expenditures, and they analyze a tax change as being equivalent to a change in the private wage rate.

Empirical Evidence

There are a large number of econometric studies of labor supply; and, at first blush, the results seem disappointing because of the wide variation in their conclusions. There has, however, been a steady progression toward more sophisticated models that incorporate an improved understanding of workers' decisions. The early studies ignored taxes and focused on gross wage rates. Only recently have studies emerged that take account of the nonlinearities and other complexities introduced by a progressive tax system with different categories of taxpayers (joint and single returns).

Aggregate time-series data on labor supply have proved to be of limited value because the information is dominated by secular trends that may be correlated with changing preferences. A much wider range of variation in hours of work, wage rates, and income is available from survey data of individual households. It is true that, in inferring effects of wage rate changes from the hours of work of individuals with different incomes and wage rates, one can never be sure that differences in other factors have been excluded. With respect to this problem, however, studies of labor supply have benefited enormously from a series of experiments operated by the government to test the operation of a negative income tax–based welfare program. Those experiments provided information on the change in work time for a panel of individuals

Burtless and Jerry A. Hausman, "The Effect of Taxation on Labor Supply: Evaluating the Gary Negative Income Tax Experiment," *Journal of Political Economy*, vol. 86 (December 1978), pp. 1103–30.

142   TAX INCENTIVES AND ECONOMIC GROWTH

who were followed over time as their after-tax wage rates were systematically varied.

In simplest form the empirical studies have related hours of work (*H*) to the wage rate (*w*), income (*Y*), and a host of demographic variables (*X*):

$$H = a + b \cdot w + c \cdot Y + d \cdot X,$$

where *a*, *b*, *c*, and *d* are parameters to be estimated. The net effect of a wage rate change is measured directly by the coefficient *b*; but separate identification of the substitution and income effects can be achieved only by associating the income effect with the response to changes in nonlabor income, the coefficient *c*. The substitution effect is thus obtained by subtraction.[13]

Results from Cross-Sectional Surveys

The empirical conclusions that emerge from the studies based on surveys of a cross section of the population are that the net labor supply effect (substitution plus income) of changes in the wage rate is small and probably negative for prime-age males, while the decisions of married women appear to be more sensitive to the wage rate.[14] Estimates of the net elasticity of the female labor supply with respect to the after-tax

13. In mathematical terms the relationship between the net labor supply effect of a change in the wage rate and its two components of the compensated substitution effect and the income effect is given by $\partial H/\partial W = s + H(\partial H/\partial Y)$, where $\partial H/\partial W$ (the coefficient *b* in the above equation) is the derivative of hours with respect to the wage rate, *s* is the substitution effect, and $\partial H/\partial Y$ (the coefficient *c*) is the derivative of hours with respect to income. In reporting results it is often more convenient to report the results in elasticity form as percentage responses: $\eta_w = \eta_s + \eta_y (w \cdot H/Y)$, where $(w \cdot H/Y)$ is the fraction of total income earned from wages.

14. The most extensive survey of the empirical work for males is Glen G. Cain and Harold W. Watts, "Toward a Summary and Synthesis of the Evidence," in Cain and Watts, eds., *Income Maintenance and Labor Supply*, pp. 328–69. The individual studies were then reviewed in two other papers that attempted to narrow the range of empirical values by assessing the quality of the study. See George J. Borjas and James J. Heckman, "Labor Supply Elasticities for Public Policy Evaluation," National Bureau of Economic Research Working Paper 299 (Cambridge, Mass.: NBER, November 1978); and Robert A. Moffitt and Kenneth C. Kehrer, "The Effect of Tax and Transfer Programs on Labor Supply: The Evidence from the Income Maintenance Experiments," in Ronald Ehrenberg, ed., *Research in Labor Economics*, vol. 4 (JAI Press, 1981), pp. 105–09. Throughout, the elasticity of labor supply refers to the percentage increase in labor supply for a 1 percent change in the after-tax wage rate.

wage rate are as large as 1.0. For males the pure substitution elasticities have ranged from 0.0 to 0.3 and the income effect from 0.0 to −0.3. The range of substitution elasticities for females has been as high as 1.2 and the income effect has varied between −0.06 and −0.81.[15] The overall weighted-average elasticity for men and women together was given the value of 0.15 in one survey by Fullerton: a 1 percent rise in the after-tax wage rate would increase hours of work by 0.15 percent.[16] Such a value has often been used to argue that taxes do not strongly affect the total supply of labor.

The emphasis in policy discussions on the net effect on labor supply may be misleading, however. A small net effect is still consistent with large absolute values for the compensated substitution and income components. While the two effects may be offsetting on total labor supply when evaluating a simple proportionate tax rate change, both effects are relevant for examining the response to a change in the tax structure. A simple head tax, unrealistic though it may be, generates an income effect, for example, but no substitution effect. The substitution effect is particularly important to the evaluation of a graduated tax rate system. If the compensated substitution effect is large, aggregate supply would be increased by a change in the tax system to raise the same amount of revenue with lower marginal tax rates—a less progressive system. This is one source of the conflict between efficiency and equity concerns that is so intense in current discussions of tax policy.[17]

The emphasis on the compensated or pure substitution effect is particularly evident in a recent study by Hausman.[18] While his results were in general agreement with those of others that the net effect of a wage rate change on labor supply was small for men, he found it to be composed of large offsetting substitution and income effects. Thus he concluded that substantial distortions of the work-leisure decision are

15. Moffitt and Kehrer, "The Effect of Tax and Transfer Programs on Labor Supply," p. 106.

16. Don Fullerton, "On the Possibility of an Inverse Relationship between Tax Rates and Government Revenues," *Journal of Public Economics*, vol. 19 (October 1982), pp. 16–19.

17. As mentioned earlier, the studies have also been criticized because they ignore the increase in public services that the tax provides. Evaluation of the benefit flow associated with the tax can be particularly critical for transfer programs, such as retirement and unemployment insurance, where the benefits are limited primarily to the taxpayers.

18. Jerry A. Hausman, "Labor Supply," in Henry J. Aaron and Joseph A. Pechman, eds., *How Taxes Affect Economic Behavior* (Brookings Institution, 1981), pp. 27–71.

introduced by the taxation of labor income. In addition, the large substitution effect for high-income individuals led Hausman to conclude that there are major efficiency costs to progressive taxation.[19]

The major surprise in the Hausman study is his finding of a large negative income effect, thus implying a large offsetting compensated substitution effect. In part, this result is a construct of his constraint in his estimation procedure requiring that every individual in the sample must have a negative income response and that the income effect can vary across individuals, with some individuals being required to have large income responses. These assumptions are not made in most other studies.[20]

Negative Income Tax Experiments

Income maintenance experiments designed to test alternative negative income tax proposals provided a unique opportunity to evaluate the income and substitution effects on work decisions within the confines of a controlled situation. Those experiments made it possible to observe the behavior of individuals over time as their effective after-tax wage rates changed. Their behavior was compared to a control group that did not receive the income payments. The evaluation of these experiments has highlighted some complex problems of their design—in particular, whether the participants' labor supply responses were distorted by their knowledge that the program was temporary. But the experiments had the major advantage of actually observing individuals' behavior under deliberately changed circumstances rather than inferring the response from observations of the behavior of different individuals under different circumstances.

In their review of the studies based on those experiments, Moffitt and Kehrer concluded that the estimated substitution and income elasticities were generally smaller and less variable than those based on nonexper-

19. Jerry Hausman, "Income and Payroll Tax Policy and Labor Supply," in Laurence H. Meyer, ed., *The Supply-Side Effects of Economic Policy* (Boston: Kluwer-Nijhoff, 1981), pp. 173–202. He reports that the ratio of deadweight loss (a measure of welfare loss) to the net income for men rises twelvefold as the wage rate increases from $3.15 to $10.00 and the percentage gain in labor supply rises about fourfold. This results because the income elasticity rises with the level of income in his model, and because the welfare loss is proportionate to the square of the tax rate.

20. See the comments by Gary Burtless following Hausman, "Labor Supply," in Aaron and Pechman, eds., *How Taxes Affect Economic Behavior*, pp. 76–83.

imental data. Substitution elasticities ranged between 0.0 and 0.16 for males and 0.08 and 0.42 for females, and the offsetting income effects ranged from 0.0 to −0.09 and 0.0 to −0.34 respectively.[21] These are substantially smaller effects than those obtained by Hausman, for example. On the other hand, the estimate of the income effect may be biased downward because of the temporary nature of the programs. In addition, the experimental sample excluded families in the top two-thirds to one-half of the income distribution. Hence they are not strictly comparable to the sample examined by Hausman.

What role should these empirical estimates of labor supply elasticities play in the evaluation of tax policy? First, the low values of the net elasticity suggest that tax rates, within the range currently in force in the United States, have relatively little effect on labor supplied by males with dependents.

For married females, however, whose earnings are viewed as being taxed at the family's higher marginal tax rate, the impact is more substantial. From this perspective, the introduction in 1982 of a special tax credit, equal to 10 percent of the secondary earner's income, may induce a significant change in labor supply, since it changes the average and marginal tax rates on the secondary earner's wage, but does not affect the net income of the primary earner. General tax rate changes, which generate large income effects as a result of changes in the spouse's after-tax income, would have a substantially smaller supply effect.

Second, the combination of supply elasticities and observed tax rates would appear to be far below the level required to create a situation in which tax revenues in a fully employed economy decline with a rise in tax rates—a claim made by the more extreme supply-side advocates. Fullerton concluded that tax rates would have to be in the range of 70 percent for such a situation to exist in the United States.[22] He points out, on the other hand, that the response to high tax rates is more complex in an open economy where labor and capital can move among jurisdictions with different rates of taxation. This is closer to the situation faced by state and local governments.

Third, a finding of a substantial compensated or pure substitution effect suggests that changes in the structure of the tax system, as measured by the difference between marginal and average tax rates,

21. Moffitt and Kehrer, "The Effect of Tax and Transfer Programs," p. 143.
22. Fullerton, "On the Possibility of an Inverse Relationship between Tax Rates and Government Revenue."

would have significant distorting effects on labor supply. While less confidence can be placed in the decomposition of the total effect into its substitution and income components, the studies generally find that the efficiency costs of progressive taxation are more substantial than previously believed.

Finally, in the earlier discussion of employment taxes, emphasis was placed on the importance of the employee's perception of the link between the tax and the benefits. That same point applies to other taxes as well. Most of the empirical studies analyze taxes as though they were pure waste with no associated benefits. Yet if individuals value public expenditures and these expenditures are closely tied to the tax they pay, the tax may have little effect on labor supply. On the other hand, if individuals place a high value on expenditures but they are unrelated to their own tax payment (a more common situation), an equal rise in taxes and expenditures has no net income effect, only a substitution effect. Thus it reduces labor supply by even more than the empirical studies imply.

Transfer Programs

Social insurance transfer programs have grown rapidly in recent decades. As shown in table 5-4, government payments to individuals for social welfare have expanded from 4.6 percent of GNP in 1950 to 10 percent in 1980. With an expansion of this magnitude, it is not surprising that the country should become embroiled in a heated debate over the programs' effect on work effort. The objectives of adequate income and security are important, but the influence of these programs on individuals' decisions to seek income through their own efforts is also significant in assessing the costs to society and in choosing among alternative means to achieve the objectives.

The ambiguity about the net effect on labor supply that is present in the case of a tax is absent in the case of transfers because the income and substitution effects both operate in the same direction. Most transfer programs consist of a lump-sum payment (basic guarantee) that is reduced as the individual's earnings increase. The rise in income coming from the lump-sum payment reduces work, and so too does the high effective marginal tax implied by the linkage of benefits to earned income, because it reduces the reward for extra effort.

Table 5-4. *Major Government Transfer Payments to Individuals as a Percentage of Gross National Product, Selected Years, 1950–80*

Category	Percentage of GNP			
	1950	1960	1970	1980
Social insurance	3.4	3.8	5.2	7.2
OASDI	0.3	2.2	3.2	4.5
Medicare	0.0	0.0	0.7	1.4
Unemployment insurance	0.5	0.6	0.4	0.6
Other[a]	2.5	1.0	0.9	0.8
Low-income assistance	1.2	0.8	1.9	2.7
Aid to families with dependent children	0.2	0.2	0.5	0.5
Medicaid[b]	0.0	0.1	0.5	0.8
Food stamps	0.0	0.0	0.1	0.3
Housing subsidies[c]	0.0	0.0	0.1	0.3
Other[d]	1.0	0.6	0.7	0.8
Total	4.6	4.6	7.1	10.0

Source: Department of Commerce, *National Income and Product Accounts*, tables 3.11, 3.16, and 3.17. Figures are rounded.
a. Excludes government employee retirement.
b. Medicaid is classified as a direct purchase in the national income accounts, but is shown here with transfers.
c. Government purchases and subsidies are included.
d. Includes supplementary social security income.

Yet the situation is not quite that simple. A few of the programs, such as social security and unemployment insurance, require a prior work history as a requirement for eligibility. Thus, for the employed, they exert a positive "entitlement" incentive to increase labor supply.[23] Some of the transfer programs have penalty provisions, such as reduced benefits, or additional qualifying provisions to limit the extent to which individuals can voluntarily become beneficiaries. In effect, through various targeting provisions, those who are most clearly expected to work are excluded from the disincentives of the transfer programs. The complexity of these provisions, together with uncertainty about the magnitude of the basic income and substitution effects, requires an assessment of the major transfer programs on an individual basis.

More than 70 percent of total transfers are accounted for by the social insurance programs. The aid to families with dependent children (AFDC) and food stamp programs, which are at the center of the public controversy over "welfare," account for only 8 percent of the total. Studies of

23. This point was made most clearly in Daniel S. Hamermesh, "Entitlement Effects, Unemployment Insurance and Employment Decisions," *Economic Inquiry*, vol. 17 (July 1979), pp. 317–32.

the effects of transfers on work incentives have concentrated on four major programs: unemployment insurance, old-age retirement, disability insurance, and low-income assistance.

Unemployment Insurance

The unemployment insurance (UI) program is the most important transfer program for the unemployed, and it has been the focal point for much of the analytical work on employment incentives.

While the effect of the program on the supply of labor is important, the policy debate has focused upon its impact on measured rates of unemployment. Critics of the system have argued that, by reducing the financial hardship of unemployment, the insurance program reduces the intensity of competition for jobs and increases the amount of inflation associated with any given rate of unemployment. To some extent, of course, this must be true. The significance of the argument depends on the quantitative magnitude of the effect. But, even if those magnitudes were known with certainty, the public debate would continue because of differing value judgments about the appropriate balance between a concern for strong incentives for job search and a concern for moderating the financial hardship of the unemployed.

BASIC FEATURES AND ISSUES. Unemployment insurance is a state-run program, and consequently the benefits, qualifications, and financing arrangements vary among the states. There are, however, some common features:

1. Benefits are related to prior (base-period) earnings with a ceiling and a floor.

2. Qualified workers must have had a minimum length of employment in a prior job and an acceptable reason for separation.

3. Benefits were tax exempt before 1979 and continue to be for those with family income below $18,000 or individual income below $12,000.

4. The system is financed mainly by a payroll tax with a ceiling on taxable annual earnings per employee (currently $7,000 for most states, but some have recently taken action to raise the ceiling substantially). Supplemental benefits (beyond thirty-nine weeks) and related programs are paid for out of general revenue.

5. According to the predominant system of experience rating, each firm's tax rate is based upon the prior year's ratio of its reserve of accumulated taxes minus benefits paid divided by taxable wages. Thus

Table 5-5. *Insured Unemployment Data, Selected Years, 1950–82*

Year	Insured unemployed as percentage of:		Benefits	
	Covered employment	Total un- employment	Weekly amount (dollars)	Percentage of average wage
1950	4.6	48.8	20.76	39.1
1955	3.5	49.1	25.04	37.0
1960	4.8	53.8	32.87	40.7
1965	3.0	43.1	37.19	39.0
1970	3.4	50.6	50.34	42.0
1975	6.0	62.3	70.23	42.9
1980	3.9	50.2	98.95	42.1
1982	4.7	38.0	119.20	44.7

Source: *Economic Report of the President*, February 1983, p. 204.

the tax rate rises automatically as the reserve ratio is drawn down. Under a full experience-rated system each firm would pay the full cost of its laid-off workers.

6. The tax rate is limited by minimum and maximum values that moderate the extent of experience rating.[24]

Some aggregate statistics on employment insurance are shown in table 5-5. First, it is important to note that less than half of the unemployed actually receive insurance. New entrants to the work force and voluntary job leavers are generally not eligible, and some job losers lack a sufficiently long period of prior employment to qualify for benefits. The percentage of total unemployment covered by insurance has also declined in recent years because more individuals have exhausted their benefits. Benefits have averaged about 40 percent of average weekly wages throughout the postwar period with a very modest upward trend. That replacement ratio is lower than the statutory rate of 50 percent primarily because of the ceiling limitation on benefits to high-wage workers.

The overall level of unemployment is the product of two separate factors: the number of spells of unemployment and the duration of each spell of unemployment. That is, unemployment would be reduced either by reducing the frequency with which workers become unemployed or by shortening the duration of each spell. The concern with the incentive effects of the UI program involves both of these factors.

24. These basic characteristics are taken from Alan L. Gustman, "Analyzing the Relation of Unemployment Insurance to Unemployment," National Bureau of Economic Research Working Paper 512 (Cambridge, Mass.: NBER, July 1980).

First, the benefit system may encourage workers to lengthen the duration of their unemployment. Most state programs limit the benefit to about 50 percent of the prior gross wage. For many workers, however, the wages are taxed and the benefits are not; therefore, the replacement of after-tax income may be substantially higher. Much of the recent controversy was stimulated by the argument of Feldstein that, on average, unemployment insurance benefits replaced 79 percent of the prior after-tax wage of the unemployed.[25] The calculation of effective replacement rates is a complex issue and it is addressed in more detail below. But replacement rates of the magnitude suggested by Feldstein imply that some beneficiaries have weak incentives to seek employment. In effect, they would gain very little net income from work so long as they remain eligible for UI benefits. Concern with this issue has led some critics to advocate full taxation of UI benefits and sharp limits on their duration, requiring earlier resort to the means-tested welfare programs. Recipients of UI are required to be actively searching for a job. Thus the system creates an incentive for discharged workers to be classified as unemployed rather than as nonparticipants in the work force. Although this may have little effect on the effective supply of labor, it drives up the measured unemployment rate.

A second controversy focuses on the issue of experience rating as a basis for setting the tax rate for individual firms. In principle, under experience rating the firm's tax rate reflects its past history of generating unemployment, as benefit payments draw down its reserve. In practice, however, the existence of a maximum and minimum value for the tax rate implies that firms at the tax rate ceiling do not pay the full cost of additional layoffs and are subsidized by other firms. If wages of the firm's employees are above the $7,000 ceiling and if the tax rate is at the maximum or minimum, additional temporary layoffs have no effect on the taxes paid into the system. It is profitable for those firms to view unemployment benefits as a component of their compensation of employees and to use temporary layoffs as an active element of their adjustment to fluctuations in the demand for their products. In addition, workers are more willing to accept jobs with a high probability of layoff because they know they will receive compensation during the period of

25. Martin Feldstein, "Unemployment Compensation: Adverse Incentives and Distributional Anomalies," *National Tax Journal*, vol. 27 (June 1974), pp. 231–44, especially p. 232. He produced even higher replacement rates for workers in Massachusetts under differing illustrative circumstances.

layoff. By stimulating more frequent layoffs the UI program adds to unemployment.[26] An opposite effect is that the program encourages beneficiaries to extend their job search to find jobs that are a better match for their skills, reducing voluntary turnover.

The early empirical work focused upon the incentives that UI benefits create for the unemployed to lengthen the duration of unemployment. In contrast, the issue of experience rating directs attention toward the incentives for employers to initiate more spells of temporary unemployment. Workers laid off by such employers, awaiting recall to their former jobs, may not actively seek alternative employment. It is argued that such unemployment is voluntary in the sense that it results from the choice of an occupation with a known expectation of layoff.

The UI program also creates some incentives that operate to reduce unemployment. The existence of the ceiling on taxable wages ($7,000 per employee), for example, encourages firms to reduce the turnover of employees.[27] Eligibility for UI also must be earned by accumulating an employment record, which creates an added incentive to find and sustain employment.

BENEFIT REPLACEMENT RATES. The assertion by Feldstein that UI benefits replaced more than 75 percent of the prior after-tax wage of the unemployed heightened concern about the program's effect on employment incentives.[28] A recent study by Vroman examined this issue in considerable detail.[29] The UI replacement rate would seem to be a relatively straightforward concept; but because UI benefits are not taxed and there are alternative methods of measuring the loss of earned income, different studies yield widely differing numbers. Furthermore, while the

---

26. The theoretical issue of experience rating is examined in detail by three authors: Martin N. Baily, "On the Theory of Layoffs and Unemployment," *Econometrica*, vol. 45 (July 1977), pp. 1043–63; Frank Brechling, "The Incentive Effects of the U.S. Unemployment Insurance Tax," in Ronald Ehrenberg, ed., *Research in Labor Economics*, vol. 1 (JAI Press, 1977), pp. 41–102; and Martin Feldstein, "Temporary Layoffs in the Theory of Unemployment," *Journal of Political Economy*, vol. 84 (October 1976), pp. 937–57. The effect of UI on the duration of unemployment—through increases in the reservation wage of the person engaged in job search—is elaborated on in Dale T. Mortensen, "Job Search, the Duration of Unemployment, and the Phillips Curve," *American Economic Review*, vol. 60 (December 1970), pp. 847–62.

27. Brechling, "Incentive Effects of the U.S. Unemployment Insurance Tax."

28. Feldstein, "Unemployment Compensation."

29. Wayne Vroman, "State Replacement Rates in 1980," in National Commission on Unemployment Compensation, *Unemployment Compensation: Studies and Research*, vol. 1 (July 1980), pp. 165–86.

152 TAX INCENTIVES AND ECONOMIC GROWTH

laws of most states call for a 50 percent replacement of base-period wages, actual experience is heavily influenced by administrative procedures and base-period wages are often not a good measure of the loss of earnings.

The official data of the Department of Labor are based on a comparison of the average unemployment benefit payment with the average weekly wage of workers in industries covered by the UI program. That ratio averages in the 0.3 to 0.4 range. The alternative measures considered by Vroman took account of taxes, fringe benefits, work-related expenses, and the ceiling limitation on benefits.[30] One of the major differences with Feldstein's study was in the estimation of the base-period wage. Feldstein assumed that the unemployed were earning only 70 percent of the average wage rate of covered workers. However, Vroman reports that the insured unemployed in 1980 previously earned a wage 10 to 15 percent above the average.

Vroman computed individual benefit replacement rates, incorporating the above adjustments for a representative survey sample of the unemployed, and obtained net after-tax replacement rates that averaged 40 to 45 percent of the base-period wage, or 45 to 50 percent if other transfers were included—substantially below the estimate used by Feldstein.[31] At the same time, there was a wide variation in individual experience, particularly on an after-tax basis.[32] This variability is the result of differences in state programs and variations in marginal tax rates as well as in the work experience of individuals.

EMPIRICAL STUDIES. Many studies have attempted to measure the effect of the UI program on the incidence and duration of unemployment, but because the newer studies have identified serious problems with the earlier work, the relevant literature is quite small. Hamermesh surveyed

30. The existence of benefit ceilings limits the replacement rate for high-wage workers. Thus, if the average benefit ratio is obtained by dividing average benefits by average wages, it is lower than the ratio obtained by averaging individual replacement rates. Vroman found this effect to account for 15 to 25 percent of the differences among studies.

31. Vroman used a mean marginal tax rate of 0.3, a work-related expenses ratio of 0.08, a fringe-benefit ratio of 0.13, and a wage inflation factor of 0.17. While the last two factors offset much of the marginal tax rate in 1980, they would not do so at other times. He also found that beneficiaries received compensation for 81 percent of the weeks they were unemployed.

32. While he obtained a mean replacement rate of 0.391 for the most comprehensive measure of after-tax income, the standard deviation was 0.216, indicating a significant number of individuals with replacement rates above 60 percent.

a large number of the empirical studies on the expected duration of unemployment and concluded that a 10-percentage-point increase in the ratio of benefits to prior wages (replacement rate) would lengthen the duration of insured unemployment by approximately half a week.[33]

Many of these studies suffer from the difficulty of accurately measuring the duration of an unemployment spell. For those based on data from the insured unemployment program, duration is limited to the period during which the benefit is received, ignoring the period after benefits are exhausted. Other surveys of the labor force truncate the period of duration for those who are unemployed at the time of the survey and also miss short spells of unemployment that fall between the survey dates.

One study by Marston confronted this issue directly by measuring the expected full duration of spells of unemployment for insured and uninsured workers.[34] In a year of relatively tight labor markets, 1969, he estimated the expected duration of a spell of unemployment at 5.6 weeks for insured workers; and he concluded that, adjusting for demographic differences, this period averages about 30 percent greater than that for uninsured workers. His results imply that elimination of the UI program would lower the overall unemployment rate by 0.2 to 0.3 percentage point. On the other hand, the extension of benefits from twenty-six to fifty-two weeks would add about 0.2 percentage point.

More recently, a study by Moffitt and Nicholson appeared to find substantially larger disincentive effects.[35] They obtained data on the work experience of a group of workers who initially received extended unemployment insurance in 1975, were interviewed in 1976, and were interviewed again in late 1977. Thus they had data on work experience over a time span that averaged 155 weeks, together with information on benefits, prior wages, potential duration of benefits, and other characteristics of the workers. By regression analysis they estimated the effect of changes in the duration of benefits and the after-tax replacement rate on the proportion of time spent working. Both of these factors were

33. Daniel S. Hamermesh, *Jobless Pay and the Economy* (Johns Hopkins University Press, 1977), pp. 32–39.

34. Stephen T. Marston, "The Impact of Unemployment on Job Search," *Brookings Papers on Economic Activity, 1:1975*, pp. 13–48. (Hereafter *BPEA*.)

35. Robert Moffitt and Walter Nicholson, "The Effect of Unemployment Insurance on Unemployment: The Case of Federal Supplemental Benefits," *Review of Economics and Statistics,* vol. 64 (February 1982), pp. 1–11.

154   TAX INCENTIVES AND ECONOMIC GROWTH

statistically very significant. Their results led them to conclude that a 10-percentage-point increase in the replacement rate or a ten-week extension of benefits would increase the duration of an unemployment spell by one week. This implies that the existence of the UI program adds five to six weeks to the duration of an unemployment spell—a far larger estimate than that of Marston.

The conclusions of the Moffitt and Nicholson study are misleading, however. They actually estimated the proportion of time during the 155-week survey period that the individuals worked—not the duration of an unemployment spell. The fraction of time employed averaged 0.48 for men, implying an average unemployment period of seventy-five weeks. Clearly this is a very unusual sample, if Marston's estimate of an average duration for an insured spell of unemployment of 5.6 weeks is anywhere near correct. While the Moffitt and Nicholson study is very important in finding a statistically significant effect of the UI program on the proportion of a time period spent unemployed by a sample of the long-term unemployed, it cannot be used to infer, in any simple way, the magnitude of effect on the duration of an average spell of unemployment or the effect on the overall unemployment rate.[36]

All the studies that focus on duration in attempting to evaluate incentives are subject to serious criticisms. The insured unemployed, who are job losers, cannot be compared with other unemployed workers who have either quit their jobs or just entered the work force. That is, the duration of unemployment can be expected to depend systematically on the reason for unemployment. In addition, as Feldstein has pointed out, to the extent that less than full experience rating induces an increased number of short-term layoffs, the system would appear to reduce the average duration of overall unemployment even while increasing the expected duration for each worker. Furthermore, a spell of unemployment could be terminated by a decision to leave the labor force as much

36. Certainly their study cannot be used, as was done in a survey by Danziger, Haveman, and Plotnick, to obtain an estimate of reduced labor supply. In the latter study five weeks was interpreted as the effect of UI on the duration of a spell of unemployment, but then it was multiplied by the average number of insured unemployed rather than the total number of spells in a year. Sheldon Danziger, Robert Haveman, and Robert Plotnick, "How Income Transfer Programs Affect Work, Saving, and the Income Distribution: A Critical Review," *Journal of Economic Literature*, vol. 19 (September 1981), pp. 995–97.

as by finding a job, so that the duration of unemployment cannot be used to infer the time required to find a new job.

A study by Feldstein avoided the distinction between incidence and duration by focusing on the probability that an individual would be unemployed at a point in time and examining whether or not the probability was affected by the availability of unemployment insurance.[37] He considered only the unemployed who were on temporary layoff (approximately 400 individuals) in a survey of 25,000 experienced workers between the ages of twenty-five and fifty-five in the private nonfarm economy. Feldstein estimated that an increase in the benefit-replacement ratio of 10 percentage points would increase the probability of being on layoff by 0.13: that is, elimination of the UI program, with its mean net wage replacement rate of 0.55, would reduce the temporary layoff component of unemployment by 0.74 percentage point, or 46 percent of the 1.6 mean value in the sample.

Feldstein focused upon the unemployment category of temporary layoffs. While it is important to identify the differing incentive effects on employers and employees in that situation, many would disagree with Feldstein's view that temporary layoffs account for a substantial fraction of total unemployment. Temporary layoffs account for a substantial proportion of persons who experience unemployment, but, because of their short durations, they account for a far smaller fraction of the total time lost through unemployment.[38]

In addition, the study was originally motivated by a concern for the effects on employers' decisions of the failure to fully incorporate experience rating in the setting of tax rates. Yet the empirical analysis excludes all measures of such effects. The ratio of benefits to earnings is of relevance to the employee but the employer should be concerned with the ratio of benefits to the tax cost. Thus one really does not know what characteristic of the UI program is responsible for the effect Feldstein reports.

37. Martin Feldstein, "The Effect of Unemployment Insurance on Temporary Layoff Unemployment," *American Economic Review*, vol. 68 (December 1978), pp. 834–46. He included within the category of temporary layoff all workers who said they were awaiting recall by their prior employer, including those with an indefinite duration of layoff.

38. Kim B. Clark and Lawrence H. Summers, "Labor Market Dynamics and Unemployment: A Reconsideration," *BPEA, 1:1979*, pp. 13–60, especially pp. 46–51.

A more comprehensive analysis of the effects of UI on employment status is attempted in a recent study by Clark and Summers.[39] They examine its influence on the flows or transitions of individuals among the three categories of employed, unemployed, and not in the labor force. Like Feldstein, they find that UI increases the flow from employment to unemployment, but they find an offsetting decline in the flow from employment to nonparticipation: that is, the existence of UI leads individuals who would otherwise be out of the labor force to report that they are looking for work. On balance, they find that a reduction of 10 percentage points in the UI benefit replacement ratio would reduce the overall unemployment rate by about 0.1 percentage point. Elimination of the program would reduce the employment ratio and the unemployment rate by 0.6 percentage point each, but the labor force participation rate would decline by 1.1 percentage points. Thus, they conclude that the major effect of UI is to increase the apparent attachment to the labor force.

One of the more surprising results of the Summers-Clark paper is that they could not find a significant role for their measure of experience rating in affecting the rate of job separation.[40] This raises questions about the connection between the theory, which emphasizes the importance of the experience-rating issue for employer decisions, and the empirical results. If variations in the level of temporary layoff are not correlated with differences in the extent of experience rating, it might be more reasonable to interpret the major empirical studies as implying the opposite flow of causation: situations of frequent layoff generate pressures for compensatory payment programs. In that case, curtailment of state UI programs would simply create pressures for private programs— a phenomenon that is evident in some domestic industries with supplementary unemployment insurance programs.

The Summers and Clark study was subject to several of the same problems as that by Feldstein, and the distribution of the effects is not fully consistent with the theoretical model.[41] It is, however, the most

39. Kim B. Clark and Lawrence H. Summers, "Unemployment Insurance and Labor Market Transitions," in Martin Neil Baily, ed., Workers, Jobs, and Inflation (Brookings Institution, 1982), pp. 279–318.

40. This result may simply reflect difficulties they faced in constructing a measure of experience rating. The survey of the unemployed does not provide such information directly.

41. See, in particular, the comments on their paper by Martin Feldstein in Baily, ed., Workers, Jobs, and Inflation, pp. 318–21.

comprehensive of the recent studies and has the advantage of examining actual transitions of individuals from one employment category to another.

In summary, the UI program lengthens the duration of unemployment spells for those who are insured, but the impact on unemployment of that factor alone seems small. The major uncertainty is associated with the effect of the program on occurrences of unemployment. If it generates a large number of short-term layoffs, the duration of an average spell would be a poor measure of the program's effect. The study by Clark and Summers suggests that the program does cause a substantial reclassification of labor market status between the categories of employed, unemployed, and not in the labor force, but that its effect on the unemployment rate is in the range of 0.5–1.0 percentage point.

If one assumes that the program does not change the total supply of jobs offered by firms, the major incentive effect is to reduce the intensity of competition for jobs among the unemployed. Thus it would increase the unemployment rate associated with any given degree of inflationary pressures. From this perspective, however, there has been only a minor expansion of the program in recent decades, so that it cannot have made a significant contribution to the worsening of the inflation-unemployment relationship.[42]

Social Security

The sharp decline in the labor force participation rates of older men creates a presumption that social security has been a contributing factor. The evaluation of the program's potential effects on retirement decisions, however, should be considered within the context of its effect on saving because the two issues are closely related. If old age and survivors insurance (OASI) is fully substitutable for private saving, it should have little effect on retirement decisions: the increase in social security wealth is offset by reductions in private saving and the individual is left with the

42. Some of the disincentives for workers in high-income families were reduced by the recent shift to taxation of benefits. On the other hand, there appears to have been a reduction over time in the extent to which states use experience rating in the establishment of effective tax rates. The duration of benefits has also been changed on a countercyclical basis but not permanently. See Robert Topel and Finis Welch, "Unemployment Insurance: Survey and Extensions," *Economica*, vol. 47 (August 1980), pp. 365–66.

same total lifetime assets that he could accumulate on his own.[43] On the other hand, if OASI does not reduce private saving, the prospect of receiving benefits after retirement encourages earlier retirement.

The simplest perspective is that social security taxes reduce the current net wage; and, if workers ignore the accumulation of future benefits, the effect on labor supply should be the same as for any other tax on wage income. To the extent that workers recognize the value of future benefits, however, the effect of the tax on labor supply will be reduced, if not eliminated. If the present value of the future benefits is viewed as equal to the current tax, there is no effect on the supply of work effort (assuming no borrowing constraints). It seems reasonable that younger workers, for whom the benefits are in the distant future, will view the contributions as a tax, while older workers will be more inclined to take account of the benefit entitlement.

This relatively simple statement of the issues, however, must be modified to take account of several special features of the rules determining benefit payments. Beginning at age sixty-two, the average worker actually faces a complex set of options. If he postpones retirement, his basic benefit is increased by 8⅓ percent for each year forgone up to age sixty-five, and it is increased by 3¾ percent for each year between ages sixty-five and seventy. In the age interval of sixty-two to sixty-five, the adjustment is almost fully "actuarially fair" in that the higher benefit almost exactly offsets a shorter period of expected benefit payment. The adjustment is less than actuarially fair after age sixty-five.[44]

In addition, having accepted the benefit, the retired worker below the age of seventy faces an earnings test that reduces the benefit by 50 percent of any income earned above a minimum. In 1982 the minimum was $6,000 and $4,400 for workers above and below age sixty-five, respectively. A further complication is introduced by a provision that

43. Strictly speaking, this assumes that the individual's desired saving is greater than that provided by social security and there are no liquidity constraints on his borrowing.

44. A detailed discussion of these issues is provided in Alan S. Blinder, Roger H. Gordon, and Donald E. Wise, "Reconsidering the Work Disincentive Effects of Social Security," *National Tax Journal*, vol. 33 (December 1980), pp. 431–42; Richard V. Burkhauser and John A. Turner, "Can Twenty-Five Million Americans Be Wrong?—A Response to Blinder, Gordon and Wise," *National Tax Journal*, vol. 34 (December 1981), pp. 467–72; and Blinder, Gordon, and Wise, "Rhetoric and Reality in Social Security Analysis—A Rejoinder," *National Tax Journal*, vol. 34 (December 1981), pp. 473–78. I benefited from the discussion in Henry J. Aaron, *Economic Effects of Social Security* (Brookings Institution, 1982), pp. 2–7, 60–65.

permits a recomputation of the basic benefit after retirement to incorporate postretirement earnings. For some retired workers with substantial earnings the recomputation of benefits may offset the reduction due to the earnings test.

The extent to which the average worker fully understands these provisions is an important qualification for any evaluation of their effect on labor force participation. It is also not possible to resolve the issue by reference to the observed decline over time in the labor force participation of older workers because the trend was evident well before the introduction of social security.[45] It would be reasonable to argue, for example, that earlier retirement is a normal result of rising living standards.

Furthermore, to date, the average recipient has received a transfer payment far in excess of his contribution plus accumulated interest because most recipients have not had a full work history under the program and Congress has expanded benefits over the years. Thus there are a large number of transitional effects associated with introduction of the program. That is particularly true of the large windfall gains for retirees that resulted from large benefit increases in the early 1970s.

The empirical studies of the impact of OASI on retirement decisions were surveyed in a recent review article.[46] The authors concluded that four studies were to be preferred in terms of the quality of both the data and the statistical methodology that were used. Of these, one study concluded that social security could more than account for the 25-percentage-point decline since 1950 in the labor force participation rate of older men. A second study found an effect half as large, and the other two studies found no significant effect on the retirement decision.

The wide disparity in the conclusions of those empirical studies is discouraging. But recent studies have used a more elaborate methodology to take account of the nonlinear effective tax schedules, and they may measure the responses with greater precision. A study by Burtless and Moffitt, for example, made use of a survey that followed the work history of older workers during the 1970s.[47] They found that the OASI

45. Aaron, *Economic Effects of Social Security*, p. 32.

46. Danziger, Haveman, and Plotnick, "How Income Transfer Programs Affect Work, Saving, and the Income Distribution," pp. 975–1028.

47. Gary Burtless and Robert A. Moffitt, "The Effects of Social Security on Labor Supply of the Aged," in Gary Burtless and Henry J. Aaron, eds., *Retirement and Economic Behavior* (Brookings Institution, 1984).

program does have significant effects on labor supply decisions, but the magnitude is relatively small. A 20 percent reduction in benefits would postpone retirement of the average worker by ten weeks. Elimination of the earnings test would raise hours worked by eight hours per week for those affected by the provision, but because only 12 percent of the retired are constrained by the provision, the average increase is only one hour.[48]

Several other studies have examined the issue of whether social security causes the elderly to withdraw from the labor force rather than focusing on hours of work. As one might expect, the existence of social security does have substantial effects on that decision; but because older workers typically have reduced hours of work at low wages, an emphasis on the labor force participation decision gives little insight into the effect on incomes or hours of work.

The complexities of the social security system as it affects labor supply decisions and the importance of distinguishing among workers of different ages is well illustrated in a paper by Gordon. He computed the effective tax rate for an average worker as the sum of income and employment taxes minus the present value of future retirement benefits that result from an additional hour of work.[49] The calculations assume that the worker is fully aware of all the provisions of social security—certainly an optimistic assumption.

Gordon found that social security in the past has provided a large subsidy to workers, but the magnitude of that subsidy is rapidly declining for younger workers. The major reason for the subsidy is that the periodic legislated increases in benefits were made available to past cohorts of retirees without regard to their previous tax contributions. For workers (with a spouse) who retired in 1975, the system in effect provided a subsidy to work throughout the working years that more than offset the personal income tax. Even for the cohort reaching age sixty-five in 1985, couples will have paid little or no net tax through the working years, as the accrued benefits exceeded the tax. Married workers who will reach

48. While it is difficult to compare the studies, it appears that effects of similar magnitude are reported by Jerry Hausman and Donald Wise, "Social Security, Health Status and Retirement," presented at the Conference on Pensions, Labor and Individual Choice, sponsored by the National Bureau of Economic Research (March 1983).

49. Roger H. Gordon, "Social Security and Labor Supply Incentives," National Bureau of Economic Research Working Paper 986 (Cambridge, Mass.: NBER, September 1982). His analysis also took account of the earnings test on postretirement earnings and the potential for recomputation of the basic benefit to reflect postretirement earnings.

age sixty-five in the year 2005 will receive benefits in excess of their payments, while single and secondary earners will pay more social security taxes than their benefits.

These results emphasize the extent to which the history of social security has been one of transition. The incentive effects on future retirees (the young) are much different from the effect on those who retired in past years. Thus, even though the system has been in existence for over forty years, it has not yet been possible to observe a fully mature system in which workers receive benefits that are closely related to the cumulative value of their contributions. Past experience may be a very poor basis for evaluating the implications of the system for the future.

Disability Insurance

The labor force participation rate of men between the ages of forty-five and fifty-four declined from 96 percent in 1965 to 91 percent by 1980. The drop in the participation rate is even larger for men aged fifty-five to fifty-nine—a fall of 8 percentage points between 1965 and 1980. In a search for explanations, considerable attention has been directed toward the disability insurance (DI) program and the possibility that high DI benefits induced workers to withdraw from the labor force.

The disability insurance program has expanded rapidly over the last decade, with a liberalization of both eligibility and benefits. Payments to beneficiaries grew from $3.0 billion to $17.3 billion between fiscal years 1970 and 1981, and the number of beneficiaries rose from 1.5 to 2.8 million.[50] After falling short of the rise in wage rates during the 1960s, the average benefit payment rose by 115 percent between 1970 and 1978, compared to a 70 percent rise in average weekly earnings.[51]

If the beneficiaries of the program were truly disabled, the labor force supply issue would not arise. It is argued, however, that disability may have voluntary elements and that the labor supply decision is influenced by the magnitude of the insurance benefits. Alternatively, the recent expansion of the beneficiary rolls can be viewed as a one-shot response

50. *Background Material and Data on Major Programs within the Jurisdiction of the Committee on Ways and Means*, House Committee on Ways and Means, Committee Print, 97 Cong. 2 sess. (Government Printing Office, 1982), p. 3.

51. Social Security Administration, U. S. Department of Health and Human Services, *Social Security Bulletin, Annual Statistical Supplement, 1980*, p. 106. The benefits are for male workers with a wife and two or more children.

by a previously existing pool of the disabled for whom the qualifying requirements were too stringent. In other words, is the rise in the number of disability insurance recipients a response to an economic incentive or a result of an administrative change in the health standards that define disability?

Several investigators have looked at the link between expanded disability insurance and the decline in the male labor force participation rate. An initial study by Parsons concluded that the disability program was a major source of the decline in labor force participation, and that the recipients were responding to the economic incentive of the ratio of the disability benefit to their wage.[52] Parsons did not, however, actually have a measure for the individuals in his sample of the potential disability benefit, which is a function of an individual's work history under the social security system. He tried to estimate the benefit by applying the benefit formula to current wages only. Thus his benefit replacement rate is simply a transformation of the wage rate divided by the wage rate, and it will be only loosely related to the true replacement rate. It will be high for low-wage workers and low for high-wage workers, a factor which is itself correlated with disability.[53]

Two recent studies, based on survey data of individual workers that included actual benefits, avoided some of the problems of the Parsons study, but they reached markedly divergent results. A study by Leonard claimed a significant statistical correlation between the amount of an individual's potential DI benefits and the probability of being a beneficiary.[54] Using a sample of 1,685 men aged forty-five to fifty-four, Leonard related the probability of being a beneficiary to measures of various personal characteristics and twenty-seven specific health conditions. The coefficients on these variables were then allowed to vary with the level of the individual's potential DI benefits.[55] He reported that an

52. Donald O. Parsons, "The Decline in Male Labor Force Participation," *Journal of Political Economy*, vol. 88 (February 1980), pp. 117–34.

53. The study is evaluated more fully in Robert H. Haveman and Barbara L. Wolfe, "The Decline in Male Labor Force Participation: A Comment" (University of Wisconsin–Madison, 1982), forthcoming in *Journal of Political Economy*.

54. Jonathan Leonard, "The Social Security Disability Program and Labor Force Participation," National Bureau of Economic Research Working Paper 392 (Cambridge, Mass.: NBER, August 1979).

55. Disability benefits are determined in a parallel fashion to that for OASI benefits, and Leonard had information on the individuals' work history to enable him to apply the benefit formula. The actual regression related beneficiary status (S) to an estimated probability of being eligible ($\hat{E}$), potential benefits (B), and a vector of health (Z) and

increase in the benefit level increases substantially the probability of being a DI recipient—an elasticity of response of 0.35 to changes in the benefit amount.

The Leonard study does not provide evidence, however, that increases in the benefit amount induce more people to move on to the disability roll. The expected benefit measure used in the statistical regressions is the product of the benefit amount and an index of health characteristics. Variations in the health status measure ensure that the combined variable would be significant even if the benefit amount had no effect: no one disagrees that workers in poor health are likely to be on disability. Evidence on the specific effect of benefits could have been obtained by including both the index of health status and its interaction with benefits as separate variables. That was not done.

The second study, by Haveman and Wolfe, distinguishes between the effect of health status and the size of the potential DI benefit.[56] They concluded that changes in the benefit payment had a relatively small effect on labor force participation. Their data sample included more detailed information on health conditions, expected labor earnings, and labor force status.

The Haveman-Wolfe results imply that a doubling of the benefit amount would reduce the labor force participation rate by about 0.5 percentage point. In contrast, Leonard concluded that the proportion of the population on disability insurance would rise by about 2 percentage points.[57]

---

other characteristics (X): $S = a + b (\hat{E} \cdot B) + \Sigma \, c_i \cdot X_i$, where $\hat{E} = \Sigma \, d_i \cdot Z_i$, and a, b, c, and d are parameters to be estimated.

The eligibility relationship is estimated from a subset of individuals who applied for the program, and then computed for all individuals. The health variables, Z_i, are binary variables that equal one if the individual has the specific health problem. If the coefficient b is significant in the status equation, one does not know if it reflects the effect of the benefit (B) or eligibility (E).

56. Robert H. Haveman and Barbara L. Wolfe, "Have Disability Transfers Caused the Decline in Older Male Labor Force Participation? A Work-Status Rational Choice Model" (University of Wisconsin–Madison, Institute for Research on Poverty, October 1981).

57. The response for the Haveman-Wolfe study is found in ibid., p. 29. Leonard reports an elasticity of 0.35 and a proportion of the male population aged forty-five to fifty-four on disability of about 5 percent ($0.05 \times 0.35 = 0.018$). A third study by Slade is supportive of the Haveman-Wolfe study, but his measures of health status are not very specific. Frederic P. Slade, "Labor Supply under Disability Insurance," National Bureau of Economic Research Working Paper 860 (Cambridge, Mass.: NBER, February 1982). A second study by Slade also found no evidence that the potential DI benefit

Low-Income Welfare Programs

Aid to families with dependent children and the other welfare programs have played a role in public discussion of the disincentive effects of government transfers that is far out of proportion to their size in the budget.[58] The four major programs are AFDC, food stamps, the earned-income tax credit, and medicaid. These programs may create disincentives for low-income individuals to seek employment because of their design and the manner in which they interact with one another.

The AFDC program is run by the states but with substantial federal funding. Each state establishes a maximum benefit, related to recipients' needs, that would be paid if the family received no income from other sources. The level of the maximum benefit varies sharply among the states. Actual payments decline from this maximum in step with the rise in "countable" income from other sources. Before 1981 federal law required that countable monthly income be defined net of work-related expenses, the first $30 of earned income, and one-third of the remainder. In theory, this would limit the effective marginal "tax" rate to no more than 67 percent. The definition of countable income is an after-tax measure in that payroll and income taxes are deducted and it includes the earned-income tax credit. Legislative changes enacted in 1981 increased the effective tax rate by limiting allowances for work expenses and child care and restricted the exclusion of one-third of earned income to the first four months of the benefit year.

The federal food stamp program also establishes a maximum benefit related to family size. The payment is then determined by subtracting 30 percent of a family's countable income from the maximum benefit level. Countable income includes AFDC payments but excludes 18 percent of earned income, day care expenses, and shelter costs in excess of 50 percent of income.

---

affected the labor force entry or exit of older workers. See Frederic P. Slade, "Labor Force Entry and Exit of Older Men: A Longitudinal Study," National Bureau of Economic Research Working Paper 1029 (Cambridge, Mass.: NBER, November 1982). The study is criticized in Haveman and Wolfe, "The Decline in Male Labor Force Participation."

58. The AFDC program has not grown appreciably since the mid-1970s. Between 1975 and 1981, the number of recipients declined by 4 percent, and median benefits in constant dollars were cut by 27 percent between 1970 and 1981. Additional cuts were enacted in 1981 legislation. The food stamp program expanded from $1.1 billion in 1970 to $10 billion in 1981, and it was cut back slightly in 1981 legislation. See *Background Material and Data on Major Programs within the Jurisdiction of the Committee on Ways and Means*, p. 128.

Table 5-6. *Monthly Welfare Benefits in Pennsylvania for a Single Parent with Two Children*

Dollars unless otherwise indicated

Earned income	AFDC payment	Food stamps	Net taxes[a]	Disposable income[b]	Implicit marginal tax rate[c]
0	318	138	0	456	0
100	224	140	6	458	98
200	130	142	12	460	98
300	35	144	17	462	98
400	0	119	23	496	66
500	0	81	44	537	59
600	0	54	83	571	66
700	0	0	110	590	81
800	0	0	138	664	26
900	0	0	176	724	40
1,000	0	0	208	792	32

Source: *Background Material and Data on Major Programs within the Jurisdiction of the Committee on Ways and Means,* House Committee on Ways and Means, Committee Print, 97 Cong. 2 sess. (GPO, 1982), p. 133. Table based on post-1981 law.

a. Includes earned-income credit and $40 allowance for transportation expenses.

b. Disposable income equals gross earnings plus food stamps, plus AFDC, minus net taxes (payroll, state, and federal income taxes).

c. Defined as the percentage of the increase in earned income that is offset by benefit reductions.

The earned-income credit provides a refundable tax credit equal to 10 percent of earned income up to $5,000; but, equally important, the amount of the credit is reduced to zero as incomes rise from $6,000 to $10,000—imposing a positive effective marginal tax rate of 12.5 percent in that income range. Eligibility and benefit levels under the various housing assistance programs are also tied to income. For those families with large medical expenses, eligibility for medicaid is also likely to be of major concern. It is very closely tied to the standards for AFDC, so that there is a sharp reduction in family medical coverage at the maximum income for AFDC assistance.

The interaction of these programs is illustrated in table 5-6 for a family composed of a single parent and two children in Pennsylvania—a state with an average AFDC benefit level. At low levels of earned income any increase in earned income is nearly fully offset by the reduction in AFDC benefits and food stamps: recipients face a marginal "tax" rate of about 98 percent.[59] After $300 per month of earned income there are no AFDC payments to reduce, and the marginal tax rate declines to about 60

59. In the first four months, the AFDC provisions are more liberal and imply a marginal tax rate of 77 percent on the first $300 per month of monthly income.

percent; but income above $500 is affected by the need to repay the earned-income tax credit, and the effective marginal tax rate continues to be more than 30 percent. In addition, at an earned income slightly above $300 per month the recipient loses medicaid benefits with an average monthly value of about $100—a factor not included in the table.

In states that have very low AFDC payments, such as Texas, the phaseout of benefits plays a smaller role and the marginal tax rate stays in the range of 50 to 60 percent. At the other extreme, under the 1981 law a single parent in New York with day care expenses for two children faces a marginal tax rate of more than 100 percent: earned income will actually reduce total income for earnings up to $800 per month.[60]

In practice, marginal tax rates may be less than implied by the illustrative examples. One study found that 25 percent of AFDC recipients with income failed to report their earnings, and for those who did, only about 60 percent of the income was accounted for.[61] In addition, at least before the 1981 law, social workers had considerable discretion in computing work-related expenses and other determinants of the payment. Thus it appears that the effective marginal tax under AFDC on reported earned income was only about half the implied rate of 67 percent.[62] The ceiling limitations on deductions imposed in 1981 reduce the degree of discretion.

The effects that the high marginal tax rates implicit in the welfare program have on overall labor supply are, as with taxes, controversial. If leisure is a desirable consumption good, the receipt of nonwage income and the high effective tax rate on wage income will both reduce the supply of labor. There is some agreement, emerging out of the negative income tax experiment, that the income effect of a simple increase in the maximum monthly AFDC benefit in the mid-1970s would

60. *Background Material and Data on Major Programs within the Jurisdiction of the Committee on Ways and Means*, pp. 131–42.

61. Hardan Halsey and others, "The Reporting of Income to Welfare: A Study in the Accuracy of Income Reporting," Research Memorandum 42 (Menlo Park, Calif.: Center for the Study of Welfare Policy, August 1977).

62. See Irene Lurie, "Estimates of Tax Rates in the AFDC Program," *National Tax Journal*, vol. 27 (March 1974), pp. 93–111. She obtained effective marginal tax rates on reported income for seven states that ranged from 0.11 to 0.41 on earned income and from 0.59 to 0.95 on unearned income. One state seemed extreme in reporting an effective tax rate on unearned income of only 0.19. Similar results were obtained by Robert Moffitt, "Cumulative Effective Tax Rates and Guarantees in Low Income Transfer Programs," *Journal of Human Resources*, vol. 14 (Winter 1979), pp. 122–29.

significantly reduce hours of work—by about one hundred hours annually
for each additional $1,000.[63] There is less agreement about the effect of
changes in the implicit tax rate, with estimates ranging from a zero effect
to elasticities of labor supply near -0.5. Because many low-income
families are headed by women, it is important to note that the estimates
of their income and substitution effects seem to lie closer to those of
married men (low) than of married women (high).[64]

Throughout much of the 1970s, a concern with the disincentive effects
of the high marginal tax rates implicit in the welfare program dominated
many of the reform efforts. In particular, the range of income over which
the benefits were paid was extended as a means of reducing marginal tax
rates—a more gradual phaseout. Of course, that also implied a substantial
rise in the number of beneficiaries as families in higher income brackets
received a transfer payment. By 1981 the number of recipients rather
than effective tax rates had become the focal point of criticism. And
since 1981 the ceiling on earned income has been sharply reduced and
the implied marginal tax rates have again increased. The program has
reverted back to the situation of the 1960s.

One of the problems with many of the earlier analyses of the program
was that they focused upon the effects on recipients and neglected to
study the impact of changes in eligibility. More recently, Levy and
Moffitt pointed out that, while the high marginal tax rate implied by a
rapid phaseout of benefits might reduce the work effort of recipients,
increasing the rate of benefit reduction reduces the number of people
who receive benefits and who are exposed to the program's work
disincentives.[65] Thus the design of a welfare program encounters a
choice between high marginal rates for a few (a rapid phaseout of
benefits) and a small disincentive for many (a slow phaseout). Any
evaluation of the incentive effects of alternative welfare systems should
examine the effect on those who are excluded but close to qualifying, as
well as the effect on beneficiaries. The net effect of variations in the rate
of benefit reduction on aggregate labor supply may be small.

---

63. Danziger, Haveman, and Plotnick, "How Income Transfer Programs Affect
Work, Saving, and the Income Distribution," pp. 993–95.

64. Moffitt and Kehrer, "The Effect of Tax and Transfer Programs," p. 137.

65. Frank Levy, "The Labor Supply of Female Household Heads, or AFDC Work
Incentives Don't Work Too Well," *Journal of Human Resources*, vol. 14 (Winter 1979),
pp. 76–97; and Robert Moffitt, "A Problem with the Negative Income Tax" (University
of Wisconsin–Madison, April 1983).

Education and the Quality of Labor

Thus far the analysis of the response of labor supply to taxes and transfers has emphasized the quantity rather than the quality of work effort. Yet in his growth accounting studies Denison estimated that improvement in the educational skills of the work force has been the source of about 50 percent of the growth in the effective labor supply since 1929.[66] Education has upgraded job skills, improved the mobility of the work force in shifting among occupations, and increased workers' awareness of the job opportunities where their productivity is greatest. Denison estimated the effects of education on the quality of labor from information on relative earnings of various educational groups. When these data were adjusted for academic aptitude and the socioeconomic status of the parents, they provided a set of weights that could be applied to the growth in cohorts of the labor force with different levels of educational attainment. The weights indicated that, relative to an eighth-grade education, completion of high school added 20 percent to earnings and a college degree accounted for an additional 40 percent.

An alternative approach has emphasized the human capital aspects of education. From that perspective the skills of labor are similar to physical capital. They reflect the accumulation of past investments in education, they depreciate, and they earn a return. Yet such investments are treated as consumption in the national income accounting framework.

A large number of studies have attempted to measure the private and social return from investments in education. When the return is measured as the gain in private earnings, the after-tax real rate of return on private costs (including forgone earnings) has generally been in the range of 10 to 15 percent—substantially above the return on physical capital.[67] Because students pay only a fraction of the costs of education, however, the social rate of return is estimated to be slightly less.

The measures of the return to education are subject to various

66. Most recently, Edward F. Denison, *Accounting for Slower Economic Growth: The United States in the 1970s* (Brookings Institution, 1979), pp. 42–47.
67. Richard B. Freeman, "Overinvestment in College Training?" *Journal of Human Resources,* vol. 10 (Summer 1975), pp. 287–311; Martin Carnoy and Dieter Marenbach, "The Return to Schooling in the United States, 1939–69," *Journal of Human Resources,* vol. 10 (Summer 1975), pp. 312–31; and the references cited in the second article.

interpretations. On the one hand, it is extremely difficult to separate the influence of education from that of "innate ability," which is likely to be correlated with years of schooling. In addition, the studies are unable to adjust for investments in informal education that may continue after formal training has been completed. On the other hand, there is a large consumption component to some education expenditures that leads to an overstatement of the amount of investment, and the measures of earnings do not include the value of fringe and nonpecuniary benefits of high-earning jobs. Furthermore, there is good reason to believe that the full benefits of innovation are not captured by private firms, yet education is an important input into that process. Thus the gains to society may exceed the private benefits.[68] The measured return has also been found to be very sensitive to unemployment and other aspects of the business cycle.

Some doubts about the benefits of higher education have been expressed recently because of evidence that the return to such investments fell during the 1970s. In particular, Freeman has estimated that the private return to a B.A. degree fell from 11 to 8 percent between 1969 and 1980.[69] This may not represent a permanent phenomenon, however, because the sharp growth in the number of college graduates in the late 1960s reflected growth in the college-age population rather than a large increase in the proportion of that group attending college. It has also been suggested that the shift in the relative earnings structure could reflect the movement of a large age cohort, the postwar baby boom, into the labor force.[70]

In any case, there has been a sharp rise in the overall proportion of the U.S. work force with at least a college degree. For this reason, it is not surprising that the rate of return should decline. In addition, since to

68. This issue of the effect of education on productivity growth, apart from its effect on labor quality, is discussed in a recent paper by Mansfield. It involves the interaction between education, research and development, and technical change. He argues that these effects are likely to be substantial. See Edwin Mansfield, "Education, R and D, and Productivity Growth" (University of Pennsylvania, January 1982).

69. Richard Freeman, "Overinvestment in College Training?"

70. Finis Welch, "Effects of Cohort Size on Earnings: The Baby Boom Babies' Financial Bust," *Journal of Political Economy*, vol. 87 (October 1979), pp. S65–S97. The deterioration of relative earnings does not appear to have continued in the late 1970s when the growth in college graduates slowed. Yet the decline also seems evident in other countries. See Richard Freeman, "The Changing Value of Higher Education in Developed Economies: A Report to the OECD," National Bureau of Economic Research Working Paper 820 (Cambridge, Mass.: NBER, December 1981).

Table 5-7. *Expenditures on Education and Job Training, Selected Years, 1955–80*[a]

	Total expenditures (billions of 1980 dollars)			Per student expenditures (1980 dollars)	
Year	Elementary and secondary education	Higher education	Government job training	Elementary and secondary education	Higher education
1955	42.4	8.9	1.2	1,207	3,756
1960	53.4	14.0	1.5	1,272	4,363
1965	76.0	22.3	2.7	1,552	4,050
1970	102.1	33.1	4.3	1,984	4,636
1975	111.1	40.8	4.6	2,193	4,522
1980	110.7	43.0	6.7	2,360	4,271

Sources: U.S. Department of Commerce, *National Income and Product Accounts;* and author's calculations.
a. Expenditures on education include private institutions. The number of students in higher education refers to degree credit students only. The data are converted to 1980 dollars using price deflators for private educational institutions. Research expenditures are excluded.

some extent expenditures on education are a form of consumption, the economic benefits of the pure investment in education appear to be equal to or greater than those on physical capital in general.

Expenditures on education in the United States are shown in table 5-7. Total investment in formal education amounted to $154 billion in 1980, or about half the expenditures on business capital. It also is evident that the United States has greatly increased the resources devoted to educating each student. In constant 1980 dollars, per student expenditures for elementary and secondary education rose by over 50 percent during the 1960s and by an additional 20 percent during the 1970s.[71] Either there has been a large improvement in the quality of such education—something not evident in the achievement test data—or these institutions have suffered a major decline in productivity. A smaller rise in per student expenditures occurred in higher education between 1955 and 1970; and over the last decade those expenditures have actually declined substantially.

There have also been significant changes in the pattern of financing for higher education, as shown in table 5-8. State and local governments fund more than half of total expenditures—in fact, their share rose from 47 to 56 percent between 1955 and 1980. The federal government, which

71. The adjustment for inflation is based on an education-specific price deflator from the national income accounts. Thus the table provides a measure of the increase in real inputs to education. Yet output has declined by many measures.

Table 5-8. *Payments for Higher Education, by Source, Selected Years, 1955–80*
Percent

Source	1955	1970	1980
Federal government[a]	0	6	12
State and local government	47	56	57
Private	53	38	31
Total	100	100	100

Source: Same as table 5-7.
a. Federal transfers and grants are deducted from private and state contributions.

had no significant role in 1955, supplied about 12 percent of total financing in 1980, primarily through direct grants to the institutions and transfer payments to individuals. Because subsidized interest payments for student loans are reported on a current outlay basis, these data understate the full extent of the federal financing contribution. The private share of the costs fell from 53 to 31 percent.[72]

Several studies have also examined the treatment of education within the income tax system, particularly as compared with investments in physical capital. An early view was that the tax system discourages investment in education because there is no allowance for depreciation similar to that for physical capital. But that analysis ignored the fact that the major cost to the individual is the earnings forgone during the period of education, which are not taxed and therefore need not be depreciated.

If forgone earnings are the only costs, a proportionate income tax encourages investment in education. The tax reduces the cost and the future return proportionately, thus having no effect on the marginal rate of return; but because it reduces the return on income from other types of capital, it encourages investment in education. With a progressive tax system the results are more ambiguous. A higher future tax rate on the income from education may more than offset the current-period advantage that the treatment of forgone earnings confers relative to investment in nonhuman capital. In addition, if there are significant out-of-pocket costs, the income tax becomes a disincentive because such expenses are not tax deductible.[73]

72. These trends may reverse in the 1980s as reduced federal payments may force a sharp rise in tuition costs.
73. These issues are discussed and the relevant literature cited in L. G. Sgontz, "Does the Income Tax Favor Human Capital?" *National Tax Journal*, vol. 35 (March 1982), pp. 99–104.

There has been almost no empirical work on the effect of taxes on investment in education. The proportion of individuals in the age cohort of eighteen to twenty-four attending college did not change during the 1970s. During that period programs such as student loans were sharply expanded. That would suggest that such decisions are less sensitive to cost than is commonly assumed. On the other hand, tuition costs also rose substantially. It may be that the net costs to the individual did not significantly change over the period.[74]

A consideration of the role of education in economic growth does suggest the arbitrary nature of the assumption of distinctions between consumption and investment and between labor and capital. The definition of saving that is often used in discussions of capital formation or in proposals for a shift to a consumption-based tax treats education as consumption and ignores the investment element.

Summary

Some readers, noting the high levels of unemployment that have plagued the U.S. economy for years, may regard as absurd an emphasis on economic policy measures to increase labor supply. The economy seems unable to find jobs for those who have already indicated a desire to work. And certainly for years to come it will be difficult to get the unemployed back to work.

It is important, however, to distinguish between the supply of labor and its utilization as reflected in the unemployment rate. In recent years the labor force has been underutilized, as economic policy has emphasized the restraint of demand and employment as a means of reducing inflation. Increased unemployment is one cost of such an effort. Indeed, unemployment must rise if increased competition for jobs is to moderate the wage demands of the employed. But it is the balance between the supply and demand for labor, and not the overall size of the labor force, that is relevant to the concern about inflation. That concern, justified or not, should not inhibit efforts to increase the demand for labor at a rate in keeping with the growth in supply.

74. For evidence of the importance of cost in decisions to attend college, see John Bishop, "The Effects of Public Policies on the Demand for Higher Education," *Journal of Human Resources*, vol. 12 (Summer 1977), pp. 285–307; and the citations in that study.

Even in the present context, incentive effects of the tax and transfer system on labor supply are relevant to several issues. Some studies have argued that the unemployment insurance system creates strong incentives for the unemployed to extend the duration of their unemployment, thereby weakening the link between increased unemployment and reduced inflation. The unemployment system does contribute to a rise in the unemployment rate associated with any given degree of inflation pressure. The overall effect appears to be an increase in the aggregate unemployment rate of about 0.6 percentage point. The overall effect is limited because only about one-half of the unemployed receive benefits . under the program. More important, there has been no significant change in the structure of the program in recent decades that would justify claims that it has contributed to a secular rise in unemployment. The maximum duration of benefits has been increased in recessions but shortened during the subsequent expansions. The ratio of benefits to wages has remained largely unchanged. A smaller disincentive effect might be expected because of recent actions to include UI benefits in the taxable income of workers in the middle and upper ranges of the income distribution. Most of the studies have focused upon the incentives that the program creates for employees to extend their spells of unemployment. Less is known about the extent to which the failure to tax firms for the full amount of the unemployment they create—imperfect experience rating—encourages excessive layoffs.

The response of labor supply to higher taxes is also relevant to current discussions of tax incentives for capital formation. If taxes on capital income are reduced to increase saving incentives, they must be offset by increased taxation of labor income, and that will change the incentives for both the quantity and quality of labor supplied. If taxes have important incentive effects on both capital formation and labor supply, the optimal design of an overall tax system becomes very complex. This is even more true when these incentive issues have to be integrated with public concerns about fairness and the distribution of tax burdens.

In some respects this review of the research has been encouraging because it suggests that the incentive effects are not as large as some of the recent public discussions would have one believe. In general, changes in tax rates, and thus after-tax wage rates, appear to have only a small net effect on the labor supply of adult men, but a more substantial effect for married women.

In some policy applications it is important to distinguish between the offsetting substitution and income effects that contribute to that net outcome. The substitution effect takes on particular significance in discussions of changes in the degree of progressivity of the tax system—comparing two situations of equal after-tax income but different marginal tax rates. Most of the studies find that both income and substitution effects are small for men, although recently that conclusion has been questioned. There is agreement on a substantial sensitivity to income and the marginal after-tax wage rate in the work decisions of women. Thus the response of family labor supply to tax changes is more difficult to predict because changes in the tax on the earnings of the primary worker can exert strong income effects on the work decision of the second earner.

The concern with the effect of taxes on labor supply is motivated in part by a belief that marginal tax rates increased substantially over the last decade. This conclusion is largely the result of changes in the number of earners per family rather than changes in tax legislation. The growing tendency toward two-income families raises the number of earners who are subject to high marginal tax rates, particularly those in families above the median income level. If the focus is on the marginal rate of a worker in a family of fixed characteristics, however, the rise is much less dramatic. It is evident that there is much more variation in marginal tax rates among workers than was formerly the case, with situations of high marginal rates occurring at both the top and the bottom of the income distribution.

The clearest evidence of a general rise in marginal and average tax rates is supplied by the increased importance of employment taxes—particularly those for the social insurance programs. It is not obvious what effect, if any, those taxes have on work effort. For the most part they represent contractual arrangements to change the timing of the receipts from labor. If social insurance taxes were abolished, workers would still seek arrangements with their employers to set aside income for retirement, medical insurance, and insurance against the risks of unemployment and disability. While there might be major changes in the distribution of such "taxes" among income classes, it is certainly incorrect to evaluate them as a tax without consideration of the associated benefits. In fact, the programs usually embody entitlement effects that induce some individuals to enter the labor force.

There does seem to be a consensus emerging from the most recent studies that the social security system encourages earlier retirement and that the magnitude of the effect is economically significant. Much less is known about the effect on younger workers. And those effects cannot be separated completely from changing attitudes toward retirement as incomes rise.

The analysis of the effects of transfer programs on labor supply differs from that of the effects of tax changes because the income and substitution effects of income transfers will normally operate together to reduce work effort. As long as leisure is a normal and desired good, receipt of a transfer, with a lump-sum guarantee plus a phaseout linked to other earnings, must unambiguously reduce labor supply. However, the magnitude of the effect is limited by the design of the program. As Lampman pointed out,

The present-day American system of transfers directs the greater part of its cash and in-kind benefits to the minority of the population who are aged (age 62 and over), disabled, or in broken families. . . . This characteristic of the transfer system means that the greatest disincentive effects are aimed at categories of people who are least expected to work. Conversely, those who are expected to work are relatively shielded from disincentives of nonlabor income and benefit reduction rates.[75]

The disability insurance program has clearly contributed to the decline in the labor force participation rates of adult males, but it would appear that this is largely a response to a liberalization of the health criteria rather than the response of workers to the change in benefits. The public assistance programs all embody very high marginal tax rates because benefits are reduced at a rapid rate as the recipients earn income from other sources. On the other hand, the rapid reduction of benefits limits the size of the population that is affected by the program, eliminating the disincentive effects for those who no longer qualify. Most of the studies of these programs appear to be too preliminary to offer estimates of the labor supply response. The negative income tax experiments, however, did indicate that there is a significant response of hours worked to change in both the basic income guarantee and the marginal tax rate and a larger response for women than for men.

Some surveys have attempted to provide an aggregate estimate of the

75. Robert J. Lampman, "Labor Supply and Social Welfare Benefits in the United States," in National Commission on Employment and Unemployment Statistics, *Concepts and Data Needs: Appendix Volume 1* (Washington, D.C.: NCEUS, 1980), p. 139.

effect of the transfer programs on labor supply.[76] They conclude that the existence of these programs reduces the aggregate labor supply by about 5 to 10 percent. The loss in aggregate output and income is substantially less because the poor and the elderly earn less than the average wage when they do work.

Finally, the role of education in improving the quality of the work force is often overlooked in the discussion of programs to expand national output. Most studies find that investments in education yield a return equal to or greater than the return on physical capital. The return on education does appear to have fallen during the 1970s, however. That decline is surprisingly parallel to the previously noted decline in the return on physical capital.

Expenditures on education increased substantially during the last twenty years. The expansion was particularly large for primary and secondary education. Recently there has been a decline in expenditures for higher education on a per student basis, following a large increase in the 1950s and 1960s.

The tax system has an ambivalent effect on investments in education. On the one hand, private educational expenses cannot be depreciated and offset against future tax income. On the other hand, many of the costs are paid directly through government expenditures, and because the students do not pay tax on their forgone earnings (a major education cost), there is no need to provide a depreciation deduction against future taxable income.

76. Lampman, "Labor Supply and Social Welfare Benefits"; and Danziger, Haveman, and Plotnick, "How Income Transfer Programs Affect Work, Saving, and the Income Distribution."

CHAPTER SIX

Implications for Economic Policy

THE sharp deterioration in economic growth since the early 1970s has been a major motivation behind the renewal of interest in economic policies to expand aggregate supply. In the public discussion of the reasons for that disappointing economic performance, mistaken government policies have been singled out as the major villain. Particular importance has been attached to the pivotal role played by taxes, which are alleged to have destroyed incentives for saving, investment, and work.

The previous chapters have provided a survey and evaluation of the empirical research on many of the issues that arise in that discussion. Such a survey highlights the many areas of uncertainty about the understanding of the growth process and the effect of government policies on it. Some conclusions do emerge, however, that should have an important influence on the current public discussion.

Capital Formation and Productivity Growth

Despite major research efforts, the causes of the post-1973 slowdown in productivity growth—a drop of 1½ to 2 percentage points in the growth rate—remain, in large part, a mystery. The studies summarized in chapter 2 have evaluated the quantitative effect of a large number of potential explanations. Among those factors are: the growth in the proportion of young and less experienced workers in the labor force, increased government regulation, the rise in energy prices, a reduction in research and development, and two major economic recessions. Yet the conclusion of the quantitative studies is that each of these factors contributes very little to the total slowdown. Other common explanations, such as a shift to a service-based economy, have been dismissed by these studies.

177

The fundamental problem with attributing the productivity slowdown to reduced capital formation is that the slowdown is not limited to output per worker alone. Instead, there has been a slowing of growth in the efficiency of *both* capital and labor. The slowdown in capital formation is not enough to account for more than a small fraction of the shortfall in output per worker. This fact is evident in a new data series on multifactor productivity (output per unit of capital and labor) published by the Bureau of Labor Statistics and shown in table 6-1.[1] The slowdown in multifactor productivity growth (1.9 percent annually for private business) is only slightly less than that for output per worker hour (2.2 percent).

Furthermore, the notion that business capital has become an increasingly scarce resource is puzzling in light of the sharp decline in the before-tax return to capital that occurred over the last decade. Even after adjusting for the influence of recessions, the real return on business capital (profits plus interest on borrowed capital) has fallen by about 25 percent (from 11 percent to 8 percent of tangible assets) since the mid-1960s. That decline is even more surprising in light of the usual argument that the effective tax rate on capital income increased during the period. A rise in the tax rate should lead firms to limit their investments to projects with a higher before-tax return.[2]

The limited role of physical capital in accounting for the slowdown of productivity growth and the decline in its own rate of return both caution against undue emphasis on capital formation in the explanation of past problems. It would be a mistake, however, to go to the opposite extreme and conclude that incentives to expand capital formation should not be an important element in government policies to improve productivity growth in the future. Many of the factors affecting productivity growth are outside the control of government, but government can influence the pace of investment. If the share of net nonfarm business output going to investment could be increased by 1 percentage point from an average of 4 to 5 percent in the 1970s (a 25 percent rise), the *level* of output per worker in that sector would rise by about 5 percent in the long run. The

---

1. The results of the BLS analysis for the total private economy are similar to those for the nonresidential, nonfarm sector discussed in chapter 2.

2. In the long run investors should be comparing the after-tax return on business capital with that available on alternative uses of their funds. Thus an increased tax on domestic business capital should ultimately be reflected in a rise in the before-tax rate of return.

Table 6-1. *Average Annual Rates of Growth in Output, Labor and Capital Inputs, and Productivity, by Major Sector, 1948–73 and 1973–81*

Percent

Measure	Private business[a]			Nonfarm business			Manufacturing		
	1948–73	1973–81	Slowdown	1948–73	1973–81	Slowdown	1948–73	1973–81	Slowdown
Output per hour of all persons	3.0	0.8	−2.2	2.5	0.6	−1.9	2.9	1.5	−1.4
Contribution of capital per hour[b]	1.0	0.7	−0.3	0.8	0.6	−0.2	0.7	1.1	0.4
Multifactor productivity[c]	2.0	0.1	−1.9	1.7	0.0	−1.7	2.2	0.4	−1.8
Addenda: supporting indexes									
Output	3.7	2.2	−1.5	3.9	2.1	−1.8	4.0	1.2	−2.8
Hours of all persons	0.7	1.4	0.7	1.3	1.5	0.2	1.1	−0.2	−1.3
Capital services	3.6	3.2	−0.4	3.6	3.3	−0.3	3.5	4.0	0.5
Combined capital and labor inputs	1.7	2.0	0.3	2.1	2.1	0.0	1.8	0.9	−0.9

Source: U.S. Department of Labor, Bureau of Labor Statistics.

a. Excludes government enterprises.

b. Change in capital per unit of labor weighted by capital's share of total output.

c. Output per unit of combined labor and capital input; equals output per hour minus contribution of capital per hour.

transition to that higher output path stretches over many years, however, and the effect on the growth rate in any year would be a few tenths of a percentage point.

It is worthwhile to attempt to increase the capital stock because society earns a healthy future return on that capital; but increased accumulation of physical capital alone will not contribute a great deal to the growth rate of productivity. In addition, the expansion of the physical capital stock should not come at the expense of other uses of resources where the returns are equally high (education and research and development, for example).

Saving or Investment Incentives?

While it might be possible to reach a consensus on the desirability of expanded capital formation in the future, there are significant disputes about how that objective might be achieved. The major issues can be illustrated by asking whether government policies should focus on expanding incentives for private saving or expanding those for investment. In other words, is the problem of a low rate of domestic capital formation the result of inadequate saving or weak demand for domestic investment?

Saving

Much of the discussion of the need for more saving incentives implies that private saving has fallen in the United States. Yet, as shown in chapter 3, the gross private saving rate has remained very stable throughout the postwar period at about 16 to 17 percent of GNP, and there is no evidence of a decline during the 1970s and early 1980s. What has changed is the composition of private saving: corporate saving (retained earnings and capital-consumption allowances) has increased, while saving attributed to the household sector—which includes nonprofit institutions and unincorporated business—has declined. Some of the factors responsible for this shift were examined in chapter 3.[3] In any

3. The flow-of-funds accounts, which provide an alternative measure of saving based on changes in asset holdings, suggest that household saving is larger (and has declined less) and corporate saving is less than that reported in the national income accounts. Given the difficulties of tracing the ownership of those financial assets, however, the

case, it is not clear that the composition of private saving has any particular significance for the issue of capital formation.

Some economists prefer to deduct from gross saving the cost of maintaining the existing stock of capital—flow of depreciation on capital-consumption allowances—to arrive at net saving; and they observe that the net saving rate has declined from an average of 8.6 percent of net national product in 1961–70 to 6.5 percent in 1981–82. But the rise in depreciation, which led to the decline, reflects a shift in the pattern of investment rather than in that of saving behavior. The composition of business investment has moved toward shorter-lived capital—equipment relative to structures—with a consequent rise in the rate of depreciation. That means that capital is being used up more rapidly and that the gross saving rate must rise to maintain the same growth of the net capital stock. But it is important to know the reasons for the shift in the composition of investment. If it reflects a change in the pattern of technology—an increased need for equipment, such as computers, relative to structures—a rise in saving is the appropriate response. If the shift is due to a distortion in the taxation of equipment relative to structures, the tax law, not saving, should be changed.

In addition, it is difficult to accept the view that a decline in private saving has become a major constraining influence on domestic investment, or that an increase in private saving would be fully reflected in an increased rate of domestic capital formation. The adequacy of saving to support a specific level of investment is relevant only to a fully employed economy, or an economy where total output is constrained by monetary policy—situations in which resources for increased investment must be provided by forgoing private or public consumption. In the presence of unemployment, an increase in investment can be financed by the utilization of idle resources. The increase in investment raises production and incomes, providing higher levels of both saving and consumption.

Even commencing from a situation of full employment, it is possible that an increase in planned saving may not lead to an increase in investment, at least in the short run. The increased supply of saving will lower interest rates and serve as a positive inducement to investment. On the other hand, the decline in consumer spending will reduce current demand and business perceptions of the need for additional capital. Lags

---

national income accounts would seem to provide a better measure of the allocation of saving. In any case, the two accounting systems do not imply a significantly different level of total private saving.

in the adjustment of wages, prices, and interest rates will lead to a transitional period of depressed output unless they are offset by other policies. If that transition is to be avoided, it is necessary to coordinate changes in saving incentives with concurrent direct actions to raise investment.

While both of these concerns about an exclusive emphasis on saving incentives raise only short-run issues of transition, the longer-term view that Americans save too little and that the low saving rate constrains domestic investment ignores the important role of world capital markets. In a situation of international capital markets, domestic saving and domestic investment are not necessarily equal: an increment to domestic saving could easily flow abroad if the return on foreign investment is above that of domestic investment, and domestic investment can draw on a pool of worldwide saving. Therefore, the adequacy of domestic saving is not necessarily relevant to answering the question of why investment in the United States is so low relative to other countries. The sharp rise in world saving rates provided by the surplus of the OPEC countries after 1973 illustrates the mechanism: the funds flowed primarily through U.S. financial institutions to finance investment in the developing countries.

There are, of course, political and institutional limits on a country's ability to finance domestic investment from foreign capital inflows on a sustained basis. In view of these constraints, while higher domestic saving may not be sufficient to ensure increased domestic investment, it is nevertheless an appropriate long-term element of a program that does do so. An effort to expand the supply of resources for capital formation should focus on increasing national saving—government plus private saving. A rise in private saving, if offset by increased government dissaving (budget deficits), does not add to the resources available for private capital formation. A tax reduction, if not matched by an equal reduction of government expenditures, requires the private sector to save the entire tax cut simply to leave the national saving rate unchanged. That is, unless the sensitivity of private saving to changes in tax rates is very high, tax cuts alone cannot raise national saving and are more likely to reduce it.

There are two ways to raise the private component of national saving through budgetary actions without losing the benefits to a large deficit: (1) cut expenditures and reduce marginal tax rates on capital income without changing the budget surplus or deficit, or (2) restructure taxes to reduce marginal tax rates on capital income without lowering total government revenues.[4] As pointed out in chapter 3, economists are very uncertain about the likely effect of such measures on private saving behavior. The net effect on saving is ambiguous from a theoretical perspective, and the empirical evidence is not convincing on either side of the issue.

Given the uncertainties surrounding private saving behavior, direct actions to shift the government budget toward a surplus are a more certain means of increasing national saving. While some economists argue that variations in the government deficit lead to compensatory adjustments in private saving and investment, the empirical studies reviewed in chapter 3 indicate that the offset is likely to be small. The general conclusion is that national saving would rise, although probably not on a one-for-one basis.[5] Thus government should look first to control of its budget balance as the primary means of ensuring an adequate rate of national saving to finance investment.

Investment

The evidence that government policies can have a direct effect on business investment is significantly stronger than that for saving incentives. One reason is that the direction of the effect on investment incentives of a change in taxes or interest rates is not ambiguous from a theoretical point of view: the income and substitution effects reinforce one another. Tax policy affects the investment decision by changing the cost of using capital in production relative to the cost of using labor. That cost of capital is composed of three basic components: the price of capital, effective tax rates, and the interest rate (adjusted for inflation). The major issue under dispute is the size of the response of investment to changes in the cost of capital, which depends upon the potential for substitution between capital and labor in production.

While there continues to be significant disagreement among the

---

4. The major proposals to achieve such a restructuring usually involve an offsetting increase in the tax on labor income.

5. It might appear that reductions in government expenditures are less likely than increases in taxes to initiate offsetting changes in private saving. In the short run that is true because private consumption expenditures adjust to changes in after-tax income with a lag: the largest initial response to a tax increase is a fall in private saving. But in the long run it depends upon the type of expenditure reductions, because the public may seek to replace the loss of public services with increased private outlays.

empirical studies about the precise magnitude of the overall investment response to changes in the cost of capital, the potential for substitution seems to be greater for investment in equipment than it is for business structures. One convenient rule of thumb that emerges from the major econometric models is that the investment induced by a tax incentive limited to new equipment (such as the investment tax credit) is roughly equal to the loss of tax revenue (a bang for the buck of about unity).

A second major finding of the empirical studies is that changes in the cost of capital have a stronger effect on the demand for residential structures and consumer durables than on business investment. A decline in interest rates, for example, increases total investment but shifts it in the direction of housing and consumer durables.

If one accepts the hypothesis that government policy can affect investment demand significantly through changes in the after-tax cost of capital, the evaluation of past government support for investment depends upon trends in both the taxation of capital income and the cost of funds. To date, the public discussion has concentrated on changes in tax rates. Yet the economic analysis tends to show that the effective tax on new investments declined in the 1970s: if there was an increase in the real cost of investment during the decade, it was the result of increased financing costs rather than higher taxes.

Much of the disagreement about prior trends in the tax rate on investment reflects a confusion between marginal and average tax rates. The average personal income tax rate on capital income in general is quite low because about two-thirds of such income is exempt from taxation (housing, and state and local government bonds) or the taxes are deferred (capital gains and retirement accounts). The income from corporate capital, however, is taxed at a high average rate, about 60 percent, and that tax rate increased during the 1970s.[6] This occurred because the depreciation allowance for existing capital was not adjusted to take account of inflation, and because the income paid by corporations to individuals—interest and dividends—is heavily taxed under the personal tax system.

Quite a different pattern emerges, however, for the tax rate applicable to income from new investments. Depreciation allowances for new investments have been liberalized by several legislative actions, and the

6. This includes corporate, personal, and property taxes.

size of the investment tax credit has been raised.[7] In addition, the provision that allows firms to deduct nominal interest costs in computing taxable income became increasingly important during the period of high inflation. Thus the effective corporate tax rates on new investment fell from 55 percent in 1969 to 33 percent in 1980, and the 1981 and 1982 tax acts will reduce that rate to about 15 percent in the 1983–86 period. Similarly, as discussed in chapter 4, the studies that examined the overall tax rate (corporate, individual, and property taxes) on new investments reported a decline from 47 percent in 1970 to 32 percent in 1983.

The most important conclusion drawn from those studies is not so much that the overall tax on new capital has declined but that effective tax rates are highly variable by type of capital asset, method of financing, and owner. That disparity of tax rates implies a potentially large distortion and inefficiency in the allocation of investment.

The evidence about past trends in the cost of financing investment is more mixed. It does seem clear that the real cost (adjusted for inflation) of debt finance declined during the 1970s. But it is not clear whether the fall in the price-earning ratio (rise in the cost of equity finance) for corporate stock reflected a decline in expected future income from existing capital because of obsolescence, or an increase in the risk premium for new investments. If the performance of the stock market in the 1970s reflected an increased obsolescence of existing capital, it did not imply an increased cost of financing new capital.

Labor Supply

Although much emphasis has been placed on the need to reduce the taxation of capital income to encourage saving, little attention has been paid to the effects of increased taxation of labor income. The response of workers to government tax and transfer programs should be a significant consideration in the design of policies to expand aggregate supply. A capital income tax distorts the consumption-saving decision; a wage tax distorts the work-leisure decision. Proposals to reduce the

7. The changes in depreciation and the investment tax credit were applicable only to new investment and actually encouraged firms to throw away old capital at an earlier date.

taxation of capital income as a means of stimulating investment must be financed by a heavier tax on wage income, and it is possible that the gains of a larger capital stock are offset by a contraction of the available labor supply. From the efficiency perspective of economics, the choice between a capital income tax and a wage tax depends upon the relative responsiveness of the two factors to after-tax rates of return: efficiency is improved by concentrating the tax on the factor whose supply is least affected.

The review in previous chapters of historical trends in tax rates indicates that it is the marginal tax on labor income rather than that on capital income that increased during the 1970s, primarily as a result of the increased frequency of multiple-earner families rather than as a result of a change in the underlying structure of the income tax system. Average tax rates also rose, but by a relatively small amount. This tendency toward higher tax rates on labor income is particularly dramatic if workers view contributions to the social insurance funds as a tax rather than saving—a view that may be held more by young workers but is likely to change as they age and become more concerned about retirement income.

The studies reviewed in chapter 5 indicate that the net effect on labor supply of a proportionate change in tax rates is relatively small. That net effect is, however, the result of offsetting income and substitution effects, and the magnitude of the pure substitution effect is substantially larger. Thus changes in the structure of the tax system that alter the marginal tax rate (relevant to the substitution effect) without altering the average tax rate (relevant to the income effect) will have a more substantial influence on labor supply decisions. That is, labor supply changes are an issue of greater concern for proposals to reform the structure of the tax system than for changes in the overall rate of taxation.

The empirical evidence also supports the notion that social security and other transfers have significant effects on labor supply. Social security does induce workers to retire earlier. That should not be surprising, since it was perceived as a desirable objective of the program at the time of its inception.

Most of the welfare programs provide a basic income guarantee that is reduced in step with earned income. The guarantee (income effect) and the very high rates of benefit reduction per dollar of earned income (substitution effect) both constitute strong work disincentives. But the economic significance is limited because of restrictions that limit benefits to those who are least expected to work and who would have the lowest wage rates and productivity if they were employed. Similarly, the unemployment insurance program contributes to a higher level of reported unemployment because it reduces the intensity of job search. Since the program has not been extended in coverage or benefit levels in recent decades, however, it cannot account for the secular rise in unemployment levels. In fact, it has been scaled back significantly in recent years.

Relevance for Policy

The economic policies introduced by the Reagan administration in 1981 emphasized the expansion of aggregate supply through increased incentives to work, save, and invest. Most of the effort was directed toward a reduction in overall tax rates as a means of achieving the lower marginal tax rates that are stressed in the analysis of economic incentives. That supply-side economic program has encountered severe difficulties, however. The administration and the Congress did not reduce expenditures in step with the cut in taxes, so that there was a large increase in the current and anticipated budget deficits. That fiscal stimulus, and the large capital market borrowing it entailed, collided with a monetary policy intent on restricting the supply of credit and economic activity to reduce inflation. The result was a sharp rise in interest rates that overwhelmed the investment incentives of the tax cut. High interest rates and recession combined to reduce rather than increase capital formation.[8] In addition, the rise in interest rates is widely blamed for raising the U.S. exchange rate, thereby weakening the competitive position of those industries involved in international markets.

Supply-side incentives were temporarily forgotten under the pressures of economic recession. But the decline of inflation and the economic recovery will revive the issues of how to increase economic growth. The focus of that policy discussion has shifted from the incentive effects of the tax reductions to a concern for the crowding out of private investment

8. The recession cannot be blamed on the fiscal program proposed by the administration. It was planned by the monetary authorities as a necessary means of reducing inflation. Some of the pressure on interest rates could have been avoided if the tax reduction had led to an increase in private saving, but, as shown in prior chapters, the empirical evidence provides limited support for such an expectation.

by the large deficits that emanate from the 1981 program. The original issue is important, however, and should not be ignored.

The contention of this study is that for purposes of promoting long-term growth the appropriate mix of stabilization policy is exactly the opposite of that which emerged from the decisions of 1981. Given the evidence that private saving is rather immune to manipulation by government, government should expand the incentives for domestic investment and provide the required financing directly by reducing its own budget deficits. This can be achieved by pursuit of a budget policy that aims for a surplus (or at worst a balance) of revenues over expenditures. Meanwhile, monetary policy should be directed to maintain investment demand sufficient to reach the desired level of aggregate output.

In addition, the discussion of the incentive effects of tax policy should be redirected away from general tax reductions toward proposals to reform the structure of the tax system. This perspective takes as given the government's need, in the absence of cyclical fluctuations, to raise enough revenue to finance its expenditures. A given amount of revenue can be raised by a variety of tax systems, however, and it would be desirable to choose one that has the least distorting effects on private decisions.

Three major categories of issues need to be distinguished in discussions of budget policy: (1) the appropriate size of government, (2) the balance between expenditures and taxes (fiscal policy), and (3) the structural characteristics of the tax system (tax policy). The first category is primarily a political issue with strong ideological associations. Fiscal policy is primarily an economic topic, and tax policy involves both economic and equity concerns. In part the current economic problem of large budget deficits arises because fiscal policy has become caught up in the battle over the size of government. Advocates of a smaller government sector argue that tax reductions are the most effective means of achieving their ultimate goal of reduced expenditures. Tax reductions attract widespread public support and the resulting deficits can be used to exert pressure for reduced expenditures. That argument may be true, but in the meantime fiscal policy is lost as a useful tool of overall economic stabilization policy. Similarly, much of the discussion of tax policy confuses the economic incentive effects of structural tax reform with the overall stimulative effect of a general tax reduction—fiscal policy.

To date, the discussion of tax reform proposals has emphasized the potential effect on saving behavior of eliminating or sharply reducing the taxation of capital income. But when the system is evaluated from the perspective of investment a second issue emerges: the distortions in the efficient use of capital occasioned by the wide variation in the tax on income from different assets. Furthermore, the evaluation of those reform proposals needs to take greater account of the labor supply implications of shifts in the distribution of taxation between capital and labor income. These issues are examined below.

Supply-Side Economics and Fiscal-Monetary Policy

It is not reasonable to judge a program directed toward increasing the long-run growth rate of the economy on the basis of short-run economic conditions. That is particularly true of the Reagan fiscal program in 1981–83. Perhaps no program could succeed in bringing down inflation without imposing the substantial short-run costs of unemployment and reduced capital formation. The recession of 1980–82 was a product of monetary, not fiscal restraint, and economic events for several years in the future will be dominated by the normal economic forces of a cyclical recovery.[9] But the budgetary actions of the 1981–82 period will shift the direction of fiscal policy for many years to come. Tax reductions motivated in part by a desire to increase private saving and investment have, in combination with higher government spending, increased government dissaving. The final result may be perverse in that national saving and domestic capital formation will be reduced rather than increased by the actions that have been taken.

MEASURES OF THE FISCAL DEFICIT. These shifting budget trends are illustrated by an analysis of the budget outlook published by the Congressional Budget Office (CBO) in 1983. Budget outlays and receipts expected under current law were projected out to the year 1988; a summary is provided in table 6-2. First, the administration's effort to redirect expenditures is evident in the rise of defense spending from 5.6 percent

9. There are two separate aspects of the debate over the economic policy of recent years. The first is an overall policy question of whether the use of a recession to reduce inflation was worth the costs in unemployment and lost output. The second involves the particular mix of fiscal and monetary policy used to achieve that target. By shifting toward expansion at a time of monetary restraint, the budget changes intensified the upward pressure on interest rates and the foreign exchange rate. Thus more of the restraint fell on interest-sensitive capital goods industries and the tradeable-goods sectors of the economy than under an alternative deflation program that would have combined a more restrictive fiscal policy with a less restrictive monetary policy.

Table 6-2. *Change in Budget Outlays and Receipts as a Percentage of Gross National Product, Selected Years, 1960–88*

Budget component	Actual			Projected change from 1981 share		
	1960	1970	1981	1984	1986	1988
Expenditures						
National defense	9.1	8.1	5.6	1.3	1.9	1.9
Social security and medicare	2.2	3.7	6.2	0.5	0.5	0.4
Net interest	1.4	1.5	2.4	0.3	0.4	0.4
Other nondefense	5.8	6.9	8.7	−0.7	−1.6	−1.7
Total	18.5	20.2	22.9	1.4	1.2	1.0
Receipts (by type of tax)						
Personal income	8.2	9.3	10.0	−1.6	−1.7	−1.7
Corporate income	4.3	3.4	2.1	−0.5	−0.3	−0.3
Social insurance	2.9	4.6	6.4	0.2	0.4	0.4
Other	3.1	2.6	2.4	−0.3	−0.8	−1.1
Total	18.6	19.9	20.9	−2.2	−2.4	−2.6
Surplus or deficit	0.1	−0.3	−2.0	−3.6	−3.6	−3.6

Source: U.S. Congressional Budget Office, *Baseline Budget Projections for Fiscal Years 1984–1988* (CBO, February 1983), tables 10, 15.

of GNP in 1981 to 7.5 percent by 1988, financed by a cutback of roughly equivalent magnitude in the share of GNP going to discretionary non-defense programs and entitlements other than social security and medical care. Total outlays, however, will increase because of continual growth in the cost of the retirement programs and higher interest payments. Thus total spending will rise by 1 percent of GNP. On the other side, revenues will decline by 2.6 percent of GNP. As a result, the underlying budget deficit in 1984–88 will exceed that in 1981 by 3.6 percent of GNP—from 2 percent to 5.6 percent.

The budget deficit projections for 1984–88 may exaggerate the magnitude of the change in fiscal policy because in part they reflect the high levels of unemployment that are expected to persist throughout the forecast period. This problem can be avoided by examining a high-employment budget projection that excludes cyclical factors. On that basis the projected deficit will exceed the average high-employment deficit of the 1970–81 period by about 3 percent of GNP.[10]

10. The high-employment budget deficit is projected to exceed 4 percent by 1985 with no change in budget policy. That compares to an average high-employment budget deficit of 0.8 percent in 1971–80. There is, however, a shift in the underlying unemployment target from 5 percent in the 1971–80 period to 6 percent in the projections. That adds nearly 1 percent of GNP to the projected high-employment deficit.

DEFICITS AND INTEREST RATES. On the demand side, current fiscal policy provides the potential for a rapid increase in economic activity. But that outcome is dependent upon a willingness of the monetary authorities to finance such an expansion. If they are not, the fiscal stimulus will translate into a higher level of interest rates and a shift in the allocation of the economy's output away from interest-sensitive capital expenditures. And the monetary authorities cannot finance indefinitely a rapid expansion of total demand without incurring an acceleration of inflation.

The effects of a budget deficit on interest rates depend both upon the economic situation in which the deficit occurs and the conduct of monetary policy. The underlying economic situation is important because of the need to distinguish between passive changes in deficits that emerge as a result of fluctuations in economic activity and structural changes in deficits that are created by legislative actions.[11] Interest rates typically fall during recessions because of a decline in private credit demands. At the same time, the deficit rises as a passive response to the decline in economic activity. Therefore, there is an inherent tendency for interest rates to fall as the deficit rises. That is not true for changes in the deficit that are the result of legislative actions.

Even legislated changes in budget deficits, however, have ambiguous implications for interest rates that are critically dependent upon the accompanying monetary policy. In an economy of high unemployment the monetary authorities should be willing to finance a rise in overall demand; a stimulative fiscal policy need not draw resources out of other uses, and with an expansion of credit supply, it may have little or no immediate impact on interest rates. But a continuation of accommodative monetary policies as the economy returns to full resource utilization implies an intensification of both actual and expected inflation. Thus a higher expected inflation rate will ultimately raise nominal interest rates, although perhaps not real rates. If the monetary policy is not accommodative to the rise in the deficit, the deficit can be expected to increase interest rates, both nominal and real, because it stimulates aggregate economic activity and adds to the total demand for an invariant supply of credit. If monetary policy is assumed to be determined independently from fiscal policy, a shift to a more restrictive fiscal policy would always

11. The Congressional Budget Office has estimated that a 1 percent reduction in real economic growth would raise the deficit by an average of $45 billion annually over a five-year period.

reduce interest rates, but at the cost of reduced economic activity and higher unemployment.[12]

The analytical procedure for evaluating the effects of the deficit on interest rates should begin with a target path for future output growth that is the common objective of both fiscal and monetary policy. Within the confines of an unchanged total output, what would be the implications of a shift in the mix of fiscal and monetary policy occasioned by a reduction in the tax on new business investment? Initially, the lower cost of capital will lead to a rise in investment. But, unless the tax reduction is financed by lower government expenditures or higher taxes on other private spending, the government has not provided the resources to produce the added investment. Thus business must compete in capital markets to draw resources out of other uses. The higher interest rates will reduce homebuilding, consumer durables, and net exports to provide a larger share of total resources for business investment. At the same time, the higher financing cost will also offset some of the tax reduction's original stimulus to business investment. If the initial tax cut was devoted exclusively to business investment there must be a net gain in investment as a share of output, but it comes at the expense of reduced homebuilding and a deterioration of the net export position.

In 1981 taxes on investment income were reduced, but the Congress also went on to enact a large-scale personal tax reduction. That raises the possibility that the total tax cut, unfinanced by reductions in budget expenditures, raised interest rates by an amount sufficient to completely offset the incentives to business investment. The personal income tax reduction increased private consumption, adding to the demand pressures that had to be offset by higher interest rates so as to maintain the target level of total demand. Such an outcome could have been avoided only if individuals saved the entire tax cut.

A further complication is introduced by the recent argument that

---

12. There is also an important sense in which the budget deficits of the 1980s are not comparable to those of past periods. In prior recessions fiscal policy actions that increased the budget deficit were perceived as positive actions to offset unforeseen declines in private demand. Those recessions were viewed as undesirable events that the government sought to avoid. But the 1980–82 recession differed in that it reflected a conscious decision of the government to slow the economy's growth as a means of reducing inflation. In that case, it makes little sense to undo with the one hand (fiscal stimulus) what was done with the other (monetary restraint). If the recession was not desired, it could have been ended at any time by altering the monetary policy that caused it.

expectations of future deficits contribute to higher interest rates today. High future deficits do imply high short-term interest rates in those future periods. If long-term interest rates are an average of the expected future short-term rates, then anticipation of high future deficits will raise long-term interest rates today. If this argument is true, it should raise the spread between current short- and long-term interest rates, depressing total investment and shifting its mix toward short-lived assets.

The basic nature of the adjustment mechanism is evident; but at present the empirical analysis is not adequate to provide quantitative estimates of the relative magnitude of resource reallocation that takes place. The existing empirical studies differ substantially in the estimate of the effect on interest rates of a rise in total demand, and the evaluation of the response of business investment, housing, and other interest-sensitive expenditures is not of sufficient precision to allow an accurate division among them. In addition, most of the econometric models emphasize a short-run perspective in which a change in taxes is partially absorbed initially by higher private saving due to lags in the adjustment of consumption to after-tax income changes.[13]

The general conclusion is that a shift to a restrictive fiscal policy would raise the national saving rate, but that much of the increased saving would flow into housing and net exports rather than business investment. There is nothing wrong with this outcome from a growth perspective if the rates of return on the alternative uses of saving are equal. There is some concern, however, that such a shift would not add to overall growth because the favored treatment of housing under existing tax laws results in a before-tax (social) return that is lower for housing than for business investment. That is, however, more properly viewed as an issue for tax policy rather than an argument against a shift in the fiscal-monetary policy mix.

There is, as well, little or no empirical evidence by which to evaluate the importance of the expectational argument about future deficits. Long-term interest rates do appear high relative to short-term rates throughout the 1979–83 period judged by historical standards, but much

---

13. An illustration of the results from these models is provided by Richard W. Kopcke, "Will Big Deficits Spoil the Recovery?" paper prepared for a conference on Government Deficits and the Economy, sponsored by the Boston Federal Reserve, October 5–7, 1983. About half of a tax change is reflected in changed private saving, and the rest is heavily concentrated in residential construction and the net export balance.

Table 6-3. *Saving and Investment as a Percentage of Gross National Product, Annual Averages, 1951–88*

Saving or invest-ment category	1951–60	1961–70	1971–80	1981–83	1984–88[a]
Saving					
Private saving	16.2	16.3	17.1	16.9	17.5
Federal government	−0.2	−0.5	−1.9	−3.9	−5.5
State and local government	−0.2	0.1	0.9	1.2	1.5
Total national saving	15.9	15.9	16.2	14.2	13.5
Investment					
Net foreign investment	0.3	0.5	0.1	−0.2	−1.0
Residential construction	5.2	4.3	4.6	3.3	4.0
Business investment	10.4	11.1	11.5	11.1	10.5

Source: U.S. Department of Commerce, Bureau of Economic Analysis, *The National Income and Product Accounts of the United States, 1929–74 Statistical Tables,* a supplement to the *Survey of Current Business* (Government Printing Office, 1977), and subsequent reports. Figures are rounded.
a. Projected. See text for discussion.

of that gap developed before the 1981 budget actions.[14] Nor is there empirical evidence from prior decades that expected future budget deficits were important to explaining the interest rate structure.[15]

THE SAVING-INVESTMENT BALANCE. The inability to specify the magnitude of the interest rate adjustments to the deficit suggests that an alternative approach of examining the aggregate implications for the balance of saving and investment may illustrate the basic issues more clearly. That is shown in table 6-3. Total national saving can be defined as the sum of private plus government saving. The rise in the deficit projected by the CBO will reduce federal government saving in the 1984–88 period by an amount equal to 3.6 percent of GNP compared to the average of the 1971–80 period. The issue is how that deficit might be financed. As one offset, state and local governments' saving might add

14. The rise in interest rates between 1979 and 1982, however, cannot be attributed solely to the rise in the deficit. Most of that increase is the result of the restrictive monetary policy, and the portion that can be attributed specifically to the deficit is a controversial issue.

15. There is some evidence that the introduction of such an expectations phenomenon does contribute statistically to explaining the behavior of rates after 1979. See Allen Sinai and Peter Rathjens, "Deficits, Interest Rates, and the Economy" (Data Resources Inc., June 1983).

an additional 0.6 percent of GNP to the national saving rate. (Their budget surplus has been rising because of a buildup of reserves in employee retirement accounts.) On the other hand, the private saving rate has been remarkably stable at 16 to 17 percent of GNP. However, the rise in interest rates and the rapid growth of incomes during the economic recovery might optimistically be projected to raise the private saving rate to 17.5 percent. Even then, national saving will have declined by about 2.7 percent of GNP. Thus the share of GNP devoted to total investment must decline in future years, given the projected deficit.

One possible response would be to finance the gap between domestic saving and investment by borrowing funds from abroad. And indeed that was an important part of the response during 1981–83: net foreign investment fell to a negative 1 percent of GNP by the second quarter of 1983. But that financing came at considerable cost as the increased foreign demand for dollars raised the exchange rate and weakened the competitive position of U.S. industry.

The high interest rates will have a restraining influence on homebuilding, but, given the rapid growth of those demographic groups with the strongest demand for homeownership, it will be difficult to hold residential construction below 4 percent of GNP. Thus an optimistic outcome for business investment would seem to be 10.5 percent of GNP, or about 1 percentage point below the average of the 1970s. Obviously, the deficit could be absorbed in a variety of different ways, but it is difficult to make any plausible allocation that translates into an economic policy promoting growth.

CONCLUSION. All of the perverse effects on capital formation outlined above could have been avoided if the tax reductions of 1981 had been made contingent on agreement by the administration and the Congress to expenditure reductions of equivalent magnitude. The proponents of the program, however, argued that either such expenditure reductions were unnecessary or they could be held in abeyance. One important reason was a political argument: the creation of large budget deficits through tax reductions was seen as a mechanism for forcing expenditure reductions. That may turn out to be true. But in the meantime it has been costly to the economy and to the objective of increasing capital formation. There is an important role for tax policy in promoting economic growth; but such actions must be undertaken within a unified policy framework that recognizes the implications of tax changes for overall fiscal policy.

A second major lesson that emerged from the 1981–82 experience is the importance of coordinating fiscal and monetary policy to achieve a common set of goals. At present, no mechanism exists to force a reconciliation between the monetary policy decisions of the Federal Reserve System and the budget actions of the Congress and the administration. The collision between a restrictive monetary policy and an expansionary fiscal policy has been costly in terms of high interest rates and a sharp rise in the exchange rate. Those costs are likely to continue to rise in future years.

The design of an appropriate fiscal-monetary policy must differentiate between two fundamental issues: (1) the appropriate target for overall economic activity and (2) the mix of policies to achieve that target. The first issue revolves around the balancing of the costs of inflation against the benefits of lower unemployment. It involves difficult economic and value judgments. However, it makes little sense to conduct fiscal and monetary policies on the basis of independent, and often contradictory, determinations of the goals they are trying to achieve. The United States has a long history of using monetary restraint at the peak of business cycle responses as a means of reducing inflation, and then adopting expansionary fiscal measures as a response to the subsequent recession and rise in unemployment. The result has been an economy that goes up and down like a roller coaster, a secular rise in both inflation and unemployment, and a continuing drift in the mix of policy toward larger deficits and monetary restraint.

The second question, the appropriate mix of fiscal and monetary policy to achieve a given target for total output, is more closely related to the subject of this book. A consideration of the responses of saving, investment, and the foreign exchange rate to interest rates and tax incentives would suggest that economic growth would be favored by a mix of policy that is tilted in the direction of fiscal restraint to provide for an increase in national saving and a monetary policy that encourages with low interest rates the pass-through of the saving into investment: that is, a policy mix exactly the reverse of that which emerged from the uncoordinated decisions of recent years.

Tax Policy

To date, the discussion of tax policy has focused on the pros and cons of reducing or eliminating taxes on capital income in general as a means of increasing the overall rate of capital formation. Meanwhile, an increasing amount of the economic research has concentrated on a second issue: the efficiency with which a given amount of investment is used. The review of that research in prior chapters emphasized the highly disparate effective tax rates for investments having different durabilities, ownership, and methods of financing. Such differences arise, in part, because of explicit legislative decisions, but much of the variation is the unintended result of changes in inflation rates and the inability of some firms to realize the full tax benefits of new investments.

TAXES AND INFLATION. As has been pointed out in several studies, inflation affects the taxation of capital income in several ways. First, depreciation allowances are based upon the original cost of the asset, and thus their value declines as inflation rates rise. On the other hand, firms are allowed to deduct interest payments, and, since interest rates tend to rise with inflation, an increasing portion of the income from capital escapes business taxation. Some of the benefit to the firm of deducting nominal interest payments is offset by the taxation of interest receipts under the personal income tax. However, because the marginal corporate tax rate exceeds that of the average recipient of interest income, the net effective tax rate on interest income is reduced by inflation. Finally, because capital gains are also not adjusted for inflation, inflation raises the effective tax rate.

The most recent studies suggest that the net effect of inflation on the overall tax on capital income is small because the deductibility of nominal interest offsets the tax-increasing effect of the other factors.[16] But that overall constancy masks great variation among assets and industries caused by differences in the relative importance of depreciation and debt finance. The tax on equipment, for example, rises rapidly with inflation while that on inventories declines.

TAX-LOSS FIRMS. There is also a significant difference in effective tax on investments by different firms. New firms, or more generally firms with tax losses, often lack sufficient existing tax liabilities against which to offset their depreciation allowances and tax credits. Firms can "carry back" current losses to recompute tax liabilities of the prior three years, or they can be carried over to future years. Since such unused tax deductions do not earn interest, however, their present value declines

16. Don Fullerton and Yolanda Henderson, "Incentive Effects of Taxes on Income from Capital: Alternative Policies in the 1980s," presented at the Urban Institute Conference on Reagan's Economic Policies and Long-Term Growth, Washington, D.C., September 1983.

with increases in the nominal interest rate. As a result, there would appear to be a differential tax treatment of the investments by new and existing firms. An attempt to respond to this problem was made in 1981 with the introduction of "safe-harbor" leasing whereby firms with no tax liabilities could, in effect, sell their tax credits and deductions to taxable firms. Public criticism of this measure led to restrictions on its use in 1982.[17]

Finally, the difficulty of measuring capital income is responsible for much of the administrative complexity of the current system. This has become the source of substantial public discontent, and it is an important motivation behind many of the reform proposals.

Proposals for Tax Reform

There have been two major lines of suggested reform.[18] The first would attempt to fix up the system by moving toward a comprehensive income tax that incorporates a measure of taxable capital income that is adjusted for the effects of inflation (indexation of the tax base). The second would abandon efforts to tax capital income and move to a consumption-based tax. These represent diametrically opposed answers to the question of whether capital income should be taxed, but both provide a means of resolving the concern about distortions in the allocation of capital.

The current personal tax system is a hybrid between an income and a consumption-based tax. This hybrid is responsible for much of the variation in effective tax rates on different types of investment. On the one hand, many forms of capital income are either exempt from taxation or the tax liability can be deferred to the point where the effective tax rate is near zero. On the other hand, interest income is taxed at high and variable rates because of the failure to index the tax base for inflation.

COMPREHENSIVE INCOME TAX. Advocates of the comprehensive income tax believe that the exclusion of large amounts of income from the tax base is the major problem of the current system. These exclusions

17. These abuses are discussed in Alan J. Auerbach and Alvin C. Warren, "Transferability of Tax Incentives and the Fiction of Safe-Harbor Leasing," *Harvard Law Review*, vol. 95 (June 1982), pp. 1752–86.

18. These two contrasting approaches are outlined in more detail, with citations, in Harvey Galper, "Tax Policy," in Joseph A. Pechman, ed., *Setting National Priorities: The 1984 Budget* (Brookings Institution, 1983), pp. 173–200.

include employee fringe benefits and transfers (in excess of contributions) as well as large amounts of capital income. These advocates would respond to the inflation-induced distortions in capital income taxation by indexing the tax base to deduct from capital gains and interest income (both receipts and expenses) the inflation premium that simply maintains the real value of the asset. The complexity of the tax would be increased by the need to adjust for inflation in measuring capital income and in-kind income (such as housing), but removing the special provisions for capital gains and other tax preferences for capital income would eliminate many of the opportunities for tax arbitrage whereby taxpayers avoid taxes by a simple restructuring of their assets and liabilities—in effect, borrowing to invest in tax-exempt or low-tax assets.[19] The revenues raised by the base-broadening measures could then be used to reduce marginal tax rates on both capital and labor income.

CONSUMPTION TAX. There are two alternative means of implementing a consumption tax, both of which begin with the previous broad definition of income. The first would simply exclude capital income from the tax base and eliminate the deduction of interest expenses. The second approach would measure total income (capital plus labor) on a cash-flow basis but allow a deduction for saving. The two concepts are equivalent for investments that earn the market rate of return and for income taxed at a single rate: it makes little difference whether the funds are excluded from taxation when they are put into the savings account (the deduction approach) or when the income is earned (the exclusion approach).[20] The first approach highlights the often overlooked fact that a consumption tax is basically a wage tax. The approach of deducting saving does maintain taxation of the extramarginal returns to capital—returns greater than those used to discount future income. In addition, the deduction of saving involves fewer transitional problems when it is introduced; in the

---

19. David F. Bradford, "Issues in the Design of Savings and Investment Incentives," in Charles R. Hulten, ed., *Depreciation, Inflation, and the Taxation of Income from Capital* (Washington, D.C.: Urban Institute, 1981), pp. 13–47.

20. The equivalence of the two approaches can be illustrated by noting that under the first proposal a dollar of wage income if deposited is not taxed, grows at a rate i for n years, and is then taxed at a rate t. The individual receives $D(1 + i)^n (1 - t)$. Under the exclusion approach a tax is paid on the income from wages, but the taxpayer gets to keep all the deposit plus interest at the end of the n years. He receives $(1 - t)D(1 + i)^n$, which is the same amount as in the first case. The two versions of the consumption tax are discussed in U.S. Department of the Treasury, *Blueprints for Basic Tax Reform* (Government Printing Office, 1977), pp. 113–43.

other method, the single exclusion of capital income from the tax base involves large windfall gains to existing wealth holders.

The deduction of saving is not as simple as the exclusion of capital income, because it initially requires a comprehensive measure of capital income. It still results in a simplification of tax reporting, however, because it uses cash-flow accounting. There is no need to measure capital gains or losses because the funds are excluded from the tax base if they are not withdrawn from the account. The use of cash-flow accounting also eliminates the need to adjust the income measure for inflation.

Nonetheless, the consumption tax is controversial. It would initiate a substantial redistribution of tax burdens, and the increased effective tax on labor income might cause offsetting reductions of labor supply and work effort. It also adopts a narrow view of capital by ignoring investments in education and other forms of capital that are reflected in higher wage rates. In addition, the consumption tax advocates assume that wealth has no value beyond its ability to support future consumption. Others believe that wealth confers power, security, and access to opportunities that are not reflected in consumption. Therefore, on equity grounds they prefer to use income as the basic measure of tax liability. One partial solution is to combine the consumption tax with an effective inheritance tax aimed at preventing the concentration of wealth. Because such a combined tax system does imply a positive tax on capital income, its net effect on saving is uncertain.

BUSINESS TAXATION. At the corporate level the contrasting approaches of income-based and consumption-based taxes are reflected in two proposed reforms. The first, suggested by Jorgenson and Auerbach, parallels the income tax by continuing to tax the income from capital, but would give firms the full present value of depreciation, based on economic useful lives, at the time the investment is undertaken, thus eliminating the problem of adjusting depreciation for inflation.[21] With economic depreciation the continued deduction of interest expenses on borrowed funds would be appropriate.

The alternative plan, suggested by Hall (among others), is consistent with the consumption tax and would allow the full value of investment to be deducted as a current expense at the time of purchase, thus

21. Alan J. Auerbach and Dale Jorgenson, "Inflation-Proof Depreciation of Assets," *Harvard Business Review*, vol. 58 (September–October 1980), pp. 113–18. They propose to use a fixed real interest rate of 4 percent to obtain the present value of the future depreciation.

eliminating completely the administrative machinery of depreciation accounting.[22] Current expensing does not imply the elimination of the corporate tax. Taxes would still be paid on any income beyond the cost of capital—extramarginal returns and income from nontangible assets such as goodwill. It does imply, however, a zero tax on the opportunity cost of capital, so that taxes do not alter the cost of capital. In addition, the tax would be applied to the total income of corporate capital: interest expenses would no longer be deductible as a business expense. As a result, current expensing implies some increase in the net tax on interest income unless it is combined with a consumption tax concept at the personal level.

Both proposals would create a business tax that is invariant under different rates of inflation and neutral in its treatment of alternative investments. In addition, the elimination of the interest deduction under current expensing would remove any distorting effects at the corporate level induced by different methods of financing—equity versus debt. Firms would earn the full before-tax return on assets and they would pay the full before-tax cost of funds. The Jorgenson-Auerbach proposal retains the interest deduction at the corporate level, however, because the underlying concept is still that of a tax on net income.

Both proposals still encounter the possibility that a firm may have a negative tax liability in some years. Thus the tax on investments of different firms could vary greatly. One solution would be to provide an unlimited carry-forward of unused deductions and allow it to grow at the market rate of interest. Alternatively, firms could be paid out of the treasury for the value of any negative tax liability, or they could sell unused credits to other firms, as in safe-harbor leasing.

Current expensing of investment at the level of the business firm is most consistent with the consumption tax at the individual level. It is possible, however, to combine current expensing with a comprehensive income tax. The purpose of such a corporate tax would be to prevent sheltering of income from the personal tax and the taxation of inframarginal returns. Under an indexed personal tax system the resulting tax on interest would not be different from that on other forms of income.

In summary, either a consumption tax or a comprehensive income tax could eliminate most of the distortions in the current treatment of

22. Robert E. Hall, "Tax Treatment of Depreciation, Capital Gains and Interest in an Inflationary Environment," in Hulten, ed., *Depreciation, Inflation, and the Taxation of Income from Capital*, pp. 149–66.

different types of capital income. The issue is not so much the form of the tax as the problem of dealing with tax preferences that arise in both cases. The comprehensive income tax is aimed at eliminating the preferences (bringing all forms of income back into the tax base); the consumption tax extends them to all forms of capital income. In addition, the consumption tax requires a higher level of tax rates because the tax base is restricted to wage income.

Conclusion

A higher rate of economic growth can make a major contribution to alleviating the economic and social problems of the United States. Yet no single explanation, such as a low rate of capital formation, can account for the slow rate of growth that has plagued the United States over the last decade. Thus one should avoid excessive emphasis on any single solution. In particular, although increased private capital formation offers a high rate of return, if a supply-side economic program that promotes such an effort comes at the expense of investments in education, research and development, and similar projects, it will not accelerate economic growth.

Second, there has been too much focus on tax incentives as a means of increasing growth while other tools of economic policy are ignored. The overall level of taxation is a decision that must be made with a full awareness of both the costs of taxation and the benefits of the expenditures they finance. But, within the constraint of a need to finance expenditures, the historical evidence does not support the view that a shift of the tax burden from capital to labor income will measurably raise the overall growth rate. Taxation does distort the saving-consumption decision of individuals, but the net effect on aggregate saving appears to be small. And the distortion of individuals' work decisions by the taxation of wages should be of equal concern.

The emphasis on increased incentives for private saving also ignores the issue of how that saving is utilized. Increased tax incentives for private saving that arise at the expense of larger government deficits offer no benefits for domestic investment. That has, however, been the result of the 1981 tax program. In addition, the recent research has highlighted the waste in the allocation of the existing volume of investment that is introduced by the disparate treatment of different types of capital income under the current tax system.

Finally, until recently a shortage of domestic saving did not appear as a major constraining influence on domestic investment. In the 1980s, however, the economy has exhibited more of the symptoms (high real interest rates and significant inflows of foreign capital) of a deficiency of saving, but the change can be traced to the spectacular increase in the government deficit rather than to a decline in private saving. It is also evident that many factors other than tax rates are critical to promoting domestic investment. These include expectations of a sustained future growth of demand for the products the new plants can produce, the avoidance of the extremes of inflation and recession, and the availability of financing at reasonable costs.

Such considerations lead to a greater emphasis on the importance for growth of reasonable fiscal and monetary policies. Specifically, a strategy to promote growth calls for a shift away from the policies that dominated the early 1980s: a combination of large budget deficits offset by a restrictive monetary policy. A more restrictive fiscal policy is the most effective means of increasing the domestic supply of saving to finance new capital investments, and a monetary policy directed toward maintaining a sustained expansion of the domestic economy offers the most effective inducement for assuring the transfer of that saving into increased investment. Tax policy has an important role to play, but it must be evaluated within the confines of an overall fiscal-monetary strategy. The greatest potential for gains would seem to lie in eliminating the distortions in the use of capital that the current tax system promotes.

Index

205

Eisner, Robert, 66n, 89n, 106, 107–08n, 109
Enzler, Jared, 85n
Evans, Michael K., 40n
Evans, Owen J., 85n

Fair, Ray C., 124
Federal Reserve Board (FRB), 123–24, 196
Feldstein, Martin, 13n, 50n, 51, 89, 91n, 93, 122n, 126, 127, 150, 151, 152, 154–56
Fellner, William, 17n, 25n, 32n
Fiscal policy, 14, 16, 17, 61, 187–88, 189–96. *See also* Deficits
Food stamp program, 147, 164–66
Franke, Richard H., 40n
Fraumeni, Barbara M., 25n, 102n
Freeman, Richard B., 168n, 169
Friedman, Milton, 7n, 85, 86n
Fromm, Gary, 101n, 108n
Fullerton, Don, 117, 118, 119, 143, 145n, 197n

Galper, Harvey, 112n, 198n
Giersch, Herbert, 14n
Gordon, Robert J., 47n
Gordon, Roger H., 158n, 160
Gotur, Padma, 86n
Gravelle, Jane, 120n
Green, R. Jeffery, 109n
Griliches, Zvi, 32, 33n, 36n
Grimm, Bruce T., 49, 50n
Gustman, Alan L., 149n
Gylfason, Thorvaldur, 79, 80

Hall, Robert E., 108, 140n, 200, 201n
Halsey, Hardan, 166n
Hamermesh, Daniel S., 147n, 152, 153n
Harberger, Arnold C., 70n, 115n, 125
Harper, Michael J., 25n, 31n, 37n
Harris, Seymour E., 122n
Hartman, Robert, 66n
Hartzmark, Michael, 134n
Hausman, Jerry A., 141n, 143, 144, 145, 160n
Haveman, Robert H., 31n, 154n, 159n, 162n, 163, 164n, 167n, 176n
Heckman, James J., 142n
Hendershott, Patric H., 108, 112n, 113–14, 116, 123n
Henderson, Yolanda K., 118, 119, 197n
Hickman, Bert G., 124n
Horioka, Charles, 126, 127
Housing: demand and prices of, 113–15; investment, 110–16, 128–29; price elasticity and supply of, 115–16; tax treatment of, 110–13, 118–19

Howry, E. Philip, 79, 80
Hulten, Charles R., 28n, 68n, 117, 120n, 199n, 201n
Hu, Sheng-Cheng, 108, 112n
Hymans, Saul H., 70, 80

Income, distribution of, 85–86
Industrial capacity, 47–50
Inflation, 6–7; industrial capacity shortages as a source of, 47–48; and interest rates, 66–67; and taxes, 7, 13, 52, 197; and unemployment, 7, 12
Interest rates: and allocation of consumption, 70–71, 73–75; and deficits, 13–14, 191–94; and investment, 12, 127–28; and saving, 70–71, 73–75, 79–84, 127–28
Investment: and economic policy, 183–85; housing, 110–11, 128–29; and interest rates, 12, 13–14, 127–28; response to change in rate of return, 21, 45–47; and saving, 60, 120–27, 181, 194–95; and tax rates, 103
Investment behavior: models of, 98–110; and rental price of capital, 101–03, 105, 110

Johnson, Lewis, 85n
Jorgenson, Dale W., 25n, 36n, 98n, 101, 102n, 106, 108, 200, 201
Jump, Gregory V., 66–67n, 94

Kehrer, Kenneth C., 142n, 143n, 144, 145n, 167n
Kendrick, John W., 25n, 32, 33, 38, 39n, 40n
Keynes, John Maynard, 3, 17, 122
Keynesian economics, 3–5; and aggregate supply, 11–12
King, Mervyn A., 117, 118n
Klein, Lawrence R., 106n
Kopcke, Richard W., 193n
Kopits, George, 86n
Kunze, Kent, 25n, 31n, 37n
Kurihara, Kenneth K., 69n
Kurz, Mordecai, 90n

Labor income, taxes on, 133–38, 185–86
Labor supply: and capital stock, 23; and disability insurance, 161–63, 175; and economic policy, 185–87; education and the quality of, 168–72, 176; effect of transfer programs on, 21; incentives, 138–41; income maintenance experiments, 144–46; and social security, 157–61; studies of, 141–42; survey results, 142–44; and tax changes, 24–25, 173–74; and transfer programs, 146–48, 173,

Taxes: and inflation, 7, 13, 197; and labor supply, 131, 133–38
Tax policy: changing views on, 5–6, 7–8; and economic policy, 21, 182, 188, 196–98
Tax rates: average, 75, 116, 133–38, 186; and capital formation, 116–20; and corporate investment, 103, 117, 127–28; marginal, 75–79, 116–19, 133–38, 186; trends in, 133–38
Tax reductions, effects of, 18–19, 189, 192
Tax reform: business taxation, 200–02; comprehensive income tax, 198–99; consumption tax, 199–200
Tobin, James, 12n, 84n, 89
Toder, Eric, 112n
Topel, Robert, 157n
Ture, Norman B., 16n, 17
Turner, John A., 158n

Ultrarationality, and saving behavior, 17–18, 87–89
Unemployment insurance (UI), 148–57;

basic features, 148–51; benefit replacement rates, 151–52; empirical studies, 152–57; and industrial capacity, 48–49

von Furstenberg, George M., 51n, 77n, 78n, 87, 89, 102n, 109n, 127
Vroman, Wayne, 151, 152

Wages, 14–15, 122, 138–40
Warren, Alvin J., 198n
Watts, Harold W., 140n, 142n
Welch, Finis, 157n, 169n
Welfare programs: effect on labor supply, 164–67; and marginal tax rates, 165
White, Betsy B., 84n
White, Lawrence J., 115n
White, Michelle J., 115n
Winter, Sidney G., 43n
Wise, Donald E., 158n, 160n
Wolfe, Barbara L., 162n, 163, 164n
Work-leisure decision, 138–41
Wright, Colin, 70n